As It Was

As It Was

Stories from the History of
Southern Oregon and Northern California

CAROL BARRETT

JEFFERSON PUBLIC RADIO
Ashland, Oregon

This book is dedicated to the countless volunteers
who since 1969 have helped build Jefferson Public Radio,
and whose dedication and spirit keep public radio
alive in the State of Jefferson.

Printed in the USA.

ACKNOWLEDGEMENTS: The publisher gratefully acknowledges the many individuals and historical societies who provided photographs for this book; and James Phillips for his editorial assistance.

Design and typesetting: Impact Publications

Library of Congress Catalog Card Number: 98-87804

ISBN: 0-9667741-0-8

AS IT WAS

TABLE OF CONTENTS

Prehistoric

Explorers and Trappers

Early Days

Early Transportation

From Trails to Roads

Gold Rush

Lost Gold

Government

Native Americans

Parks

Disasters

Growing Up In a Small Town

Prohibition

Depression Years

Wartimes

❧❀❧

AS IT WAS

INTRODUCTION

AS IT WAS
TITLE: Grants Pass Sewers
DATE: September 1, 1992
SOURCE: Rogue River Courier (Grants Pass)
          via Grace Blanchard, Josephine County Historical Society

NARRATOR: Welcome to "As It Was," a look at the history of Southern
Oregon and Northern California.

I'm Hank Henry.

ON SEPTEMBER 1, 1992, listeners to Jefferson Public Radio (JPR), Southern Oregon University's regional network of public radio stations, heard the first installment of *As It Was*, a radio series devoted to the history of Southern Oregon and Northern California. The script above comes from that very first broadcast.

Initial work on the radio series had begun months earlier, after the Southern Oregon Historical Society (SOHS) approached JPR with the suggestion of a radio program devoted to the history of the region. The Historical Society offered JPR the services of a volunteer researcher and writer named Carol Barrett.

A program like this certainly met with JPR's mission to provide stimulating cultural and information programming and to promote lifelong learning. While SOHS focuses its activities primarily on Jackson County, Oregon, JPR staff thought it was important to create a series that would include the entire region served by Jefferson Public Radio: the counties of Southern Oregon and Northern

California which form the mythical State of Jefferson, which in turn gives JPR its name (for more on the State of Jefferson, see page 87).

After Carol met with JPR staff, we decided to move ahead. Carol even had an idea for a name for the series: *As It Was.* Naming a radio series is often the toughest task of all, but even with that problem solved we weren't quite ready for the airwaves. We still had a few small details to attend to, among them finding a host and a producer for the program. Jefferson Public Radio has always relied on a diverse and talented group of volunteers to maintain its programming services, so we began a search for volunteers who could give life to the series.

Hank Henry

We invited veteran broadcaster and former Jackson County Commissioner Hank Henry to be the voice of *As It Was,* and he immediately agreed. Hank's voice was already instantly familiar to many people in the region, because prior to his tenure as County Commissioner he served as News Director of KMED-TV (later KTVL), Channel 10, from Medford, and anchored the station's evening newscasts. He also had a long career in radio before moving to television, having worked at stations in Portland, Roseburg, and Klamath Falls. In fact, Hank's presence on the local airwaves for over twenty years gave us a host who was himself well versed in the region's history.

The next step in creating the series was to find someone to do the studio work: the scheduling, recording, editing and dubbing needed to transform Carol's scripts and Hank's voice into a daily radio feature.

Those duties fell primarily to two volunteers from JPR's News Department, Bob Davy and John Clarke. Bob Davy, a retired Emmy Award-winning television producer, sailed right into the project, editing scripts, arranging recording sessions, and giving the project solid organization. For the first couple of years of the program, John Clarke assisted Bob. John is a retired surgeon, and JPR staffers used to joke that this made him uniquely qualified to cut and splice recording tape.

Bob Davy

Through the efforts of Carol, Hank, Bob and John, *As It Was* has become a daily presence on Jefferson Public Radio, and a favorite of listeners. The 2½-minute program has aired weekdays on all three of Jefferson Public Radio's program services, Classics & News, Rhythm & News, and News & Information since its debut. As this book goes to press, over 1,200 original episodes of *As It Was* have aired on Jefferson Public Radio, with more to come.

When Carol Barrett suggested that the *As It Was* scripts might make for interesting reading in book form, this, too, seemed to fit with JPR's mission. While JPR's primary activities show up on the radio dial, over the years we have branched into other media; first with our member's magazine, *The Jefferson Monthly*, which publishes regional feature articles, opinion, literature and cultural reviews, and later with JEFFNET, JPR's non-profit Internet service provider. While this is the first book ever published by JPR, we believe it serves not only to preserve a record of a successful radio series, but will bring the stories of *As It Was* to new audiences who may not have heard the radio program.

We never intended the radio series *As It Was* to be a comprehensive history of the State of Jefferson. Rather, we hoped to tell stories that would give a sense of the colorful, varied—if sometimes disquieting—history of the region, and thereby give us all a richer sense of what it means to live here. While the series tells stories about the flavor of early pioneer life, or amusing anecdotes of unusual characters, *As It Was* has never shied from the less pleasant aspects of our history and has included stories about the racism against Native Americans and the Chinese, the frontier violence, the sometimes life-threatening hardships encountered by the region's early residents.

This book, taking a cue from the radio program, doesn't aim to do more than tell good stories. In preparing this book, Carol went back through all the over 1,200 scripts and picked those that had special significance to the region's history, or were particularly amusing stories—and she included some personal favorites. So you might read this book cover to cover, but it's probably just as enjoyable to browse through the chapters and the photographs—many of which Carol Barrett located through private collections, and are published here for the first time.

While the stories collected in this book bear witness to the strength and resilience of the residents of the State of Jefferson, this book itself is testimony to the inspiration, care and dedication of the volunteers who have helped build Jefferson Public Radio—and *As It Was*. ≈

JOHN BAXTER
Director of New Media
Jefferson Public Radio
October, 1998

CHAPTER 1

PREHISTORIC

Mesozoic Era

ONE HUNDRED MILLION years ago Oregon was underwater with the coast of the Pacific Ocean off to the east somewhere in the neighborhood of Boise, Idaho. There was no high Cascade Mountain range. This was the Mesozoic Era. The fossil beds of Eastern Oregon and Northern California show the kinds of life that lived there. When the waters receded and land appeared, the area had missed the whole age of the dinosaurs.

About 70 million years ago the animals that made their home in this area were: massive pigs, fat rhinos and miniature three toed horses. These and other fossils appear most distinctly in the John Day fossil beds but also throughout eastern Oregon and California. At Merrill, Oregon, near the California line, a crew digging an irrigation ditch found some interesting fossil bones. They were determined to be the remains of an enormous camel about twice the size of the Arabian camel.

The Cascade Mountains appeared as a result of volcanic eruptions that are still going on. They effectively cut off the migration of animals from east to west.

Great Moments in Oregon History, edited by Pintarich; *Ancient Tribes of the Klamath Country,* Howe; *Oregon Oddities,* WPA

Ice Age

THE PACIFIC COASTLINE was greatly affected by the ice age. Fifty thousand years ago, the last ice age was at its height. It is thought that until this time no humans lived in either North or South America. As the water from the oceans evaporated into the air, the moisture fell back down to earth in the form of snow, which compacted into ice. The snow and ice didn't melt but just kept building up until most of North America was covered with ice. In our area ice did not cover everything. It crept down from the mountains leaving parts of the valleys uncovered.

So much water was taken from the oceans to form this ice cover, that the oceans were four to five hundred feet lower. This is why there was continuous land between Northern Asia and the present day Aleutian Islands and Alaska. It is here that many animals and humans migrated to North America.

Before the ice was completely gone, Indians lived east of the Cascade mountains. They brought dogs with them and they hunted with spear throwers.

Why did they venture into this unknown area? We will never know.

The History of Jackson County, Medford *Mail Tribune*, March 3, 1979.

Fossils – 1869

THE FIRST MASTODON fossils in Oregon were found on March 13, 1869. Since then other mastodon bones have been found throughout our area. The chalk material deposited in the strata with the fossils provided later Indians with a base for white paint which they used for body decorations.

It is thought that the earliest men arrived around 25,000 years ago but the oldest record in Oregon is 11,000 years. These early Indians relied for food on the mammoth, bison, horse and later species of camels and saber-tooth tigers. They killed these large animals by throwing flint tipped spears.

Ancient Tribes of the Klamath Country, Howe; Artifacts, SOHS

Prehistoric Horses

THE MOUNTAINS BETWEEN Southern Oregon and Northern California are some of the oldest in the two states. Fossils tell us that an early horse lived here forty million years ago. This horse was only as large as a sheep. It had four toes on its front feet and three on its back. As volcanoes formed, the terrain became harsher and the horse adapted by learning to run faster and to eat a larger variety of food. It also grew larger and lost his side toes. After millions of years, all that remained was a single toe or hoof. Eventually the horse became extinct until the Spanish reintroduced it to our area.

Copper Paladin, Palburg.

CHAPTER 2

EXPLORERS AND TRAPPERS

Norse Explorers?

DID NORSE EXPLORERS ever reach the Rogue River Valley? Some people thought so. A man named Upsjon, a Norwegian scientist, lectured in Spokane, Washington in 1924. He claimed that a party of Norse explorers crossed the American continent in the year 1010 AD. He further claimed that they went as far south as the Rogue River Valley.

Stones have been found with "runic" letters carved on them. These are similar to the runic alphabet used in ancient times, especially in the Scandinavian countries. Mr. Upsjon claimed he had seen some of these that are peculiar to Norse writing. In some cases, zodiac signs and the year, month and day are included.

According to Upsjon, the Norse men spent a winter on Puget Sound. The Indians were not friendly so they traveled south as far as the Rogue Valley. Here they also spent some time but their trail after that is not mentioned.

There are certainly stones that have been found with strange inscriptions, but few people seem to believe in the theory of early Norse explorers.

Rogue Valley Communities (selected writings)

1492	1513	1752	1775
Oct 12 – Columbus sets foot in the new world	Jean Ponce DeLeon establishes the 1st colony in U.S., St. Augustine, Florida.	French and Indian War	Battle of Lexington and Concord

Ferrelo – 1543

WE TEND TO THINK of Oregon history beginning with the Lewis and Clark Expedition. It is easy to forget the hunters, trappers and big fur business that preceded them. And who was Ferrelo?

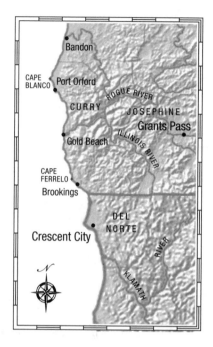

Mendoza, the Viceroy of Mexico, equipped Cabrillo for a sailing trip of exploration up the Pacific coast of North America. Always looking for ways to expand the Spanish claims in the new world, San Miguel Cabrillo was commissioned to make detailed charts and maps along the way. The maps that he drew were so well done, they were used by all who followed. Unfortunately Cabrillo died on January 3, 1543 before completing the trip. Ferrelo was his pilot and took command of the expedition. It is thought that he sailed up the coast as far as the 42nd parallel and would have been the first white man to see Northern California and Southern Oregon.

Oregon, Horner

Port Trinidad – 1775

THE GOVERNMENT of Mexico kept pushing exploration further up the Pacific Coast. The ship *Santiago,* under Captain Bruno Heceta, sailed north from Monterey. On June 10, 1775 it anchored near a promontory and a detachment went ashore. They took possession of the land in the name of Spain. It being the Sunday of the Holy Trinity, they named the harbor Port Trinidad.

The ship remained at anchor for nine days while they took on water and made repairs. They made a cross and placed it on the promontory, piling rocks around it. In 1817, forty-two years later, when the British schooner *Columbia* sheltered in Trinidad harbor, the cross was still standing. After describing the friendly natives, the captain wrote. "We saw a cross on shore fixed there by the Spaniards many years ago…"

Lower Klamath Country, McBeth

1783	1789	1792	1797
End of the Revolutionary War	Apr 30 – George Washington becomes 1st president	Kentucky becomes 15th state. Postal Service is established	Mar 4 – John Adams becomes 2nd president

Crescent City in 1857
SOURCE: Del Norte County Historical Society

Hudson Bay Company – 1670

THE HUDSON BAY company is remembered in many different ways but here is one you might not have heard.

On May 2, 1670 Charles II of England issued a charter to the Hudson Bay Company. It wasn't until a hundred years later that it became the dominant faction on the west coast.

The company sold heavy woolen socks for cold winter wear. The socks came up to the knees and were very thick. Eventually the toe would wear through. The practice was to cut off the part with the hole and sew it up across the end again. As a new hole appeared, it was cut off again and the toe resewn. The socks would last until warm weather in the spring but by then the sock might not come above the tops of a man's shoes.

Oregon Folks, Lockley; *Oregon Oddities*, WPA

1801	1803	1805	1809
Mar 4 – Thomas Jefferson becomes 3rd president	Louisiana Purchase	Lewis and Clark winter in the Astoria area	Mar 4 – James Madison becomes 4th president

Captain George Vancouver – 1792

THE SPANIARDS FIRST saw the Pacific Ocean in 1522. They sent many expeditions northward in search of the water connection they believed existed between the Atlantic and the Pacific oceans. They called this waterway the Strait of Anian.

Spanish galleons began sailing south along the coast as they returned from their trading trips to the Philippines but they stayed well out to sea to avoid the dangerous rocks and currents. The Southern Oregon and Northern California coast still remained relatively unknown.

On April 24, 1792 Captain George Vancouver anchored his ships, the *Discovery* and the *Chatham*, just south of Cape Blanco at present day Port Orford. He named the cape for his friend the Earl of Orford. Indians paddled out to the ships and wanted to barter for iron and beads. The sailors described them as 'friendly', a term those following disagreed with.

Captain James Cook had surveyed this area of coast previously but Vancouver's records were more precise and his was the reference for years after. It was also the basis of England's claim to the Pacific Coast from San Francisco to Puget Sound.

After Vancouver's voyage, fur traders from many countries plied up and down the coast. Finally the hope of finding a waterway across the continent was given up.

A Guide to Oregon South Coast History, Doughit

Black York – 1804–1806

THE SECOND AFRICAN–AMERICAN in Oregon came with Lewis and Clark. York seems to be the only name for William Clark's slave. He was called "Black York" when he accompanied his master on the Lewis and Clark expedition in 1805. He was a man of great strength, a skilled hunter who knew how to live off the land. He had some knowledge of French and acted as a translator. Add to that his height of six feet two inches and you can imagine what a great curiosity he was among the Indians who called him "Great Medicine." He enjoyed showing off his strength and skills. It was said that Indian children followed him everywhere and the Indian women fought over him.

In 1811 York was given his freedom and a six horse team with wagon for his part in the Lewis and Clark trip. The enlisted men of the expedition received three hundred and twenty acres of land and double pay.

How York's life ended is a mystery. There are many stories. Jesse Applegate said he met an Indian of mixed blood who claimed he was a son of Black York.

A Peculiar Paradise, McLagan

1812	1817	1821	1825
War with Great Britain	Mississippi becomes 20th state	Northwest Fur Company absorbed into Hudson Bay Co.	Mar 4 – John Quincy Adams becomes the 6th president
	James Monroe becomes 5th president		

Fort Ross – 1812

RUSSIA WAS ONE of the early claimants to the northwest coast of the United States. They claimed as far south as Fort Ross, California.

Fort Ross was established in 1812 to be used as a base for hunting, fishing and trade with the Spanish and Indians. The Russian–America Company had forts north along the coast all the way to the tip of the Aleutian Islands. This southern post was to raise and buy food for the northern settlements, while, at the same time, hunting the sea otter. Gardening became successful with the raising of cabbage, lettuce, pumpkins, watermelon and potatoes. They also harvested apples, pears and cherries. Chicken, pigs and horses were kept.

Bricks were manufactured, but the buildings were mostly of logs, constructed to house and provide for 25 Russians and 80 native Alaskans. It was meant to protect the inhabitants from the Spanish who also laid claim to the area. The men intermarried with the Indians and produced a multicultural society.

The Aleuts paddled their kayaks in search of sea otter. As many as a thousand pelts might be turned over monthly. Each one was worth $150.

By 1841, when the sea otter had been depleted, John Sutter bought the settlement for $30,000 worth of wheat.

Medford Mail Tribune, August 23, 1993

The Rock – 1815

ALEXANDER RODERICK MCCLOUD is generally considered to have been the first non-Indian to reach the South Umpqua Valley. But, listen to this story.

Back in the 1920s a young couple packed their supplies on a few horses and went for a vacation in the forest between Diamond Lake and Crater Lake. There were no roads and few trails. They stopped for the night at a spot where the husband had been before. There he refound the rock that he had been shown on a previous hunting expedition. On it was cut the date *1815*. Below it was cut *8 and 10*. Below that was the name *Mr. S. Vanauken* and below that, the initials *G.R.*

When this rock was brought to the attention of the South Umpqua Historical Society, they investigated the history of the carving. Their first attempt involved digging deeply around the rock to be sure that it did not mark a burial spot. They found that the rock was indeed a large boulder and not part of an outcropping.

Next, they began wondering about the initials *G.R.* They noted that during the war of 1812 guns had the same initials signifying *George Rex*, meaning King George III of England, who was still king in 1815 when the rock was carved. Was someone trying to claim this part of the land for King George?

Or could S. Vanauken have been a trapper? If so he would have been with the Northwest Fur Company, a British company who later merged with the Hudson Bay Company. When contacted, the Hudson Bay Company found no record of anyone named Vanauken but noted that it was still possible he might have been working for them in a temporary capacity.

We will probably never know the story.

One of the most intriguing questions that comes to mind is: Are there other rocks out there with Vanauken or other names and dates carved on them?

Pioneer Days in the South Umpqua Valley, 1974

David Douglas – 1826

DAVID DOUGLAS WAS the botanist for whom Douglas County, Oregon and the Douglas fir tree are named. He lived at Fort Vancouver, the Hudson Bay Company headquarters. In October of 1826 he went by himself up the Umpqua River in search of a particular tree he had heard about. He wrote in his diary:

> About an hour's walk from my camp I was met by an Indian. . . . With my pencil I made a rough sketch of the cone and pine I wanted and showed him it . . . when he instantly pointed to the hills about fifteen or twenty miles to the south. As I wanted to go in that direction . . . he seemingly with much good-will . . . went with me. At midday I reached my long-wished for (pine) and lost no time in examining and endeavoring to collect specimens and seeds. New or strange things seldom fail to make great impressions and often at first we are liable to over-rate them. . . . I now state the dimensions of the largest one I could find that was blown down by the wind: Three feet from the ground . . . 57 feet 9 inches in circumference . . . extreme length 215 feet.

Douglas Fir
Abies douglassii

The tree Douglas had discovered was the sugar pine. He made the mistake of trying to secure a cone by shooting one off the tree. Immediately eight Indians appeared, weapons in hand. Douglas was able to calm them with offers of tobacco if they would help him find a pine cone. The minute they went off in search, he grabbed his things and left.

The Douglas fir, not the sugar pine, insures that David Douglas will always be a familiar name in the Pacific Northwest.

Land of the Umpqua, Beckham; *Talking on Paper,*
Applegate and O'Donnell

Sugar Pine
Picea grandus

Alexander Roderick McLeod – 1826

THE HUDSON BAY COMPANY men were always exploring and their records show that Alexander Roderick McLeod and a small band of trappers, with their Indian escorts, camped at Coos Bay harbor on October 25, 1826. They were searching for beaver.

In the summer of 1828 Jedediah Smith and his men approached Coos Bay from the south. Coos Bay was one of their stops on a long and arduous trip of exploration.

The next record of importance is December 1851 when the coastal steamer *Captain Lincoln* sailed up from San Francisco with men and supplies for Port Orford. They battled treacherous winds off Coos Bay and became disabled. Although they kept the boat afloat for several days, it finally grounded. The men were able to get ashore and, over the next few days, unload a great deal of the ship's cargo. They formed Camp Castaway on the peninsula and waited out the winter. Shortly after the wreck, settlers found the area and the small town of Marshfield (Coos Bay) emerged.

Coos Bay, The Pioneer Period, Beckham

Peter Skene Ogden
at Klamath Lake – 1826

HISTORIANS ARE INDEBTED to Peter Skene Ogden for keeping a detailed diary of his trip of exploration for the Hudson Bay Company.

On December 11, 1826, Ogden reached the eastern shore of the Upper Klamath Lake and camped there for several days. His job was to search out the geography and conditions of the area. While doing that, the men were to trap as many beavers as possible, hoping to leave the streams so barren later trapping would be discouraged.

The Klamath Indians were friendly and helpful to Ogden. They furnished canoes for his men to cross the Klamath River and they traded fish and dogs for the trappers to eat.

Ogden reported that there were hot springs all around the area but they found few beaver. The men were disgruntled with the poor results but as they followed the west side of the Klamath River downstream, conditions improved. Snow and storms finally halted travel and they made camp for a time. Trappers were sent out to the nearby streams, mapping their course and trapping beaver.

First Over the Siskiyous, LaLande

Ogden in the Rogue Valley – 1827

BECAUSE OF HIS CAREFUL diary, we know that January 24, 1827 is the exact date Ogden arrived in the Rogue River Valley. These were the first known whites in the valley. Ogden lead the party of twenty eight, accompanied by several Indians and over one hundred horses. This was the company's first foray into the area, the last unexplored region in North America south of the 49th parallel. There was still the belief that one of the Oregon rivers drained the great Salt Lake and this they were to prove or disprove conclusively.

Peter Ogden noted that the Indians were friendly and had a domestic cat. He presumed it must have been traded from coastal tribes.

From this time on, the north–south Indian trails were used by whites, but it was 25 years before people saw the possibilities of living in the area.

History and Prehistory of the Rogue Valley National Forest, U.S. Forest Service

Ogden at Table Rock – 1827

PETER OGDEN STAYED one week on the Rogue River near Table Rock and Gold Hill. The Indians came into camp to make peace. Gifts were handed around, Ogden giving the Indians about two dozen buttons. When the ceremony was over, the Indians performed a dance for the explorers.

The week's stay allowed parties to go out and explore the upper streams emptying into the Rogue, Antelope Creek, Little Butte Creek and Sam's Creek. Men may have gone up as far as present day Fish Lake. The beaver hunters came in with fifteen skins, bringing their total count to one thousand. When they headed north, up the Rogue, they were stopped by heavy snow. They turned around and went back down stream as far as Grants Pass.

First Over the Siskiyous, LaLande

Ogden at Grants Pass – 1827

OGDEN REACHED WHAT is now Grants Pass on March 8, 1827. Here three trappers, who he had sent ahead, returned with information from native Takelma Indians. The Indians spoke of rivers well stocked with beaver to the north. This was enough to persuade Ogden to cross the Rogue and head in that direction.

What makes Ogden's account of March 8 interesting is that his men had found the Takelma with axes and knives. The Indians were able to tell them that they had traded for them with the Umpqua to the north. The Umpqua, in turn, had gotten them from the Hudson Bay Company. They were prized possessions and the first white man's goods these Indians had.

First Over the Siskiyous, LaLande

Ogden With the Pit Indians – 1827

OGDEN'S MEN WERE traveling through Modoc country on May 8, 1827 when about 20 Indians visited him. The Modoc, even then, were known as wild and uncommunicative. However this visit was friendly. They had come to warn Ogden to avoid the paths along the stream he was following. They told him they had dug deep pits to trap wolves and deer. Ogden did not change his direction but he was on the lookout for anything resembling a pit. Nevertheless, three men fell in with their horses. One valuable horse was killed. The holes were described as up to 30 feet deep, some with pointed stakes in the bottom. They were so numerous Ogden wondered why they hadn't lost more men.

Peter Ogden named the river Pit (sometimes spelled "Pitt") River and the Indians became known as the Pit Indians.

Ancient Tribes of the Klamath Country, Howe

Who was First?

IT IS THOUGHT Jean Baptiste McKay was the first white man to enter the territory that is now Siskiyou County. But was he?

It is recorded that McKay camped near Sheep Rock in Shasta Valley. The question of who was first arises from the following story.

E. Watson obtained a ranch on the Salmon River's south fork. There was a large, very old pine tree lying on the ground when he arrived in 1867. The tree was cut up and a bullet was found in the very center. It was from a smooth bore gun and must have been lodged in the tree when it was a sapling. There were no scars, such as would have been made if the bullet had passed through the wood. The tree was estimated to be at least a hundred years old. That would have been about 50 years before McKay came into the area. The Indians didn't possess any fire arms at that time. So who shot that bullet into the pine sapling in the late 1700s?

Saddle Bags in Siskiyou, Jones

Jedediah Smith – 1828

JEDEDIAH SMITH BECAME a fur trader at the age of twenty-two but it was his trips of exploration to the Northern California, Southern Oregon coast for which he is best known.

Smith was only twenty-nine at the time and the first American to venture into the area. A natural leader of men, Smith, was well known when he started out from Utah in 1826. He and his men wintered in California and didn't really start the expedition until the last day of 1827. He lead nineteen men and one Indian boy. The only trails were Indian paths, so two men were sent ahead every morning to start clearing a wide enough road for the three hundred horses he had brought. Traveling down the Klamath River to its mouth, they reached the Pacific Ocean on June 8, 1828. From there they followed the shore line north.

These coastal explorations were well documented and have been compared in importance to the Lewis and Clark expedition.

A Guide to South Oregon Beach History, Doughit

Jedediah Smith State
Park placard
PHOTO: Carol Barrett

Smith Crosses the Umpqua – 1828

THE JEDEDIAH SMITH party crossed the Umpqua River and made camp. A group of fifty or more Kelawatset Indians came to trade. There was a crisis when Smith's men tried to recover a stolen axe. It appeared to be settled. Nevertheless, when Smith left camp the next morning with two of his men, he gave orders that no Indians were to be allowed into camp. These orders were not obeyed. When Smith turned back from exploring up the Umpqua River, the Indians fired on him and the two men with him. They hid in the woods and made their way back to a hill on the bank opposite the camp. From here they could see the devastated site. Everyone was dead.

Smith and his men headed north and eventually got to Fort Vancouver. There they met Arthur Black, the only man who survived the massacre.

Jedediah Smith's journey was well documented by diaries kept by both himself and his men. These were recovered when the massacre site was revisited. For some reason, Smith's information was not published, so his explorations remained relatively unknown, and his original journal has disappeared. He did leave behind secondhand information of the Indians and their way of life, and many detailed maps and geographical descriptions.

A Guide to South Oregon Beach History, Doughit

Old Fort Umpqua – 1836

ON JULY 1, 1836 John McLoughlin, the Chief Factor of the Hudson Bay Company, ordered William Rae to find a site for a trading fort.

The spot selected was an open meadow on the banks of the Umpqua River. It filled one of the requirements, that there be sufficient land to grow vegetables. It also had the advantage of being on a route the Hudson Bay Company had used for years.

For fifteen years this post was maintained. The gardens flourished and were the first to introduce many vegetables and several varieties of apples.

Johnson King was the last commander of Fort Umpqua. He made a trip to Fort Vancouver with a load of furs in November 1851. While there, he received word that fire had destroyed the entire fort complex.

Trade continued for a few years until the Hudson Bay Company pulled out of Oregon Territory entirely.

Land of the Umpqua, Beckham

Hunter's Life

TALLMADGE WORD WAS a hunter and trapper. He worked in Oregon in the 1840s. It was a hard life as we can tell by his letter to his brother:

"A hunter's life is a dog's life ... exposed to all kinds of danger and hardships and but little gained at last. But men soon get so accustomed to it that in a short time they fear neither man ... musket or the (Devil) and there is so much nature ... romance and excitement in their way of living that they soon become much attached to it. It is much easier for a white man to become an Indian than to reverse the thing."

1829	1836	1837	1841
Mar 4 – Andrew Jackson becomes 7th president	Mar 6 – Battle of the Alamo. The Republic of Texas is formed, Sam Houston, Pres.	Jan 26 – Michigan becomes 26th state	Mar 4 – William Henry Harrison becomes 9th president. Dies of pneumonia Apr 4
	June 15 – Arkansas becomes the 25th state	Mar 4 – Martin Van Buren becomes 8th president	John Tyler becomes 10th president
		Queen Victoria is crowned and reigns until 1901	

Tallmadge Word goes on to tell how hunters caught crickets for food.

"Early in the morning when the crickets…climb to the top of weeds in great numbers…that the sun may get a fair chance at them…they are easily captured by jarring them off into a basket and then roasting them with hot stones. Feathers…guts and all. (They) make very good eating when one gets used to it."

Talking on Paper, Applegate and O'Donnell

Willamette Cattle Company – 1837

THE WILLAMETTE CATTLE Company was formed to purchase cattle in California and drive them north over the Siskiyou Mountains to the Willamette Valley. The company hired Ewing Young to head the drive. He had already been responsible for driving a herd of horses north. Young hired men and boarded a ship which took them to California, arriving in March 1837. Here his troubles began. His first step was to petition the Mexican governor for permission to buy the cattle and take them out of California. He chased officials up and down the San Francisco Bay area before he got the needed papers authorizing him to buy seven hundred head of cattle to be taken to Oregon. He was to obtain these from various missions, which necessitated driving the growing herd from one mission site to another.

Once gathered together, Young and his men drove the cattle north up the Sacramento River and over the Hudson Bay trail. They arrived in the Willamette Valley in mid October. They had been on the trail five months. While 200 head of cattle were lost, some had been replaced and Young arrived with 600 head. Most of these were sold for $7.67 each.

Until this time almost all the cattle in Oregon had belonged to the Hudson Bay Company, who would not share them with the settlers.

The South Road, Its Development and Significance, Nichols

Charles Wilkes' Men – 1841

ON JULY 14, 1841, one of the vessels of the Charles Wilkes Expedition was lost at the mouth of the Columbia River. Wilkes was on his way home from the South Pacific and Antarctic. When the ship was lost he decided to send Lt. George Emmons with thirty-nine men overland from Astoria to Fort Sutter, California. They were to explore along the way, especially the Sacramento River area. With the party went twenty-two women and forty-four children. They also had seventy-nine horses.

1842	1843	1845	1845
Preemption Land Claim Bill	First large wagon train over the Oregon Trail	Mar 3 – Florida becomes the 27th state.	Mar 4 – James Polk becomes 11th president
			Dec 29 – Texas becomes the 28th state

In October the company reached the Shasta mountain range. In his journal Emmons wrote,

"Near the encampment a mountain range shoots up in sharp conical points and needle-shaped peaks. One of these peaks almost overhangs the valley presenting a gray surface of rock two thousand feet high."

This was Castle Crags in the upper Sacramento valley. Emmons thought the valley "worthless and useless" although they did find "evidence of gold."

W.B. Brackenbridge was a botanist in the party. He took back with him over one hundred living plants and seeds. These formed the core of the United States Botanical Gardens in Washington D.C.

Shasta County, Centennial History

Langsford Hastings – 1843

LANGSFORD WARREN HASTINGS dreamed of founding a California Republic. He would be the president.

Hastings came west in 1842 and worked for a year with John McLoughlin founding Oregon City. The next year he headed for California and arrived at Sutter's Fort in July 1843. He worked for John Augustus Sutter as California's first lawyer.

Returning east, he wrote and published an *Emigrants' Guide to California*. Hastings tried to persuade the Mormons to come to California rather than Utah. While he failed in this, he managed to divert many others by way of the "Hastings" cutoff.

In July 1846 Mexico gave California to the United States and any plans for an independent republic were lost. Hastings was still looking for power. A staunch southern sympathizer, he almost won over Jefferson Davis to a plan for securing Arizona and California for the Confederacy. When this failed he lost interest in California and turned his sights to Brazil.

Shasta County, Centennial History

Wagons Over the Mountains – 1844

TWENTY-SIX MEN, eight women and seventeen children with eleven wagons headed west in 1844. Elisha Stevens was their leader and a determined group they must have been. They were from the plains and knew nothing about mountains

1846	1846	1846	1847
June – Applegate Trail laid out and opened	June 15 – Oregon treaty with Britain sets the 49th parallel as the N boundary of Oregon. They give up claim to Oregon.	War with Mexico. Ends in 1848 Dec 28 – Iowa becomes 29th state	Mormons, led by Brigham Young, settle at Salt Lake City

when they left Missouri Flats. Wagons couldn't go over the rugged Sierra Mountains but this party didn't know that so they kept pushing on, widening the paths and opening the trail. Finally they left six of their wagons at what was later known as Donner Lake. The other five wagons were unloaded and hauled over a thousand foot high granite slope going a foot at a time.

These were the first wagons over the Sierra Mountains and the momentous date is thought to be November 25, 1844. This was the beginning of the California Trail. Five wagon trains used the trail the next year with a hundred following the year after.

They Saw the Elephant, Levy

Reading/Redding – 1844

PIERSON BARTON READING arrived in Northern California in 1843 and became one of the area's most outstanding citizens.

Reading joined a large party of emigrants in 1843. At Fort Hall those heading for California broke off from the main wagon train. Reading went with a group who blazed a new trail from Fort Boise to Sutter's Fort.

In May 1844 Reading applied to the Spanish governor for a grant of land along the west bank of the Sacramento River. It contained 26,000 acres. Here he lived, planted cotton, tobacco, fruit trees and raised cattle and horses. He had no neighbors but kept a huge lantern on the roof of his house to signal a welcome to any travelers in the area.

When gold was discovered, Reading went to Sutter's Fort. He thought the gold bearing soil conditions similar to parts on his own holdings. When he got home, he found he was correct. He discovered gold on Clear Creek at a spot known as Reading's Bar. A similar bar in the Trinity area is also called Reading's Bar. Here he later washed $80,000 worth of gold.

The town of Redding was named for Pierson Reading. An attempt to correct the mistake in the spelling only caused confusion and "Redding" won out.

Shasta County, Centennial Edition

Klamath Exploring Expedition – 1850

A STOCK COMPANY was formed in San Francisco and named the Klamath Exploring Expedition. But, when they sailed up the coast, they passed right by the Klamath River and went on to the Rogue River.

It was the schooner *Samuel Roberts* that set sail from Sausalito on July 7, 1850 and spent fourteen days reaching the mouth of the Rogue. A whale boat was sent out to explore the entrance but it was wrecked and two of the crew drowned. The other three were captured by the Indians as they reached shore. The captain of the schooner decided to risk entering the harbor to rescue the three crewmen. This they were successful in doing but from there on, they had trouble with the Indians.

Ox teams
SOURCE: Coquille River Museum, Bandon Historical Society

Still intent on exploring the Rogue River, nine men were sent out. Those left behind had to be on constant guard as the Indians crowded around the ship and stole everything they could find, even tearing chunks of copper off the ship's sides.

The party exploring up the river found it to be a series of rapids. They would get out of the boat and pull it up the rapids while wading knee deep in the water. All the while the Indians were stealing from the boats as they pretended to help. Finally the explorers gave up and went back the few miles they had been able to go up the river.

Deciding that the Rogue River was not suitable as a way to reach the gold fields, the *Samuel Roberts* went off to explore the shore line further north.

The Historical Development of Southern Oregon 1825–1952, Guest

⇒ 1848 ⇐	⇒ 1849 ⇐	⇒ 1850 ⇐	⇒ 1850 ⇐
Feb 2 – Treaty with Mexico cedes New Mexico and California to the U.S.	Mar 4 – Zachary Taylor becomes the 12th president.	July 10 – Millard Fillmore succeeds Taylor	Sept – The Donation Land Claim Act goes into effect (DLC) If a man was living in the
Mar – Discovery of gold at Sutter's Mill	Oregon Territory organized by Congress. Joseph Lane governor.	Sept 9 – California enters the union	state before 12/1/1850 he is entitled to 320 acres of land. If married, 640 acres. Men arriving after 12/1/1850 receive 160 acres or if married 320 acres.
May 24 – Wisconsin becomes the 30th state.			

Chapter 3

Early Days

(to 1890)

North–South Road

INDIANS TRADED UP and down the Pacific coast, but inland there is little evidence of trading between California Indians and those in Oregon. Thus there was no heavily traveled trail over the Siskiyous. Peter Ogden was the first white man to find his way over the mountains.

The early Hudson Bay Company men trapped the rivers down as far as the Siskiyous and the Klamath Basin but they didn't see any reason, or practical way, to cross into California. The next man to cross over was Jedediah Smith who came up from California over the Siskiyous and reached what became the Oregon line on June 23, 1828. But he didn't leave a path for others to follow.

In 1837 the Mexican governor granted the Hudson Bay Company a license to trap in California. These trappers were the first to make a definite trail south. A few years later, cattle were driven up from California and this further developed a trail or crude road.

It seems that the first emigrants to use the road south were a group of fifteen travelers who attached themselves to an official exploring party. In 1841 they crossed the boundary mountains. Mrs. Walker was with this group and became the first woman in the Sacramento Valley and the first white woman to reach California over land.

It took gold to create a need for improving the north–south trail. Not only were prospectors and miners rushing south, but now large numbers of mules were packing supplies from the Willamette Valley. As demand grew, so did the road, until it was improved enough for wagons to be brought over the mountains.

With more permanent settlers, the stages began running north and south. They required better year around roads. Finally the automobile reached the west coast and necessitated better and wider roads.

Covered wagon, Grave Creek
PHOTO: Carol Barrett

Through all this, the route over the Siskiyou Mountains varied very little and can still be followed on old Route 99 and Interstate 5.

The South Road: Its Development and Significance, Nichols

Isolation – 1847

THE EARLIEST SETTLERS felt a great aloneness and a great loneliness. Everyone who came west left friends and family behind. The families at home worried, and those who left must have often felt a longing for home and familiar faces. The many who settled on rural land might not even see any other people for weeks on end. Thomas Smith, a pioneer, speaks about it like this:

"Previous to the time I started for Oregon, I had never been away from home one week at a time. I left home on the ninth day of April 1847, and never heard a word from home until some time in June 1850, (three years later) and then the letter I received was eighteen months old. My father heard of a man who was coming to this coast and rode 25 miles to get him to bring a letter to us. He brought it to California and by some means it got to Oregon City and my brother heard of it and sent for it, and after he read it gave it to a man that was going to the mines, and he brought it from Eugene to Winchester, Douglas County and charged me a dollar for so doing."

Everyone was enduring the same isolation. Looking back, Thomas Smith said, "I consider it one of the greatest privations a pioneer had to encounter."

Ashland Tidings (Excerpts Vol 8) February 17, 1896

Phoenix, Oregon – 1851

WHEN SAM COLVER came to the Rogue Valley there were only 26 settlers in Southern Oregon. He and his wife, Huldah, took out a donation land claim in what is now Phoenix, Oregon in 1851. For the first two years they lived in a small log cabin. Colver envisioned building a large house that would act as a center for community activity. What he built was known as the block house and was the local refuge during the Indian uprisings.

There were many unmarried men in the area and women were at a premium. Kate Clayton, who was hired to cook for the men working at the nearby mill, was the only unmarried girl. At twenty she had the reputation of being a perpetual talker. She would carry on an animated conversation with half a dozen men at the same time. The term "gas" or "gassy" was then slang for talkative. One evening the subject of the town name came up and the idea of naming it Gassville, in honor of Kate, was suggested. Since that was determined to sound too insignificant, it was changed to Gassburg. And Gassburg it was called for 20 years. It wasn't until the post office was established that the more dignified name of Phoenix was decided on. Even so the natives continued to use the name Gassburg for many years.

Southern Oregon, O'Harra; *State of Jefferson*, Bradford
Reminiscences of Pioneer Days, Stearns

Louis Remme's Great Ride – 1855

IN 1855, LOUIS REMME drove a herd of cattle to Sacramento and sold them for $12,500. He deposited his money with the banking firm of Adams and Company. While he was eating his breakfast, he read in the newspaper that the parent banking company had failed.

Remme rushed to the Adams and Co. bank but already the doors were closed with people lined up hoping to get their money back. Then Remme had an inspired thought. There were no trains and no telegraph. Maybe the Adams and Co. bank in Portland hadn't heard of the closure. Portland was 700 miles away.

Remme ran and got aboard a steamer headed 42 miles up river. Here he got a horse and began his ride to Portland. Occasionally, along the way, he stopped for a fresh horse. He went through Yreka, then Jacksonville, across the Rogue River and on to Eugene.

1852	1853	1854	1857
Napoleon reigns until 1870	Mar 4 – Franklin Pierce becomes the 14th president	June – Oregon California line is surveyed	Mar 4 – James Buchanan becomes 15th president
Feb – Gold is discovered in Jacksonville at Rich Gulch	Rogue Indian war begins and continues to 1856		

Remme made it to the Portland branch of the Adams and Co. bank just a few minutes before the steamer *Columbia* docked with the news of the bank closure. He and one other man were the only two to get their money. He had come 700 miles in five and a half days with only ten hours sleep.

Siskiyou Pioneer, 1977

Pioneer Clothing

THE EARLIEST PIONEERS didn't waste a single thing.

The problem of clothing was serious. The few items brought over the trail from the east were well worn by the time people had used them for the seven or eight months crossing. Serviceable jackets were made from tents and the canvas that had covered the wagons during the trip. They might be lined with a patchwork of woolen scrap material to give it extra warmth.

Buckskin was used for men's clothing and shoes, the main problem being that when buckskin got wet it stretched, doubling in size. When it dried out again the leather had to be reworked to make it pliable.

A blanket with a hole cut in the middle acted as a coat. This was usually homespun. Old sweaters and socks were unraveled and reknit. Old clothes were taken apart, washed and remade. Scraps were always kept for quilts or patches.

Old metal spoons or other tableware were melted down to make buttons. A mold would be carved in soapstone and the molten metal poured into it.

Gradually fabrics were brought into the larger towns and a seamstress could make good money. It was some time before ready made clothing was available. Even so, many of the thrifty practices were still used.

Oregon Oddities, WPA

U. S. Army Fort Umpqua – 1856

THE UNITED STATES Army built Fort Umpqua on the north spit, adjacent to Umpqua City, Oregon. This is not to be confused with the old Fort Umpqua the Hudson Bay Company built.

Fort Umpqua was established on July 28, 1856 and took the place of old Fort Orford. Many of the Fort Orford buildings were torn down and the lumber moved by ship to the new site to be reconstructed. The new fort housed 79 enlisted men and five officers.

1858	1859	1860	1861
May 11 – Minnesota becomes the 32nd state	Feb 14 – Oregon becomes the 33rd state	Dec 20 – South Carolina secedes	Jan 29 – Kansas becomes the 34th state
	Aug 29 – Siskiyou Mountain Toll Road is opened		Mar 4 – Abraham Lincoln becomes the 16th president

The fort had a two story block house, two laundry buildings, a bakery, mess, guardhouse, powder magazine, hospital and barn in addition to the men's quarters. The officers were allowed to have their wives with them so their quarters were quite elegant by comparison. They had lath and plaster walls and a fireplace inside, while outside, a large veranda overlooked the Umpqua River. This didn't compensate the men for the isolation of the fort. The women were dubbed unpleasant gossips and the men took to cards and drink. Gold mining had dwindled and commerce was irregular so there was little to do. The only activity was rounding up Indians who had strayed from their reservations. Pretty as the scenery was, the climate was monotonous and dreary. Meteorological reports found it to be the wettest post in the country with 73 inches of rain in 1858.

Life was so boring at Fort Umpqua that desertion became a problem. With the tension building up to the Civil War, most of the troops were sent elsewhere. By May 1861 only one officer and 14 men held the fort.

Fort Umpqua was ordered closed June 27, 1862.

Land of the Umpqua, Beckham

Pack train
SOURCE: Fort Jones Museum

Fording the Stream

FORDING STREAMS WAS dangerous. Here is W.A. Latta's story.

"We didn't know that the river was up till we got there. It was at this river that I came near losing my life. We had traded rails to a man on Deep Creek for a big male ox.... I kept the ox tied to a tree with a cable chain. But one morning I went out to feed and found him gone.... So I went to the house and told mother not to wait breakfast for me for the ox had left dragging twenty feet of cable chain.

"I followed his trail, through woods and briar thickets to the ford on the river. The river was high but he had swum it, so I stripped off my duds and I tied them in a bundle and fastened them on my back so I could swim over and get him.

"I got on his back to ride and planned to take him back the same route he had come. The water was too swift. I had my boots on and if it had not been for that cable chain around his head and over my shoulders, I could not have stuck on him, for when he started down stream with the current, his nose was all you could see. He stood nearly straight up and down and I was now in the water up to my neck. The best I could do...was to hold tight to the ox. We drifted with the current until we reached the ferry embankment. I got out with the ferry man's help. We saved the bull but I tell you that broke me of ever riding an ox in the river. They try to reach bottom with their hind feet."

Letter written by Latta

Divorce – 1858

WHEN NANCY JUDSON wanted a divorce from her husband, it took an act of the legislature of the Territorial Government. It was November 1858. Nancy's petition reads in part:

"I humbly beg of the legislator of Oregon to grant me a bill of divorcement for I cannot live with Mr. Judson. He misuses me in every shape he is capable to doing. He has knocked me down and scolded me and demeaned me in every shape and lied (to) me as bad as any one could lie on another and does not provide for me nor the family as he ought to do, but has squandered all that father has given me and has squandered everything we have in the world and has mortgaged my land and his and it is all gone and he is not able to support me nor the children.... I have not lived with Mr. Judson since the first of last December 1857 from that time to this I have had to support myself as best I could.... I have three children, one little girl ten years old...one boy seven years old...and the youngest a little boy.

"Now if it will please you honorable body to give me a bill and give me the children I will ever pray.

"I ever remain your humble friends."

Nancy Judson

Curry County *Echoes*

Rock Point – 1859

ROCK POINT IS a town on the Rogue River, which has come and gone. Here the river flows from east to west through a dirt bed. When it comes to Rock Point there is an abrupt change in the flow due to huge rocks on both sides of the river. Once past the point it changes back to a dirt bed. It is easy to see why the location became a geographical landmark in the early fur trading days.

In November 1859, John B. White opened the post office at Rock Point and is considered the town father. It was an important stage stop and later a station for the train between Portland and San Francisco. In the 1800s when gold was being mined nearby, it was at its height and held a store, hotel, livery stable, blacksmith shop, saloon, school house and telegraph office. It boasted a permanent population of 200 people.

The closing of the Rock Point Post Office in 1912 signaled the end of the town. Gradually the buildings were abandoned and Gold Hill became the focus for development.

Oregon Geographic Names, McArthur; *Rogue Valley Communities, Selected Writings*

Joseph Lane – 1860

JOSEPH LANE WAS the first Territorial Governor of Oregon. He became a hero as an Indian fighter in the Rogue Indian War and when Oregon became a state he was one of our first two senators to Washington. One would think he was an ideal leader but to many he became a threat.

Lane had always been loudly pro-slavery. This was a stand that appealed to many, especially in Southern Oregon. He was also an ambitious man and had his eye on the presidency of the United States.

The Democratic Party of 1859 was split on its position towards slavery. Delegates to the national convention were hotly contested. To be pro-slavery was to be pro-Lane. In the final outcome Lane was only able to control the Oregon delegates from Lane, Douglas and Jackson Counties. They were instructed to go to the national convention seeking the consideration of Lane for the office of either president or vice-president. On June 18, 1860 two sets of candidates were selected by the Democrats. Breckenridge was nominated for president and Lane for vice-president as candidates on the pro-slavery Democratic ticket. Stephen Douglas ran as president and Herschel Johnson as vice president for the Baltimore faction of the Democratic party.

On election day 1860, the Breckenridge–Lane ticket was a close second to Abraham Lincoln. The defeat ended the memorable and often spectacular career of Joseph Lane.

A General History of Oregon Prior to 1861, Carey

Camp Lincoln – 1860s

BECAUSE OF THE influx of miners and the ill feeling with the Indians, Camp Lincoln came into being. On the extreme northern end of Elk Valley, it was next to the turnpike which led over the mountains of Southern Oregon. The camp was abandoned in the winter of 1869–1870.

One of the most memorable dispatches from Camp Lincoln was sent to San Francisco by way of Jacksonville. It read:

"At 2 pm yesterday the steamer *Brother Jonathan* struck a sunken rock and sunk in less than an hour with all on board except sixteen persons who escaped in a small boat . . . the only survivors of the ill-fated ship. No trace of the vessel is left. I was out last night on the beach with fourteen men . . . shall keep a party out on the beach. General Wright, family and staff are supposed to be lost. Full particulars by mail."

Thos. Buckley
Capt. 6th Infantry C.V. Commanding

Pioneers of Elk Valley, McBeth

Civil War – 1861

OREGON SEEMED FAR away from the eastern struggle over slavery but many settlers had come west to escape just this problem.

The opening gun of the Civil War was fired at Ft. Sumter in April 12, 1861. It took 18 days for the news to be brought by steamer to the west coast.

A proclamation by President Lincoln called for 75,000 men. Troops were rapidly withdrawn from the west to fight back east. Less than 700 remained in Oregon, charged with controlling the Indians.

When Lincoln's order came, Gov. Whiteaker was Oregon's Territorial governor. He argued that the south could never be conquered and that Oregon's geographical situation exempted it from the demand for troops. However, troops were needed to keep the Indians away from the sprawling settlements.

A campsite was selected in the woods about one mile south of Gassburg (Phoenix), Oregon, on the banks of Coleman Creek. Log barracks were erected in the fall of 1861. Stables, officer's quarters and a storehouse were added. As fast as the volunteers were recruited, they began work clearing ground for a drill field.

While these, and other western troops, never fought in the Civil War, they were part of the Union Army and maintained the peace with the Indians.

General History of Oregon Prior to 1861, Carey

Camp Lincoln
SOURCE: Del Norte County Historical Society

Lt. Col. Maury – 1861

THE CIVIL WAR began in October 1861. Troops stationed in Oregon were gradually withdrawn. On October 23, 1861 the War Department appointed five men to recruit a cavalry. Among these men was Rueben F. Maury of the Bear Creek Valley, Jackson County. He was given the rank of Lt. Colonel and the task of recruiting in the Jacksonville area. It was a thankless task.

The terms offered the recruits were not attractive. There was no incentive for service on the home front. Patriotism for the northern cause was not strong and the pay was minimal. Every man had to furnish his own horse. He would receive $31 per month. At the end of his service he would also be awarded 160 acres of land and a $100 bounty. For men who lusted after gold, this seemed unacceptable. It was spring before the ranks were filled. These men were stationed at Camp Baker near Phoenix and were referred to as "Baker's Guards."

A.J. Walling
General History of Oregon to 1861, Carey

Desertion From Ft. Crook – 1862

BEFORE AND DURING the Civil War, forts were scattered throughout our area to protect the white settlers from the Indians who still fought to hold their lands. Such a fort was Fort Crook in Shasta County, California.

Life at the fort was dull and tiresome. Many deserted. One such desertion was described in the Shasta *Courier* of October 4, 1862.

"A few days ago a sergeant was sent as escort to the mail carrier to Red Bluff. At Cow Creek he told the mail carrier that he had left his pistol at a house some distance back on the road. (He) returned, promising to overtake the mail carrier shortly. He has not been seen since."

This soldier was just one of many. At that time half of the soldiers had deserted Fort Crook. The company of a hundred was down to fifty men.

During the Civil War, 78 percent of the men serving in the Union Army were from fifteen to eighteen years old. Ages ranged from ten years old to the oldest, who was forty-four. Perhaps homesickness can be added to boredom as an explanation for the large number of desertions at Fort Crook and other isolated posts.

Joe Mazzini's Excerpts.

Homestead Act – 1862

ABRAHAM LINCOLN SIGNED the Homestead Act on May 20, 1862

The Donation Land Act of 1850, that had brought so many men west, offered a married man 320 acres of land. When it was no longer in effect, people resorted to 'squatting' on land to establish their claim. This was perfectly legal. Congress had passed "Squatter's Rights" laws allowing people to live on public land. Eventually, to acquire ownership, a small fee was required.

Once the entire present day United States was surveyed, a more formalized means of parceling out land was possible. The Homestead Act said that any person who was a head of a family or who was twenty-one and a citizen, was entitled to a quarter section of unappropriated public land after January 1, 1863.

There had been much opposition to this bill. Representatives from established states feared that their states would be depopulated as residents fled west for free land. Others feared that speculators and monopolies would get control of large sections. Those who got the biggest benefit, however, were the makers of farm machinery. Now that people held large sections of land, mechanized equipment was profitable. New plows were manufactured that plowed deeper and wider. The McCormick reaper was designed, a twine binder and threshing machines soon followed. Barbed wire was invented and became a key industry.

One million, six hundred thousand people filed homestead claims on over 270 million acres.

The Homestead Law, Department of the Interior, BLM

O'Shaw homestead. Note gunports in cabin wall.
SOURCE: Larry McLane

Fort Klamath Supplies – 1863

FORT KLAMATH WAS established on September 5, 1863.

At the time the fort was to be set up, the towns of Jacksonville and Ashland were competing with each other to be the largest, most influential town in Southern Oregon. Jacksonville's influence was stronger and the site of Fort Klamath was selected to make Jacksonville the source of supplies for the fort. It was a poor location. Furthermore, it required a road to be built across the Cascade mountains. Rather than survey the best route, Col. Drew had his men build the road following a network of Indian trails. The distance was 95 miles and the road was only open July, August, September and October. It was completely blocked by snow the other months of the year. This poorly selected route was replaced two years later by a second road.

1861	1863	1865	1867
Apr 12 – Bombardment of Ft. Sumter and beginning of the Civil War	Jan 1 – Emancipation Proclamation	Apr 9 – Lee surrenders	Mar 1 – Nebraska becomes the 37th state
	Fort Klamath is established	Apr 14 – Lincoln is assassinated, Andrew Johnson becomes 17th Pres.	
	1864, Oct 31 – Nevada becomes the 36th state	Dec 18 – 13th amendment abolishes slavery	

Mail from Ft. Klamath was delivered and sent twice a month by pony express to and from Hornbrook, California where it met the stage.

With the establishment of Linkville (Klamath Falls) provisioning Fort Klamath began to change. Linkville received its supplies either from Yreka or across the mountains to the Bear Creek Valley and into Jacksonville, a route that roughly follows Rt. 140 today. This route was usually open the year around.

As Linkville grew, the demand for supplies both for the fort and for the town grew. The route to Yreka became increasingly important. Here there were fewer mountains to cross and snow was less of a problem. Yreka was supplied by the railroad making everything much cheaper.

Klamath *Echoes*, 1968

Treason – 1865

IN APRIL 1865, Ridgely Greathouse was indicted for "wickedly and traitorously" planning to wage war against the United States. One of the 22 Californians to be named, the news shocked his fellow citizens in Yreka. The Civil War was going on and Greathouse, an ex-Kentuckian, was a strong southern sympathizer. One of the other indicted men had approached Jefferson Davis, the president of the confederacy, saying that he and his friends would outfit a pirate ship in California. The ship would patrol the Mexican coast and capture a Pacific mail line steamer carrying gold to Washington. Not only would the confederacy have the gold but another ship to add to their fleet which, in turn, would sail the entire Pacific sinking trading and whaling vessels wherever they could.

Jefferson Davis approved the plan. A third man was taken into the conspiracy, whose job it was to recruit twenty fighting men. Meanwhile, Greathouse and his friend bought a vessel, stocked it with provisions, plus the needed gunpowder, rifles, cutlasses and two twelve pound shot and shell cannons.

Ready to set sail, the navigator failed to show up. At dawn the U.S. Sloop-of-war *Cyane*, arrived and took over the pirate ship. The navigator had reported the scheme when he was first recruited.

Greathouse was tried and received a sentence of ten years and $10,000 but he was soon released under the General Amnesty Act after he swore his allegiance to the United States.

Siskiyou County *Centennial Edition*

1869	1876	1877	1881
Mar 4 – Ulysses Grant becomes the 18th president	Aug 1 – Colorado becomes the 38th state	Mar 4 – Rutherford Hayes becomes the 19th president	Mar 4 – James Garfield becomes the 20th president
			July 2 – Garfield is shot
			Sept 20 Chester Arthur becomes the 21st president

End of the Civil War – 1865

NORTHERN CALIFORNIANS BEGAN celebrating the anticipated end of the Civil War early in April 1865. When the news was flashed to Yreka, telling of Lee's surrender at Appomattox, April 9, 1865, it was a Sunday. The news was announced from the pulpits. There was a parade the next day and one hundred guns were fired in Yreka's plaza.

On April 14, less than a week later, President Lincoln met with Speaker Colfax, who was leaving Washington on a trip to the West Coast. He told him,

> "Mr. Colfax, I want you to take a message for me to the miners when you visit. Tell the miners for me, that I shall promote their interests to the utmost of my ability, because their prosperity is the prosperity of the nation. . . . we shall prove, in a very few years, that we are indeed the treasury of the world."

This was the last President Lincoln ever spoke about the West Coast. At 10:20 that night he was shot.

Saddlebags in the Siskiyous, Jones

Strange Funeral

MR. F.J. KUNTZ WAS the official undertaker at Fort Jones, California. He had begun as a wheelwright but branched out into the undertaking business. In his day, anyone could assume the job, with or without training. Felix Kuntz, his son, went to college, learned the profession and took over from his father.

At the time of our story, Mr. Kuntz, senior, was elderly and the son was away on vacation. Colonel Benton, a resident of the community, died. The elderly Mr. Kuntz was asked to conduct the funeral. Not feeling up to preparing the body he delegated the work to two men who obviously had little or no experience.

At the funeral, the friends and family of Colonel Benton marched up the aisle to pay their last respects to the body. The first person in line, peered into the casket and exclaimed, "He's not there." Hearing this, the wife fainted and the mourners were unsure what to do. It turned out that the untrained men had placed the body in the coffin in reverse so that all that was visible were Colonel Benton's covered feet.

The congregation was asked to leave for a short time while the body was reversed. This done, the ceremony continued.

Siskiyou Pioneer, 1960

1885	1886	1889	1889
Mar 4 – Grover Cleveland becomes the 22nd president	Sept 14 – Geronimo captured. The last important Indian War.	Mar 4 – Benjamin Harrison becomes the 23rd president Nov 2 – North and South Dakota become the 39th and 40th states	Nov 11 – Washington becomes the 42nd state

Civil War soldiers' graves in the Jacksonville cemetery
PHOTO: Carol Barrett

The Deckers

IN 1894, TWO BOYS climbed into a small cave about a mile south of Yreka, California. The cave was not empty. In it were two skeletons, one a child and one an adult.

Now our story goes back twenty-nine years earlier when George and Margaret Decker arrived in Yreka. They had two children and a third was born the next spring. The family lived in the hotel while George hired out as a ranch hand. He went to work for a Mr. Goodrich and stayed at the ranch during the week. The separation from his wife caused problems and the couple split up, each taking a child and sending the third to the wife's sister. Margaret was embarrassed by the separation so George promised to get her out of town quietly and off to her brother, Ben Mitchell.

Meanwhile Mr. Goodrich, George's boss, died; leaving a wife with the ranch and George to manage it. At the end of a year the two married.

⇢ 1890 ⇠	⇢ 1893 ⇠	⇢ 1896 ⇠	⇢ 1898 ⇠
July 3 – Idaho becomes the 43rd state	Cleveland begins his second term	Jan 4 – Utah becomes the 45th state	Apr 25 – Spanish American War. Ends December 10.
July 10 – Wyoming becomes the 44th state	⇢ 1894 ⇠	⇢ 1897 ⇠	
	July 4 – Republic of Hawaii is established	Mar 4 – William McKinley becomes the 25th president	

The ranch prospered and when the second Mrs. Decker died, George became the sole owner of a beautiful ranch. He was a respected member of the community. That is, until the two skeletons were found in the cave.

Decker was arrested. The case caused a sensation. The defense lawyer went in search of Ben Mitchell, Margaret Decker's brother, with whom she was supposed to be living. On May 17, 1894 the lawyer announced he had found Mitchell and Mitchell would arrive in town on the stage coach that day. The crowd pressed close as a white haired man stepped out of the coach and spoke to them, saying he wanted to introduce them to his sister, Margaret Decker. As the crowd cheered, Margaret appeared waving to friends she hadn't seen for 29 years.

George Decker was released. But who were the two skeletons in the cave?

Siskiyou Pioneer, 1993

Borrowed Horse

THE LANGE BROTHERS owned one of the fastest horses in Siskiyou County. One day a friend of theirs asked if he could borrow the horse as he had to make a quick trip to Yreka. The day after his "trip" the sheriff arrived at the Langes' cabin. It seems the stage had been held up near Mill Creek and the driver, who was with the sheriff, recognized Langes' horse.

There was a gun hanging on the cabin wall. The sheriff asked the driver to identify it as the one in the holdup but the driver denied it, saying the bandit had a much larger gun. The brothers then took the two men down to the river and showed them their profitable mining operation. They claimed that they were well off and had no need to hold up a stage.

Even now, the Langes were not suspicious of the friend. They told the sheriff they had loaned their horse to someone and that he was in Yreka. As it turned out, three men were caught and charged with the stage robbery. The Langes' friend was one of the three. He confessed that he had wanted a fast horse so that he could ride to town so quickly people would think he couldn't have been at the scene of the holdup.

The brothers got their horse back, but it is thought that the gold dust taken from the stage is still buried somewhere near the head of McKinney Creek.

Siskiyou Pioneer, 1963

꧁꧂

CHAPTER 4

EARLY TRANSPORTATION

Callahan – 1852

MATHIAS CALLAHAN WAS moving his family from Trinidad to Yreka, California when they reached a swollen branch of the Scott River. In crossing, Mrs. Callahan's horse lost its footing and she floated down the river until her dress caught in the branches of an overhanging tree. She was pulled to safety but the strain brought on the premature birth of a son.

Both mother and baby were too ill to continue the trip. They stayed at the ranch of a Frenchman who had taken them in. They liked the spot so much they bought the ranch for two mules and some supplies.

This was the winter of 1852 and gold seekers were passing their door regularly, stopping to ask for supplies and lodging. Callahan opened a store. Next he built a large log cabin as a hotel. Others settled down around them and soon the town of Callahan was born.

Siskiyou Pioneer, 1964

Cole Station – 1855

COLE STATION WAS a stage stop that straddled the California–Oregon border.

In 1855, two brothers acquired land claims high in the Siskiyous. Rufus Cole built his home just north of the present town of Hilt, California and it became the stage stop on the toll road between Redding and Roseburg.

The stage between the two cities took an average of 54 hours. This covered the distance still needed to join the north–south railroad. The stages carried passengers between the two rail heads. The toll road was used until 1887 when the railroad was completed and stage service was discontinued.

Charles Darby home – Griffin Creek Road, Jacksonville
SOURCE: Ruth Minear Alborn

Cole station remained. The ranch was sold by the Coles and was used for grazing horses and cattle. At one time, prize Morgan horses were bred there with the Cole station used as a bunk house. It still stands today.

Southern Oregon Historical Society *Sentinel,* Sept/Oct 1991

Oregon-California Stage Company – 1860

EARLY STAGES WITH mail to Southern Oregon and Northern California were an erratic semi-monthly delivery, until the Oregon–California Stage Co. was awarded a contract for daily mail between Sacramento and Portland.

The Concord coaches that were installed used four or six-horse teams depending on the incline over which they must pull. The coaches were painted a light yellow or gold with olive green trim. Stenciled on the sides they announced, "Oregon and California Stage Co." and "U.S. Mail–Wells Fargo and Company." A canvas rack at the rear carried the baggage but the driver carried the Wells Fargo money box. The Concord was considered comfortable at the time but the hard seats were stuffed with straw and inadequate canvas curtains were unable to keep out the rain or dust.

On September 15, 1860 the first stage left Portland. At the same time, three coaches left Sacramento with passengers and mail. During the dry months of the year the trip could be made in as little as seven days.

The Oregon and Californian Stage Co. kept about 6,000 horses. Thirty-five drivers were employed to drive twenty-eight coaches. They were expected to go at a rate of eight miles per hour with ten minutes allotted at each stop to pick up and deliver along the way. The driver was changed every 45 miles.

When November came, with its continual rain, the handsome Concord coaches had to be replaced by more substantial coaches and the schedule was lengthened.

History of Jackson County, Tucker; *Umpqua Valley Oregon,* Minter
History of the Rogue River Valley, Pioneer Period, Gilmore

Stage Ride – 1863

NELLIE MEACHAM'S FATHER, A.B. Meacham, built a stage stop and brought his family to live there.

When Nellie was older, she looked back on those stage coach days.

"For real excitement in travel, the stage coach of old days perhaps was more thrilling than motoring is today, for roads at that time meant one-way going with turnouts at quite remote distances; and when the snow around the summit of mountains was at a level of six feet or more, the body of the stage (was) perched on a couple of great shaky bob sleds. With hot bricks at our feet, and soft, fine, well-lined buffalo robes for warmth, the freezing air making breath frosty as it escaped, we couldn't but wish we were all safely at home and in nice warm beds."

Getting up the steep roads was slow.

"Even with eight fine, husky horses, a stop was made every few rods to let the heavy-breathing, sweating animals rest."

Papa Was A.B. Meacham, thesis of Lornel Jan Morton

Carrville Hotel – 1861

JUST NORTH OF Trinity Center, California, James E. Carr bought property in 1861. Since Carr was the manager of the mule express trains of the California and Oregon Stage Road, it is natural that the home he and his wife built would become one of the most popular hostelries along the road. While Carr became involved in several mines, the family kept the hotel in operation. In fact, the family ran it until the 1940s.

In April 1917 fire completely destroyed the hotel. It was rebuilt, designed as much as possible like the original building. It was a two and a half story structure with a two story veranda across the front. In addition to the hotel there was a post office, mercantile store, freight depot, blacksmith shop and saloon.

After the restoration, the buildings were run as a summer resort and pack station. A frequent visitor was President Herbert Hoover. Hoover had been a mining engineer on the North Fork of the Trinity River in his younger days and knew the area well.

Trinity County Historical Sites, Trinity County Historical Society

Billboards – 1865

A TRAVELER GOING from Portland to San Francisco by stage in October 1865, wrote with interest about the boards nailed to trees and placed so they were visible to the passing stages. One he noted read:

> "Whoever needs a good pair of pants, and does not want to be swindled by unethical merchants, should make a point of seeing Messrs. Duesenberg, Moses and Alexander in Portland. Parisian elegance at ridiculously low prices our specialty."

Quite a mouthful for a billboard, but stages and horses averaged about six miles an hour. Not only was there time to read such an ad but boredom would welcome even this diversion.

Huge letters on a fence advertised, "Red Jacket Bitters, elixir against death!"

Madame Proserpina, a fortune teller in San Francisco, offered to provide written testimonials to prospective customers.

The most common sign, in big white letters, suggested, "Unk Weed Remedy for fevers."

This particular product seemed to pop up on every fence, large tree, boulder, and on pigsties and houses. Some were varied to read, "Buy it! Buy it! Unk Weed Remedy! Oregon Rheumatic Cure."

Oregon East, Oregon West, Trautmann

The Same Driver

FRED LOCKLEY'S *Voices of the Oregon Territory* tells the story of a stage driver who had once been a miner. This man had suffered a terrible mining accident in Virginia City, in which he lost an eye, lost all his teeth and was badly scarred. To add insult to his considerable injuries, the medicine he had taken made his hair fall out. When he came out of the hospital he bought a wig, some false teeth and a glass eye, and started a new job driving stage.

According to Lockley's source, some Indians once stopped the one-eyed driver's stage and deliberated whether they should kill him. The driver, understanding their language (and his predicament), took off his wig and handed it to one of the Indians. The driver's bald head astonished the Indians.

The driver then took out both sets of his false teeth and handed these over to the Indians' leader. As if that wasn't enough, the driver then took out his glass eye and handed it to the Indian—who was by now terrified. He and his companions ran off, leaving behind the wig and false teeth.

Collecting the teeth and wig, the stage driver continued on his journey.

Reprinted in the *Oregon Journal*

Jones House Stage Stop on the Oregon–California road
SOURCE: Kerbyville Museum

Robber's Roost

ONE OF THE NOTORIOUS stage coach routes was the one over Topsy Grade. The grade was a long precarious climb from the Klamath River to the crest 1,000 feet above. There were several stops along the way for fresh teams of horses. No passengers were allowed to ride up top with the driver for fear the lurching stage would throw them off. The greatest fear came as the stage passed "Robber's Roost." It was the ideal location for a single bandit to hold up a passing stage.

The "Roost" was nothing more than a large boulder high enough to hide a man and six feet across. It stood right next to the road. One incident occurred as a stage, bound for Klamath Falls, pulled up the grade. A bandit stepped out, gun in hand, his face covered by a bandanna. He demanded everyone to "throw 'er down and be quick about it!" The passengers obeyed. The outlaw rode away with his loot and tossed an object back toward the stage. The object proved to be a piece of bark, whittled into the shape of a pistol and used in the hold-up.

Pages From the Past, Drew

"One Eyed Charlie" Parkhurst

ONE OF THE MORE noted stage drivers coming north from Sacramento was "One Eyed Charlie" Parkhurst.

"One Eyed Charlie" died in 1879 after thirty years of driving stage. He had warded off at least one holdup attempt and had a reputation as a heavy drinker who was always seen with a wad of tobacco in his cheek.

When Charlie died it was discovered that "he" was a "she." For those thirty years Charlotte Parkhurst had successfully disguised her identity. As a result, she also holds the distinction of being the first woman to vote in the United States. This she did in 1868 in the disguise of a man. In retrospect, the stage coach era seems romantic. However, travel was slow, dusty or muddy, jolting and either too hot or too cold. For a woman to have driven for so many years belies the term "weaker sex."

The Mythical State of Jefferson, Sutton

Last Stage to Roseburg – 1882

WITH THE COMING of the Oregon and California Railroad, stage coaches no longer carried the U.S. mail. With the loss of the mail routes and many passengers, north-south coaches disappeared. August 12, 1882 was the last pickup in Roseburg, Oregon. With the town band playing and a large group of townspeople cheering, the stage driver, Tom Burnett, picked up the last sack of mail, shook the reins of his six horse team, and dashed out of town. Thus ended a colorful era.

Stages going north and south were an uphill, downhill affair. As one stage passenger tells it:

"We reached the Calapooya Mountains . . . the driver bade us to walk in pouring rain, to spare the horses. . . . We staggered through puddles and in gushing rain, across the mountains."

It was routine for travelers to get out and walk when the going got tough. To walk twenty miles on a hundred mile trip was not unusual. Women were usually exempt from this.

In places the black soil was so sticky it packed itself between the spokes of the wheels. Every few hundred paces it was necessary to stop. The driver would order a passenger out to take his turn cleaning out the mud.

Umpqua Trapper, 1975, Vol XI #2

Ruggles Brothers' Holdup

JOHN BOYCE WAS driving the stage from Shasta, California to Redding on May 14, 1892. Just before Middle Creek, two masked men came out of the brush and demanded that Boyce throw down the box. "The box" was for valuables and was always kept up with the driver. Just as Boyce threw down the box, shots rang out and he was hit in both legs. A passenger was killed, another wounded and both robbers were wounded, one seriously.

Despite his wounds, the driver was able to take the stage a mile into town before he collapsed. The box he had thrown out contained little but there had been over $3,000 in a safe inside the coach.

The robbers were the Ruggles brothers. Charles, the more seriously wounded, was found hiding in the woods. His brother, John, was caught six weeks later and

Cole station
SOURCE: Southern Oregon Historical Society

the two were jailed in Redding. Without waiting for the benefit of law, a band of masked citizens raided the jail, broke open the safe holding the keys to the cells and escorted the two prisoners out of jail to a gallows tree near the railroad yard.

No one was tried or even accused of the double hanging.

Shasta County *Centennial Edition*

꧁✤꧂

CHAPTER 5

FROM TRAILS TO ROADS

Early Roads – 1847

IT IS HARD TO VISUALIZE this country without any roads. Building them was a number one priority. In December 1847 a law was passed giving judges control over the care and superintendence of the roads within their own counties. These judges were appointed by the territorial government and, in many counties, were the most important government officials.

The 1847 law required each male resident between the ages of 21 and 50 to work two days every year to build and maintain public roads. He was required to appear at 8 a.m. with any tools the superintendent directed. Work was still being done with a pick and shovel. In 1850 the work time was raised to three days a year. Any male could pay the superintendent $2 a day if he didn't want to work. Over and above this, a tax for roads was levied at a rate not to exceed 10¢ per $100 of the appraised value of property.

The next improvement was the use of plows to loosen the dirt which was then smoothed by a log drag. Financing the building and maintenance of roads was partly solved by authorizing an individual or company to do the job. They, in turn, could be repaid by charging a toll for use of their road. Such a road was the Siskiyou Mountain toll road, later known as the Dollarhide toll road.

The first paved road in Southern Oregon was a section of Route 99 from Central Point to Phoenix.

History of the Rogue River Valley, Pioneer Period, Gilmore; *History of Jackson County*, Tucker; *The Mythical State of Jefferson*, Sutton; *Josephine County Historical Highlights I*, Hill; Southern Oregon Historical Society *Sentinel* Newsletter, March 4, 1980

Evan's Ferry – Spring 1851

DURING HIGH WATER, early travelers swam across the Rogue River holding onto the tail of their horse. The site of one of these crossing points was first known as Tailholt. We know it now as Rogue River, Oregon.

Road to Montague from the north
SOURCE: Paul and Leah Reichman

As pack trains began transporting goods from the Willamette Valley to the gold fields of California they traveled on the trail that was started by the Indians, later used by the fur traders and still later by the Applegate Trail. Because crossing the Rogue River was a problem, the first settlers in Southern Oregon were men who provided ferry service.

The earliest ferries started in the spring of 1851. One of these was Perkins' ferry, established by Joel Perkins, who built the first house in Jackson County. The ferry was later known as Long's ferry and Vannby's ferry. Long's barge was controlled by ropes and a rudder by which the swift current caused the ferry to be pulled to the opposite bank. A loaded wagon was charged $1.50 to cross. A passenger paid twelve and a half cents.

Another ferry was the Evans ferry at the mouth of Evans Creek. Davis Evans, known as "Coyote" Evans, built two cabins about where I-5 now crosses the Rogue River. His ferry consisted of three hewn logs thirty inches in diameter with the ends rounded up. These were covered top and bottom with two inch planks that were caulked with pitch. A cable fastened at one end to an oak at the mouth of the creek then stretched across to a gravel bar which was built up with rocks to anchor the other end. A double pulley and winch were used to pull the boat back and forth.

When a covered bridge was built in 1868, the old ferry was abandoned.

The Historical Development of Southern Oregon, Grant;
History of the Rogue River Valley, Gilmore; *The Mythical State of Jefferson*, Sutton

Jacksonville/Crescent City Wagon Road – 1853

IN FEBRUARY OF 1853 the schooner *Pomona* arrived at what was to be Crescent City. Men came ashore and surveyed the area, dividing it into lots. Within a year, the town was a substantial size.

Pack trains began carrying goods to the mines in the Illinois Valley and the Rogue River Valley. It represented a great savings in time and money bringing supplies to the valley miners. Even on these undeveloped trails, mules could carry two hundred pounds. Owners were charging ten to twelve cents per pound to transport goods. A round trip took eight or ten days to cover the 110 miles. At the height of operations, about 3,000 mules were used in rotation.

In Jacksonville, a 100 pound sack of flour sold for $33 but it is said the buyer rarely got his 100 pounds. While being transported, rain wet the sacks and the flour inside. This would harden up into stiff dough, which would soon mold, leaving only the center fit to use.

Highway 199 deviates only slightly from the original Jacksonville/Crescent City road.

History of the Rogue River Valley, Pioneer Period, Gilmore; Klamath *Echoes*, 1973
Reminiscences of Pioneer Days, Thompson

Mule Train – 1850s

WHILE MULES WERE the easiest pack animals to use, packing a train of mules was still very hard work. Every pack mule needed the following:

Two blankets
A swinging rope
A lariat, or rope with a hook
Two gunny sacks
A cover for each pack it was to carry

The total cost for this equipment was about $75 per animal. The mule itself cost about $200.

When a pack train made camp at night, each mule was unloaded and the load placed on the ground beside him with the pack saddle in front of it. Any sores, from the rubbing of the pack, had to be attended to before the animal was let out to graze. In the morning the bell mare was led to the head of the line and each mule lined up in front of his load and reloaded. The bell mare led off, usually ridden by a boy. The mules would follow the bell.

While mules were important, it was the equipment that took the most time and effort to maintain.

History of the Rogue River Valley, Pioneer Period, Gilmore

Crescent City–Grants Pass stage. Passengers are posed in front of the largest redwood along the road.
SOURCE: Larry McLane

Rogue River Trail – 1855

THE ROGUE RIVER TRAIL begins at Graves Creek, Oregon and goes to Illahe. For most of the river's length, it is impossible to travel in the river valley. Instead, the trail goes along the mountain ridges. There is evidence that this route was used long ago by the Indians to reach preferred fishing locations.

During the Rogue Indian wars, soldiers used the trail. George Morey and his wife, Edna, found a marked soldier's grave dated 1856. This and other dates were chopped or cut into the old trees along the route. Part of the trail is on BLM land that has since been logged over and lost.

Along the trail, place names remain that call up a picture of early times. You cross Whiskey Creek, Booze Creek, Rum Creek and two little creeks the locals know as Gin Creek and Wine Creek. It is thought that these were named by a prospector named Cy Whiteneck. It is said that every time he ordered supplies, 10% was bacon and beans and 90% was whiskey. Horse Sign Butte, Jack Ass Creek and Mule tell other stories.

Battle Bar got its name during the Rogue Indian War. On October 9, 1855, Indians started down the north side of the Rogue River attacking the white settlers as they went. They wintered on the bar and the following April, soldiers engaged them in one of the principal battles of the conflict.

George Morey, Gold Beach

Oregon Coast Roads – 1850s

OREGON'S UNIQUE STRIP of coastal dunes is 38 miles long. It stretches from Siuslaw River to Coos Bay.

The Indians that we refer to as coastal Indians, lived largely along the lower river banks. The forests were dense and made routes difficult with only narrow foot paths. When a group wanted to trade or raid another village, they would make use of the beaches as the quickest, easiest way to travel.

When whites came to the coast they also used the beaches. This was the only place a wagon could be drawn or a horse ridden. In the 1850s many stage lines operated along the shore. The stages were nothing more than open wagons built with wide tires. The trip was considered jarring and monotonous. Later auto-stages were an improvement only in that they were faster. Riding them added the possibility of bogging down in areas of soft sand.

In 1914, Vern Gorst, an innovator in aviation, mounted an airplane engine and propeller on a Hupmobile chassis and added pontoons to create an amphibious automobile. Probably a first, but the coming of the railroad in 1916 brought the end to beach travel.

Guide to Oregon South Coast History, Doughit

Beach Travel

ONE OF THE smooth roads for travel along the beach was the route between Coos Bay and Winchester Bay. To call service "regular" would be an error as the time of departure and arrival depended on the tides. Leaving Coos Bay might be anywhere from 1 a.m. to 10 p.m.

Halfway along the beach, the stage came to Ten Mile Creek. Even crossing at low tide, the creek came up to the coach's axles. This was not the only way the beach could be dangerous.

On December 9, 1907 the stage left North Bend. On board were young and old men, women, and even an 18 month old baby. The driver was proceeding toward Ten Mile Creek when suddenly a large wave came rushing in and washed over the coach. A log, carried in with the wave, smashed into the front wheel and the coach tipped over in the cold water. The horse became frightened, broke loose and ran up the beach with the driver still hanging on to the reins. As the wave receded the undertow threatened to carry the coach out to sea but two men were able to jump out, right the stage and pull it to higher ground before a second wave hit. Shakily, everyone watched as the carriage and their baggage were washed away. When the driver returned with the horses, the women mounted and the travelers resumed their trip up the beach. An hour and a half later, they arrived at Jarvis Landing.

The Coos Bay Region, Doughit

Beach travel
SOURCE: Curry County Historical Society

Siskiyou Mountain Wagon Company – 1858

WITH THE FORMATION of Jackson County, one of the first actions of the commissioners was to press for the improvement of roads. The government had no means of financing road improvements so it had to be done by private means. The builder of the road was repaid by the tolls that he could collect.

The Territorial Legislature passed an act forming the 'Siskiyou Mountain Wagon Company'. They were to construct and maintain a road over the Siskiyou Mountains. Lindsay Applegate and several of his grown sons worked on the road and after its completion, Applegate bought the franchise.

The toll road was completed in August 1859 and open for business. By now Oregon had become a state and the state established the toll rates. A horse and rider went through for 25¢. A buggy was $1.25. A wagon and two teams paid $3.50. A drove of hogs was $3. Freight wagons were either pulled by six or eight yoke of oxen or by six span of horses. They were able to travel up to 50 miles in a day over level sections of road. Long trains of 50 to 80 pack mules were often used but they could make only 18 to 20 miles in a day. They were preferred in bad weather as they were sure footed and stood up under constant travel, whereas horses had to be rotated and double teamed if the terrain was steep.

Keeping the road in condition took a lot of labor. There were constant mud slides, washouts and winter snow.

The Applegate family operated the toll road for nine years. The final owner was Henry Clay Dollarhide, who ran the road for 40 years before selling out to the county, which turned it into a public road.

Southern Oregon Historical Society *Sentinel*, Sept/Oct 1991;
Prehistory and History of the Jackson-Klamath Planning Unit

Shasta-Scott Valley Turnpike – 1860s

THE NAME "TURNPIKE" is a pretty fancy word to use for a dirt road only wide enough for one carriage, but in the 1850s a turnpike meant any privately built road for which the owner could charge a toll. Such a road was the Shasta–Scott Valley Turnpike. In fact, it may have been the first such road in Northern California. It went over Fort Jones Mountain. The toll gate was located beside the hitching rack in front of Forest House near Yreka.

The second gate was between Robber's Rock and the Fort Jones summit. "Yank" Johnson was the toll gate keeper here and he lived in a cabin by the road. He added to his income by carving briar pipes. A contemporary account says, "He keeps constantly on hand good liquors, wines, cigars, pies, spruce beer and cool water."

In 1864 money was raised to pay the owners $3,000 and make the Shasta-Scott Valley Turnpike a free road.

Siskiyou *Pioneer*, 1965

Military Road – 1873

LOCAL REPRESENTATIVES IN Washington found that if they called a road a "military road" they were more likely to get Congress to finance it.

The early roads that connected the coastal harbors to the upland valleys could legitimately be considered "for military purposes" as supplies needed to be brought to the various valley forts. There was never enough money to build a really good road or even to survey properly the best route. One of these roads was between the Umpqua Valley and the coast. It was essential in its time. This road followed a rough trail made earlier by a Coos Bay pioneer. It twisted and wound its way through the Coast Range. From the first, the road carried stages and hauled the U.S. mail.

In 1873, when the Umpqua Valley–Coast road opened, it took 24 hours to make the trip one way and cost a passenger $5. Only six passengers could fit into the early coaches. Five stops were made to change drivers. Forty-two horses were required as it took up to eight to pull the coach over the steeper inclines. In the dry season the horses churned up a cloud of dust that swept back into the coach. In wet weather the surface was rutted and muddy.

Today the route is little changed as it goes from Coos Bay to Roseburg.

In Search of Western Oregon, Friedman

First Cross Country Auto Trip – 1903

COL. H. NELSON JACKSON was a restless man. He had just returned to San Francisco from Alaska, where he had been prospecting. On a whim he bet a man $50 that he could drive across the United States in ninety days.

In 1903 cities like Boston wouldn't even allow automobiles inside the city limits and South Dakota banned them from the entire state. Undeterred, Jackson bought a two cylinder, 20 horsepower Winton. It was a chain driven car with the steering wheel on the righthand side.

Sewall Crocker, an experienced chauffeur and mechanic, joined Jackson in the transcontinental venture and the two men took off from San Francisco May 23, 1903 at 20 miles per hour. The plan was to follow the wagon roads when possible, trails and creek beds when necessary, and go cross-country, improvising when all else failed. They carried a 20 gallon emergency gasoline tank, a rifle, pistols and canvas clothing.

On June 2 they approached Lakeview, Oregon. The town had been warned to expect a car going through at ninety miles an hour. Instead, the Winton limped in asking for a blacksmith shop. They had already broken a spring. Many people had never seen an automobile so the whole town came out and staged a celebration. The men left behind a punctured tire with a discarded inner tube of real rubber. It was cut in one-inch wide strips and sold to the boys for sling shots.

At one celebration in Idaho, the men acquired Bud, a bull terrier who went the rest of the way with them. The dog would sit in the seat beside the two men wearing goggles just like they did.

The block and tackle proved Jackson's most useful tool. One day they resorted to it 17 times to hoist them out of mud holes. Another time they went 16 hours without seeing a human being.

Chicago was the first stop where the men slept under a roof. From there on east the going was easier. They reached Fifth Avenue, New York on Sunday, July 16, 1903. The trip had taken 63½ days, far short of the 90 days Jackson had allowed for.

Schminck Museum *Scrapbooks* #4, #5, #12, Lakeview, as told by Carl Pendleton

First Car in Klamath Falls

THE FIRST CAR IN Klamath Falls was a Pope–Tribune. Harry Peltz, Sr. purchased the car in Portland and had it shipped as far as Ager, California. Mrs. Peltz described the road up Topsy Grade as definitely not for automobile use. In many places they had to fill in the deep ruts with rocks so the car would not get hung up in the center.

Once in Klamath Falls, the only way gas could be bought was through Baldwin Hardware. It came in five gallon cans. Tires had to be ordered from San Francisco or Portland. One year the car was unused all winter because a part didn't come before the winter snows.

When spring came, Harry Peltz decided to try a trip to Bly, sixty miles away. It took a whole day and resulted in a broken spring, but at Bly he was a sensation. No one had seen an automobile before and the whole town turned out.

Klamath River Ferry, 1920s
SOURCE: Paul and Leah Reichman

Poor Harry ran out of gas on the way back to Klamath Falls. On his return
he said he could see no possibility of there ever being a passable road to Bly.

Klamath *Herald News*, August 5, 1962

Redwood Marathon of 1927

ONCE THE REDWOOD Highway was completed, the towns along the way envisioned it becoming a lucrative tourist route. The plan wasn't working out. What
they needed was a publicity stunt to advertise the road. A foot race was decided
on. It was to go from the city hall in San Francisco, to the city hall in Grants
Pass. The winner would win a bucket of gold valued at $5,000.

One of the contestants was Jim McNeil. For the race, he went by the name of
"Great White Deer." He was number eight. Great White Deer had been athletic,
but for the past five years he had driven a mail route. He was very out of condition. His training began in the fall of 1926. He weighed 236 pounds. By spring
he was down to 218 pounds. When he weighed in for the race, on the twelfth of
June, he was 198 pounds.

We would like to tell you that Great White Deer won the Redwood Marathon
and the $5,000 but he didn't. Red Robin came in first. Nevertheless, it was a
memorable event for Great White Deer. He had his shoes resoled three times.
He was knocked down by a car and he had his picture taken with Myrna Loy. It
took him eight days, two hours and two minutes to run 482 miles.

Siskiyou *Pioneer*, 1969

CHAPTER 6

GOLD RUSH

Pre-rush

THE SPANISH, WHO HAD sought gold from the time of Columbus, found gold in California but ignored it.

Indians had been digging in the placers for years but only in a small way. They didn't value gold in the same way white men did. When the Mexicans came to California, they gathered the Indians around the Jesuit missions, demanding that they attend school and work for them. Jesuits knew about the nearby gold and considered it a distraction. They wanted the Indians to learn to tend cattle and farm. It was here they thought the future wealth of the region would be. Neither were they interested in iron or silver mining. Both minerals were abundant in the area.

The Mexicans lost their war with the United States and gave up California.

As soon as the gold rush began, the Indian workers were in demand. Teams of fifty or a hundred would be set to working the river bars. At first they were paid little but as the demand for their services rose, so did their pay. Some even formed their own companies.

The Gold Mines of California, Robinson

Lassen Trail – 1847

LASSEN TRAIL INTO California was described as a "holy terror," the "Death Route" and "Lassen's Horn Route."

Peter Lassen was associated with Captain John Sutter in the development of the Sacramento Valley. He obtained a tract of land and laid out a town. In 1847 he went back east to find people who would come and settle in the town he had laid out.

Lassen brought his emigrants along the usual route west, taking the Applegate Trail until it got to Goose Lake. This is really the beginning of the Lassen Trail.

The trail crossed forty miles of desert between the Humboldt Sink and the Carson River. Good grass was scarce for the livestock and in several places wagons had to be let down canyon walls. In spite of these difficulties the trail was much used during the gold rush of 1849 and then almost abandoned.

A young girl tells about her trip on the Lassen trail:

"Early in the day a cow I had always claimed as mine dropped down and I could not make her get up. I never can forget how bad I felt. I wanted to be brave and not show it. . . . A couple of men came and got her up. I ran along and picked up pieces of grass that other people had dropped until I had a little bunch. I would coax her along until she would not follow along. I kept that up until about three in the afternoon. Father had gone ahead to see if he could find water. He returned and said he had but it was boiling hot. . . . my cow fell down again. Father said if I would leave her he would fetch water and come back for her. When we arrived at the springs we heard a cow bell, and looking back, saw my cow coming as fast as she could walk. It was all they could do to keep her from running into the hot springs."

The Modoc Country, Laird

Earliest Miners – 1848

THE MEN WHO WERE already settled in Oregon and California had a head start when gold was discovered at Sutter's mill. In Portland, Oregon the rumors began in August and were soon confirmed. Quickly a wagon train was made up of 150 men and 50 wagons. They followed the old trappers' trail south to the base of the Siskiyou mountains. From there on only pack animals had traveled. It was necessary to widen the road as they went, but gold fever speeded the work. These were the first wagons to cross the mountains.

The men arrived in the Sacramento Valley on October 31, 1848, giving them a distinct advantage over the easterners. It is estimated that two-thirds of the able male population in Oregon went to California that summer and fall. These early arrivers were largely successful in finding gold. In many cases it was not in large enough supply to make it worthwhile. The temptation to sell out their claims to the newcomer was great.

Many of these men returned to the Willamette Valley to make more money raising produce and transporting food to the influx of miners. Prices skyrocketed in the mining camps, making the hazards of transportation well worthwhile.

110 Years With Josephine, Sutton

California – 1849

IN 1847 THE POPULATION of California was 15,000 non-Indians. By 1850 there were over 90,000, a 600 percent increase in three years.

$1,000 nugget from Stovepipe mine
SOURCE: Larry McLane

By March, 1849 the gold rush was on and 17,000 had already boarded ships for California. The first steamer arrived on February 28, 1849. Appropriately it was named *California*. On board were 365 people. Some were families with small children. All had endured wild storms, threats of scurvy and near starvation.

Meanwhile others were headed overland for the gold fields. The trails were soon lined with wreckage and the discarded items from those going west. A man named James Abbey counted what he saw over a fifteen mile stretch of the trail. There were 362 abandoned wagons, bones of 350 horses, 280 oxen and 120 mules.

These first people to arrive in the gold fields were largely well disciplined solid citizens who formed law abiding groups. It was those who followed who caused the rough and wild reputation of the mining camps.

In the first days of gold mining, a hard working miner averaged about $50 a day in gold.

California, WPA American Guide Series

Miner's Equipment

THE EARLY PROSPECTORS and miners were individualists who often went out into the wilderness with little equipment. But here are the basic items that were suggested.

Two pair of heavy blankets.
A buffalo robe or a blanket lined poncho.

A canvas bag, with
    a suit of strong gray woolen clothes
    a pair of brown jeans
    a change of wool underwear
    wool socks and heavy boots

Added to this was a felt hat, handkerchiefs, buckskin gauntlets and toilet articles.

Also needed was a breech loading rifle or shotgun and a revolver, ammunition, a knife and canteen. Plus a tin box of matches, a compass and field glasses.

In another canvas bag should be a frying pan, coffee pot, tin cup, spoon and fork. Basic foods were bacon, flour, beans, coffee, salt and yeast.

For prospecting the miner would need a pick and prospecting pan made of iron and an iron spoon for melting metals.

Last but most important was a surefooted mule with saddle, straps and ropes to carry all this equipment.

Filing a Gold Claim

WHEN GOLD WAS DISCOVERED, Mexico had just lost its war with the United States and given up California. The United States government had never had to deal with gold mining regulations. In fact, Congress hadn't established any laws for the new territory. It was up to the miners themselves to govern the gold fields. At first, when there were few miners, the men just wandered around searching for gold and mining wherever they wished. As the area filled up, late comers demanded a share. Meetings were called. Rules were adopted to give title to claims and restrict the size of any single man's holdings. One person was usually chosen as a recorder. It was his job to see that the rules were followed and the titles registered.

With this system, the size of a claim varied according to each location, how rich the area was, the number of people who were involved and how hard or costly the ground was to work. The man who first discovered gold at any particular site, got first choice and was usually allowed two claims.

A miner would mark his claim with stakes, a sign, a pile of rocks or a ditch. He would then pay one dollar to file the claim and must work it in order to hold on to the title. Disputes soon erupted as men traded or sold their claims. These were settled by the recorder or at further meetings.

In 1866 the Federal Mining Act was passed. It recognized the validity of local mining rules as long as they didn't conflict with federal or state laws.

Bancroft's Works, XXII History of California, Vol VI; *A History of Placer Gold Mining in Oregon,* Spreen

Weaverville – 1850

WEAVERVILLE WAS ONCE called the Shangri La of California. Early miners found the area in 1850 and swarmed over the land. Their homes were cloth tents or shelters made of hides stretched over four posts that had been driven in the ground.

Chinese miner
SOURCE: Fort Jones Museum

All through the 1850s the town was buzzing with activity and was the county seat at a time when Trinity County included Del Norte, Humboldt and Klamath Counties as well. At first everyone built wherever they pleased. Finally a town was laid out, water brought in from East Weaver Creek and freight mule trains ran to Shasta, Yreka and what is now Uniontown.

In the fall of 1851, Weaverville had its first post office which went into operation when Mr. Weed brought in two letters carried in his hat. In 1853 a hospital and school were built and four brick buildings were underway. Always fearful of fire, these buildings were of brick with a one foot layer of dirt spread between the ceilings and the tin roofs. Iron shutters covered both windows and doors.

1854 brought the first newspaper, the Trinity *Times* and Weaverville was well established and on its way.

Trinity County Historic Sites, Trinity County Historical Society.

Scott Valley – 1850

STEPHEN MEEK, A TRAPPER for the Hudson Bay Company, claimed that he and others found gold on Scott Bar as early as 1836. The finders thought it was gold but didn't realize its value and were much more interested in obtaining beaver.

Scott River is a tributary of the Klamath River and some of the richest gold mining was in this area. It wasn't until the fall of 1850 that John Scott discovered the river which was named for him. He and his men also found gold but there were so many Indians nearby, they didn't stay. The next year many large parties of prospectors came to the area and real mining began.

The largest gold nugget found in Northern California was found at Scotts Bar and weighed 187 ounces. Here is the story as told by the miner who found it.

"I was nearly down to bedrock. Possibly there was a foot or fifteen inches of earth yet to remove.... At the next stroke of my pick it encountered... something which stopped the pick, but which felt slightly yielding as though I had hit a bar of lead.... It seemed incredible that it was gold.... (I) unearthed a wedge-shaped chunk covered with a black slime. Picking it up, I knew by the weight that it must be gold."

The majority of gold found here was very coarse with nuggets valued at about $100 each. The bar brought wealth to many miners.

The Scott River post office opened March 1856. The name was not changed to Scott Bar until 1906.

Siskiyou *Pioneer,* 1978

Gold Bluff – 1851

ABOUT MIDWAY BETWEEN the mouth of the Klamath River and the Trinity River is Gold Bluff. The bluffs are about 300 to 500 feet high. Gold was found in the black sand below the bluffs in 1850, but it wasn't until January 1851 that the gold rush began.

It was thought that storm waves beating against the bluff washed down the gold bearing quartz. One wave would seem to bring the gold to the surface and the next wave would bury it. The constant action with the sand ground the gold fine. It was claimed that one pound of course sand contained ten dollars worth of gold. But how did one get to it? No one could devise a way.

Not only was the gold hard to separate, but the beach was only uncovered part of the year—and then only at low tides. All commercial efforts to mine the gold failed. Finally work was abandoned.

Lower Klamath Country, McBeth

Randolph Gold

THE TOWN OF EMPIRE, which is now part of Coos Bay, was a thriving community when gold was discovered at Whiskey Run. The two French men who made the find tried to keep it quiet, but the news leaked out. A trail was cut through the forest to Randolph, a new gold camp. Soon everyone was headed down this narrow trail to Whiskey Run. Empire was almost deserted.

Randolph became a town of tents and shacks. Every night the saloons were filled with men. During the day they worked, taking gold out of the black sands along the beach by running it through sluice boxes. In the fall of 1853 there were over a thousand men there.

A big storm swept through the area. The sluice boxes were washed away. More importantly, the black sand that held the gold was washed away, or covered up. The miners waited around, thinking another storm would wash the gold bearing sand back on shore. Soon news of other gold strikes reached town and the men drifted away, leaving Randolph deserted.

Life and Legend in the Coos Bay Area, Coover.

Beach Gold – 1852

JUST THE NAME, Whiskey Run, conjures up visions of those early, hard living, mining days. The first claim is said to have produced $8 to $10 worth of gold in each pan. At that time gold was valued at $27.67 per ounce.

The euphoria was short lived. Gold could be found almost anywhere on the beach but only a small area produced enough to be profitable. Waves kept changing the conditions. A claim might be filed for a rich spot only to have a storm appear and rearrange the sands.

Patches of gold can be found all the way from Coos Bay south but the largest deposits are near the mouths of rivers and streams. They also extend inland where, centuries ago, wave action occurred.

Gold Mines of Southwest Oregon, Mayo

Deadwood – 1851

SOME OF THE OLD mining camps had very imaginative names. Others, like Deadwood, were names used over and over again. There are eight Deadwoods listed in the book titled *California Mining Camps* by Erwin Gudde. One was in Siskiyou County, ten miles north of Fort Jones. Gold was discovered there in 1851. From the start it promised to be a thriving town. The first trading post was joined by boarding houses, hotels, saloons, a bakery and blacksmith shop. A rich strike was found just below the camp. The whole area was highly developed by placer mining. Dredging was done also, but only a few underground mines were developed. For awhile it looked like Deadwood would be selected as the county seat but Yreka won the vote.

Fire destroyed most of the town in 1861.

If you look on the map, you won't find any place named Deadwood. All eight are gone.

California Gold Camps, Gudde; Siskiyou *Pioneer*, 1982

Happy Camp – 1851

THE NAME HAPPY CAMP, California has a pleasant sound but Happy Camp hasn't always been happy.

In the late spring of 1851, a group of about thirty assorted prospectors made their way up the Klamath River, working the gravel bars as they progressed. It was hard going and in July, when they found an especially promising spot, at the mouth of Indian Creek, they decided to settle down. Being grateful for this beautiful and likely spot, they named the place "Happy Camp" and the name has remained.

The men were well provisioned and started making ready for the winter. By spring, however, other prospectors, less foresighted, had joined them and many nearly starved before supplies could reach them. The Indians didn't take well to this intrusion into their territory and were very hostile.

In the spring the camp was almost deserted as small companies went out along the river in search of gold. Sometimes as few as six people were left in the town. Nevertheless, Happy Camp was the base of supplies for miles around and the men had a place to return to. It wasn't until 1858 that a post office was established.

California Gold Camps, Gudde

Banking

WITH MINERS COMING to town with sacks of gold, someone was needed to store the gold. The merchants and saloon keepers were the first to fill the need. Express companies transported funds to the larger banks in California for the miners. Finally bankers began to take on the job.

The term "banker" would seem to require some experience but such was not the case. All a banker needed was a safe he could locate in a good solid building. There were no rules or regulations to meet. Gradually people recognized who were the honest and businesslike owners. In Yreka, it was E. Wadsworth who opened the first bank. In Jacksonville it was Cornelius Beekman. Later, these private banks merged with other banks and incorporated.

Siskiyou *Pioneer*, 1969

Lost Soldiers – 1852

THE STORY GOES that a group of soldiers became lost in the mountains and didn't find their way out until they were nearly starved. In fact they were so hungry that finding gold was of secondary importance to them. This may be why a fabulous ledge of gold was not clearly marked.

It seems that in 1852, one Private Martin Manley noticed gold when he threw himself down to drink from a stream. He unearthed several nuggets with the tip of his sword and returned to the others who were less interested in the gold than in finding their way out of the mountains.

When Manley was discharged from the service two years later, he went directly to where he thought he had marked the ledge. Though he tried over a long period of time, he was never able to find its location. Rumors still persist that somewhere south and west of Camas Valley there is a ledge, by a small stream, that holds nuggets of gold.

Oregon Oddities, WPA

Lifting Rock – 1852

CECILVILLE WAS ONCE the most hell raising mining town in Northern California. It isn't even on the map today.

The one thing that remains from Cecilville is the "Salmon River Lifting Rock." This rock was mined out in 1852 and blocked a miner's sluice box. The miner, who was proud of his strength, found he couldn't budge it. Part of the problem was its size but mainly it was because of its rounded shape.

This miner began challenging other nearby miners, betting that they couldn't move the rock. Many tried but no one could. They finally got bars to help roll the rock out of the way. The men ended by rolling the rock near the hitching post in Cecilville and there it stayed for the next 75 years.

The reputation of the rock spread. Men priding themselves on their strength came from up and down the Salmon River to give the rock a try. No one succeeded until 1906. Two miners were both able to raise the rock a few inches off the ground. Again in 1930 it is rumored a Forest Ranger lifted the rock. That lift was never verified.

The Salmon River Lifting Rock remained in place with grass almost hiding it as the buildings of Cecilville fell or were torn down. Finally the Siskiyou County Historical Society rescued the rock and put it on display in their museum. If you go to see it, don't expect a thing of beauty. It looks just like any other rock.

Siskiyou *Pioneer*, 1983

Sailors' Diggings – 1852

SAILORS' DIGGINGS WAS the name given to a wide area, the center of which was Waldo, Oregon.

During the Southern Oregon gold excitement in 1852, five sailors deserted their ship at Crescent City and started for the mines. They bought supplies and followed an Indian trail heading for Jacksonville. In a few days they found themselves hopelessly lost. They stopped for the night beside a creek high in the Siskiyous. Two ambitious men began digging and struck gold. It was to be one of the richest mining areas in Oregon. Here the first water rights were obtained and it was the first place hydraulic mining was used in Oregon.

In 1856 Waldo became the seat of government for Josephine County. By then the whole area of Sailors' Diggings may have had a population of 4,000 plus another 200 Chinese, who were not included in population figures.

By 1915 gold had run out and the population of Waldo was down to 100, but the depression of the 1930s brought renewed efforts to extract gold. In July 1937 water was piped to the deserted townsite. The town itself was the only area not yet mined. High pressure hoses cut away at the foundations until the whole town had disappeared down the sluices. The old brick and stone building that had been the center of Waldo remained although the foundation had been cut away. Now only a historical marker shows us its location.

Oregon Oddities, WPA; *In Search of Western Oregon*, Friedman
Sailors' Diggings, Street

Lost and Found Cabin – 1854

IN SAN FRANCISCO the Adams Express Company Bank failed in 1854. It was the result of the bank officers absconding with the bank's assets.

Apparently the looters tried to get away by sea but the sailors on the boat took their money and escaped on shore. Two of these sailors were said to have been seen in Jacksonville. However, they disappeared into the mountains, built a cabin and buried the treasure. After one of the men died, the other took a few thousand dollars and went back east. He kept his secret until he knew he was dying and then told Charles W. Owens.

In 1906, Owens came west to Medford in search of the lost cabin. J. M. Howard was noted for knowing every hill and valley in the area. The two men joined to look for the lost cabin. They searched and searched with no luck. Owens gave up and went to Portland. But not J. M. Howard. He took it as a personal challenge and kept on looking. Owens had minutely described the cabin. It was on the banks of a mountain stream which ran over a series of cascades. In June 1912, Howard came into Jacksonville with the news that he had found the cabin. It was rotting and almost hidden in 50 years growth but otherwise just as described.

Howard was convinced that near the cabin he would find a fortune. All he had to do now was to find Charles Owens.

Medford *Mail Tribune* (Abstracts, Vol 1)

Paradise Flats – 1855

IN THE KLAMATH National Forest, standing all by itself, is the Catholic Church of Paradise Flats.

The town of Bestville had been started in June 1850 by miners from Trinity. Captain Best was one of the members of the group. These early miners took out as much as eight dollars worth of gold for every bucket of dirt.

Father Florian Schwenninger, a Benedictine monk, came from Austria to build a Catholic church in the wilds of northern California and he chose Bestville, at Paradise Flats, as the spot. With him he brought a painting of the crucifixion. The priest supervised the building of the church, doing much himself, including building the altar.

In 1857 the first mass was said from the small church. Nearby gold was playing out and it was decided to move the town to Sawyers Bar. The church remained where it was. Known as the "Miner's Church" it is the oldest Catholic church in northern California.

Siskiyou *Pioneer,* 1982

Big Ditch – 1856

THE EASY GOLD had been taken and many miners had gone on to newer fields. The population of Yreka was shrinking. What they needed was more water.

The Yreka ditch was under construction. Also known as the "Big Ditch," it brought water nearly 100 miles. The ditch was two feet deep, four feet wide at the bottom and six feet wide at the top. Construction had started in 1853. The men working on the ditch had earned $2.50 a day plus board. Some made as much as $3 a day. A good worker could dig 16 feet every day.

When the ditch was completed on March 1, 1856, water was let in but the flow didn't reach Yreka for quite awhile. Leaks appeared and had to be corrected. Animal holes siphoned off water and had to be filled. Debris had collected in the ditch over the two and a half years of construction and had to be cleaned out. Finally the water reached Yreka. Now there was water enough for hydraulic mining and once again Yreka was booming.

Saddle Bags in Siskiyou, Jones

Quartz Mining

IT WASN'T UNTIL all the easy gold had been mined that the miner became interested in quartz mining. Gold bearing quartz had been found earlier but the difficulty of extraction was too great to interest the individual men. What was needed were organized companies.

In Siskiyou County the first quartz mill to be operated with a profit was opened on Indian Creek about 1859. The process involved tunneling into a mountainside until a vein or ledge was located. The ore had to be blasted into small pieces. In the early days, all the drilling was done with a pointed steel tool driven into the rock with a sledge hammer, called a "single jack." One man would hold the drill while the other swung the hammer. One inaccurate swing could shatter a man's hand for life.

A miner who knew explosives could mean success to a venture. Blasting powder was put into the drilled holes. They would be drilled as a series and ignited in sequence. If done properly, the whole face of the tunnel would shatter. Ore cars then took the rock outside where it was sorted. The gold bearing rock was then taken to the stamping mill.

Gold Mining in Siskiyou County 1850–1900, Stumpf

Arrastra

AN ARRASTRA WAS ONE of the simplest ways of grinding gold bearing quartz. It was a method adopted from the Mexicans.

A circular bed was carefully paved with smooth stones. It could be anywhere from eight to twenty feet across with a low wall around it. In the center was a post from which two arms projected. One was long and went over the wall to where a mule could be harnessed to it. The other arm connected with a slab of granite. As the quartz came from the mine, it was broken into small pieces with sledge hammers. These pieces were placed on the stones and slowly ground to dust as the mule circled the arrastra, dragging the slab.

It would take five or more hours to grind the quartz small enough so that no piece was more than one inch in diameter. All the while, water was being added to keep it moist. When the mix was ready, it was the consistency of thick cream. Quicksilver (mercury) was added and more water poured on as the grinding continued. During this time, the mercury combined with the gold and settled to the bottom. A gate was opened, the water flowed out and the gold and mercury were recovered.

This was not the end of the operation. Now the metals were put in a retort which was heated to distill out the mercury, leaving only the pure gold.

Gold Mining in Siskiyou County 1850 to 1900, Stumpf

Orleans Bar – 1856

THE MINERS WERE WORKING peacefully with the Chinese at Orleans Bar until late June, 1856.

The Chinese were not allowed to stake new claims for gold but they could buy a claim already worked. A company of men had done just that in the fall of 1855. The claim was on the North Fork of the Salmon River. For nine months the Chinese worked the bar with only modest results but in June they struck rich pay dirt. Suddenly the white men, who had sold them the claim, took it back. The Chinese sued the men and regained possession. As soon as the judge left the area, the white men again jumped the claim and drove the Chinese away.

A posse of citizens tried to enforce the judge's ruling and got the claim back for the Chinese. In doing so one miner was killed and the others arrested.

No record is found of the trial of these men and the assumption is that they went free. However, the Chinese got their claim back, which was unusual in these early mining days.

History of Del Norte, Bledsoe

Discovery at Gold Hill – 1860

MANY DISCOVERIES OF gold have conflicting stories surrounding who, when and where they were found. This is one.

Mr. X, a man whose name is lost, and James Hayes were hunting stray horses, on January 8, 1860. Mr. X picked up an interesting piece of quartz and put it in his pocket. He didn't linger in the area because he was a wanted man being hunted in Jacksonville. He hurried on to Yreka. There he showed the quartz to his friend George Ish and told him he had found it on a ledge near Jacksonville, Oregon. Ish knew gold when he saw it, so immediately started out in search.

Meantime, James Hayes, who had been with Mr. X while hunting the horses, apparently knew nothing about the gold laden quartz. He was plowing a field when Ish found him. Ish enlisted his help and together they relocated the ledge. The next day they filed claims with several other men.

This ledge on Gold Hill was two feet wide and twenty feet long. The vein went fifteen feet deep and produced over $100,000 in gold. Other claims were found in the area but none were as good as that ledge on Gold Hill.

Rogue Valley Communities, Throne

Gold Hill

THE TOWN OF Gold Hill was laid out in 1884 but it wasn't incorporated until 1895. The coming of the railroad and the building of the depot signaled its importance in the area. At one time they had a huge pavilion where basketball games were played and the County Fairs were held. But Gold Hill essentially remained a gold mining town. Small deposits, and some not so small, kept being found in the area. Many legends persist of these 'good old days'. One such tale is about the Rhoten Brothers.

It seems the Rhoten brothers had struck it rich on their Gold Hill mine and were in Medford giving a party at one of the saloons. At closing time they bought the saloon in order to keep it open all night. The next morning they gave it back to the owner.

Rogue Valley Communities, Throne

Hydraulic mining
SOURCE: Kerbyville Museum

Sam Clary – 1860s

SAM CLARY WAS A stubborn character. He wasn't going to have anyone digging under his mining claim.

Clary had come from New York and gotten the surface mineral rights for a hillside patch. People termed it the Potato Patch because gold came out in chunks when you pulled the grass. Meanwhile, another miner found a quartz vein that led under Clary's claim. Clary would not sell. He was happy just pulling grass and banking a total of $18,000. The claim with the quartz vein sold and resold but no one could get Clary to give up his rights even though he was threatened and beaten up several times.

Sam loved to gamble. He would come into town with his buckskin pouch full of gold. He banked some and kept out about fifty dollars for the nickel slot machines. His eyesight was poor, so he held a miner's candle up by the little window in the slot machine so he could see the colors. He got tired easily, so he hired a man to pull the crank. The saloon customers would congregate to watch Clary play. This generated so much business, the owners encouraged Clary by giving him twenty-five nickels for every dollar.

Back at the gold mine, a man named Hazlett started a tunnel on the other side of the gulch and got to the vein under Clary's claim. He took out about $30,000 in gold when he decided to sell out and go to Alaska and the Klondike strike. Jillson was the new owner and finally Sam Clary agreed to sell his rights to Jillson. The resulting mine produced about $750,000.

Siskiyou *Pioneer*, 1957

Whiskeytown

IT WOULD BE HARD to exaggerate the amount of drinking that went on in the early gold camps. Drinking was the miner's recreation. Places were given names like Drunkards, or Brandy but by far the most popular was Whiskey. There were Whiskey Diggings, Whiskey Flat, Whiskey River and Whiskey Terrace. The one we are interested in is Whiskeytown.

Whiskeytown grew up where Whiskey Creek and Brandy Creek emptied into Clear Creek. It is said that a barrel of whiskey dropped off a mule and burst open, dumping whiskey into the creek. When the town grew, a post office was established and the name changed to Whiskey Creek. Later the name was changed to Blair. Still later, to Stella and later still to Schilling. But everyone knew the place as Whiskeytown. It was a pretty wild town for awhile.

In 1853, one of the barkeepers got tired of the insults of a resident. He pulled out his gun and shot him dead. That was too much, even for Whiskeytown. The onlookers seized the barkeeper and hanged him to the nearest tree.

Bancroft

Democrat

PAT O'HALLORAN WAS a prospector and miner. Like most, he went into town weekends and got drunk. One night, as he started home, it was dark and he fell into a mine shaft about 40 feet deep.

The next morning someone heard Pat calling and went to help. With a bucket and windlass two men began pulling him up. As Pat approached the surface he recognized the preacher as one of his rescuers. The preacher was a leading Republican in the area and Pat O'Halloran was a staunch Democrat. He ordered them to lower him down the shaft again, saying he would wait until they could get enough Democrats to pull him out.

Siskiyou *Pioneer*, 1964

Fred Beaudry – 1870s

THE LIFE OF Fred Beaudry is a rags to riches story. Beaudry came from eastern Canada and made money mining gold and silver in Colorado before coming to Trinity County California in the 1890s. He had started as a blacksmith and often accepted an interest in a mine in exchange for his work. Enough of these mines worked out to make him a very rich man.

When Beaudry came to California he developed the La Grange Mine west of Weaverville. It became a massive project, one of the largest in the world. The story is told that when Beaudry started out he went to the local storekeeper to see if he had any picks and shovels. When asked how many he wanted, Beaudry said, "Five hundred each." He always thought big.

When the La Grange mine was sold, it brought three million dollars.

Along Our History's Trail, Hayden

Rogue River Gold – 1870s

BY THE EARLY 1860s gold had run out in the Jacksonville area and the town was shrinking in size and importance. Many had speculated that there must be gold in the bed of the Rogue River. Thus far it had been too swift and deep to mine, but it was speculated that all that was needed was a diversion dam. David Birdseye decided to take on the task. Birdseye had a good reputation in the community, so when he went around to raise money for the project many were willing to mortgage their homes for a chance at the promised riches.

In spring when the water went down, work began on the dam. With only horses and men it was slow work and as fall neared the end was in sight. Fate took a hand in the form of early fall rains. For days it rained and the waters rose. The dam was washed out.

David Birdseye sold his profitable store and packing business to pay off his debts but he never recovered from the loss nor did he find out if there was gold in the riverbed of the Rogue River.

Interview with Nita Birdseye

China Ditch – 1891

EASY, SURFACE MINING had played out and men left the Southern Oregon gold fields for richer areas. They sold out to men like Gin Lin, a Chinese "boss," who acquired many parcels of land along the Applegate River. He put his crews to work on a ditch starting at the mouth of Yale Creek and running to his diggings four and a half miles away. This area is still known as "China Ditch."

Over 200 laborers worked on the water way. In October 1891, they tunneled the final 400 feet at the Myrtle Creek end. At its most productive time, the resulting mining operation employed several hundred men and shipped more than $85,000 of gold to the mint in less than nine months. Remnants of China Ditch remain today.

The Umpqua Trapper, Fall 1968

Chinese Junk
SOURCE: Del Norte County Historical Society

Gold Dividing Line

THE OLD SOUTHERN PACIFIC Railroad Line coming over the Siskiyous from Redding to Roseburg is roughly the same as the dividing line between the old and the new mountain formations. All the land to the west of the rails belong to the "old" formation. The land to the east has been covered and disturbed by volcanic action.

It is in the old formation that gold is found. Intelligent miners caught on to this fact and began to search along this division. Gold was found as far north as the Umpqua River. The rivers themselves carried particles of gold that had been washed from the gold bearing quartz rock at higher elevations.

Other things were found at this joining of the old and new mountains. Things like fossilized mastodon bones, elephant fossils and fossils of sea life. This proved that there was an ocean shore in this area long before the mountains were formed.

Siskiyou *Pioneer*, 1957

Gold in the Wash

ONE OF THE TRAVELING entertainers who frequented the gold mines, Signor Blitz, was visiting a mining camp in Shasta County, California. He had a large audience for his magic act. With a flair, he removed a handkerchief from his pocket, threw it into the air, caught it and removed a twenty dollar gold coin. He challenged the miners, "Can anyone do that?"

One of those watching him was Old Pete, a miner who had the reputation for never having worn anything but the same mining shirt since he arrived in camp. Pete went up on the platform, removed his shirt and dipped it in a bucket of water. He wrung it out and declared he had produced $37.50 in gold dust and a 15 percent solution of subsoil. When he asked, "Kin you do that?" the magician didn't accept the challenge.

Shasta County *Centennial Edition*

Lost Brother-in-law

BARNEY TILDEN RECEIVED a letter on September 4, 1896 that cleared up a family mystery twenty years old. The letter was from Barney's brother, who was a miner working about ten miles south of Jacksonville. He and two friends came across a skeleton lying in a large rift on a quartz ledge. Only the skull and shoulders were uncovered, so the men began digging to see if they could identify the man. Here is what the miner wrote his brother:

> "I was amazed, yes, stricken with indescribable terror, when I found it impossible for me to avoid realizing that the remains before me were those of your long missing brother-in-law Tom. There is no question of the identity for on the left little finger I discovered the identical amethyst that mother gave him on Christmas Day, 1873.... I found by his side a package of molded papers.... among those were two of your letters and the rest from Mollie.

> "The most fearful thing...was an indelible pencil scrawl on the face of a loose letter, closely resembling Tom's handwriting, reading 'I was murdered by John R___' and then followed by a scrawl which could not be read.... An examination of the skull disclosed that it had been fractured."

Many people, particularly miners, were lost in the woods and never heard from again. At least Tom Barney was found, but his murderer was never discovered.

Ashland *Tidings* (Excerpts Vol 8) September 1896

Persistence

ROBERT CUMMINS AND a friend were prospecting when they picked up a good trace of gold in the Hungry Creek area west of Hilt. They followed the trace up the mountain. It was steep and very hard work but the signs of gold bearing quartz were encouraging. Imagine their disappointment when they reached the top and found a hole in the ground where someone had already found gold.

Cummins was not easily discouraged. He figured that the trace had been good and the hole was not big enough to account for the amount of gold they had found. The two men went to work. When they had dug down to the ledge they began to clear it off and found a lump in it. When they dug it out they tried to break it open but it barely cracked. It was being held together with $1,200 worth of gold.

Backyard Gold – 1926

BILL BRADFIELD WAS seventy and his mother, who kept house for him, was ninety when Bill struck it rich. Mother and son lived in a log cabin near Riddle, Oregon. Bill loved to prospect and was working his Ash Creek claim. His mother complained that he wasn't helping her with the chickens and keeping the elk grass out of the chicken yard.

One day Bill ran into Riddle where his friend owned the meat market. Gasping, he told his friend to cut the wires that were wound around his wrist. Each wire closed the mouth of a dirty canvas sack and each sack held a quart glass jar full of gold flakes and nuggets. Together the men weighed the gold on the meat scale. It weighed twelve and three-quarter pounds.

What Bill had found was a single pocket of gold. There was enough there to keep him digging and panning happily. His only problem was that he had to carry the dirt to the Silver Park springs to get enough water for panning. But he wasn't complaining.

Where did Bill find this rich pocket? In his own back yard, when he finally helped his aged mother dig up the clumps of elk grass.

Pioneer Days in Canyonville, 1969

Galice Gold – 1912

GOLD WAS STILL being discovered as late as 1912. Rumor spread that a vein had been found near Galice, Oregon. The find was on the Victor Mining property not far from town. It was said to be in a very rich vein of decomposed quartz. It was discovered on the surface, appearing about five inches wide but visible for one hundred feet, still on the surface. It was estimated that the ground for four feet on either side of the vein would contain enough gold to be worth working also.

On May 22, 1912 a second shipment of bullion came to town. This shipment contained fifty-five ounces and eleven pennyweight of gold. It had been hand mortared from six pail loads of the decomposed quartz. Each pail held two gallons. Gold brought $18 an ounce at the time, which worked out to be a $1,000 worth of gold from twelve gallons of dirt.

Rocker box preferred by depression miners because it required little water.
SOURCE: Larry McLane

Depression Gold

DURING THE DEPRESSION of the 1930s, interest in small gold mining operations revived. Men who were out of work began looking for gold in areas that had been abandoned as unprofitable. The price of gold had risen to $35 an ounce. A man found he could make a few dollars with only a shovel, a pick and a gold pan.

Sterling Creek, a tributary of Little Applegate Creek, was a popular area. The owners of the Sterling Mine leased out plots. Men and women were assigned frontages of 24 feet and allowed to go away from the creek for an unlimited distance.

In 1942, with the advent of World War II, Congress declared gold mining nonessential.

Gold Mines of Southwest Oregon, Mayo

Bad Luck

PROSPECTORS ARE ETERNAL OPTIMISTS. One prospector was traveling in rugged, wild country in southwestern Oregon. He tried to lead his burro around a mountain side. There was no path and the burro's pack caught on a small oak tree, causing the animal to lose his footing and roll down the steep hillside. He came to rest on a narrow ledge about 100 feet below. The contents of the pack were strewn down the mountain side.

The prospector rescued his burro and tied him to a tree. As he was gathering up the scattered equipment he noticed some of the dry leaves catching fire. It seems his coffee can of matches had broken open and the friction of their falling caused several to ignite. He tried to put out the fire but found it spreading. The burro was cut loose to save himself if possible.

Going out of the woods, the prospector met the Forest Service coming to investigate the smoke. They found the burro. He had again fallen, this time to his death in the gorge of Silver Creek some 1,500 feet below.

It took the Forest Service 24 hours to put out the blaze. Everything the prospector owned had gone up in flames. The firefighters collected $7.50 to tide him over.

When last heard from, the man had made enough money to outfit himself again and head for the mountains.

U.S. Forest Service Radio Script, August 28, 1936

Poem

WILLIAMSBURG WAS A mining town in Josephine County, Oregon. After it was deserted, Sam Simpson wandered through it nostalgically. He sat down on the hillside and wrote the following poem.

> Like a golden pheasant sunning
>> Upon a bushy hill.
>
> October flaunts her plumage
>> Of bronze and amber still.
>
> While an ancient mining village
>> At the foot of the slope awaits.
>
> Like a beggar rudely hustled
>> From fortunes shining gates.
>
> Silence where life was stormy.
>> And sadness where life was gay.
>
> A court of desolation
>> And a kingdom of decay.
>
> The camp once crowned with conquest
>> Now pays the vassal dues.
>
> While all the bannered seasons
>> March o'er the Sisk-i-yous.

Newspaper Article by Fred Lockley.
Southern Oregon Historical Society file

CHAPTER 7

Lost Gold

Benjamin Bonney – 1845

BENJAMIN BONNEY WAS seven when he found gold. He lost it because no one thought it important at the time.

The Bonney family started out in the same wagon train as Samuel Barlow in 1845 but at Fort Hall they were talked into heading for Sutter's holdings in California. Sutter was anxious to get as many American settlers as possible and was offering big inducements.

Benjamin tells this story:

"At the foot of the Sierras we camped by a beautiful, ice-cold, crystal-clear mountain stream. We camped there for three days to rest the teams and let the women wash the clothing and get things fixed up.

". . . we put in three delightful days wading in the stream. It was October and the water was low. . . . On one gravel bar I saw what I thought was wheat, but when I picked them up I found they were heavy and the color of dull yellow wheat. I took one of the pieces . . . into camp with me. Dr. R. Gildea asked me for it. That evening he came to my father and showing him the dull yellow metal . . . said, 'What your boy found today is pure gold.'. . . My father . . . didn't pay much attention to him."

Dr. Gildea got Benjamin to fill an ounce bottle with the gold. At Sutter's Fort Dr. Gildea died. It wasn't until gold was discovered that Benjamin's uncle went back to stake out a claim where the young boy had found the gold. Philosophically, Benjamin remembers, "but it had already been staked out and proved to be a very rich ground."

Across the Plains by Prairie Schooner, Bonney

Dunbar and His Lost Gold – 1856

NEAR MARSHFIELD (Coos Bay), Oregon, about 1856, a man named Dunbar accidentally discovered a boulder of gold-bearing quartz rock. He described the boulder as having been pried out of the side of a mountain. He packed it out on his horse and headed for Fort Orford. Here he shipped the rock to San Francisco where he sold it for $2,700.

Hoping that there might be more gold where the boulder came from, Dunbar and some friends formed a company and went back to search for the ledge. The area was densely wooded with thick undergrowth. Before the men could find the location, Dunbar's health gave out. He returned to San Francisco and died soon afterward.

Sluice box

Many went in search of the gold ledge. While never discovering a spot that exactly filled the description, other claims were filed. It was found that a belt of gold-bearing quartz ran for twenty miles southeast to northwest, roughly parallel to the coast. At the height of mining, there were 100 gold mines along the strip. Presumably one of these must have been where Dunbar first found the gold boulder.

Pioneer History of Coos and Curry County, Dodge

Fort Grant

DURING THE CIVIL WAR, Fort Grant was built to house the new Southern Oregon recruits. It was about a mile south of Phoenix, Oregon on the banks of Coleman Creek. Local prospectors, cattlemen and others used the paymaster as a banker and deposited money with him. The money was made up largely of five, ten and twenty dollar gold pieces as currency was almost unheard of. Periodically the paymaster would take the money into Phoenix and deposit it in the bank.

The paymaster kept this money, along with the government funds, in a large iron kettle which he buried in a hidden spot. One day he suffered a stroke and was unable to talk. He tried to draw a map showing the location of the buried kettle but he died before he could make himself understood. After his death, the earth all around the camp was probed but nothing was found.

Fort Grant was abandoned shortly after the paymaster's death and presumably the treasure is still buried somewhere in that iron kettle.

Oregon Oddities, WPA

Nugget Tom – 1871

"Nugget" Tom had a small gold claim in Curry County. He kept wondering if there was a lode of gold above his claim. But Tom was in his seventies and getting a little lazy. Nevertheless, he finally decided to see what he could find. It was the fall of 1871. He set out, working his way uphill but he felt as though someone was watching him. He kept going and came to a ledge where he hammered off a piece of quartz that was rich in gold.

When Tom didn't return, his friends searched and found him at the foot of a cliff, unconscious but still with his gold quartz. Even when Tom regained consciousness he wouldn't talk. He was convinced someone had pushed him over that cliff.

Twenty years later, two prospectors decided to try again to find Nugget Tom's lost gold ledge. They did find a rich ledge which they worked during the morning. They knocked off for lunch and were starting back to work when one of the men saw this 'Thing' throwing their gear over the side of the hill. They later described it as neither man nor beast. It was big, stood erect and had yellow fuzz over its body. Though they shot at the thing, their bullets had no effect.

Was this an early sighting of 'Big Foot' or just a wild story made up around a camp fire?

Curry County *Echoes*, 1975–1976, Vol II quoting the *Oregonian*, Nov. 9, 1947

Lost Saddle Horn – late 1870s

According to legend, three road agents held up a stage near present day Rogue River, Oregon, in the late 1870s. The three hid out in an old abandoned mining tunnel up Foots Creek. Here they had a quarrel and one man killed the other two. With the loot all to himself, the lone man decided to bury the bulk of the money at the foot of a madrone tree. In order to identify the location, he put an old iron saddle horn in a fork of the tree.

The outlaw went to Idaho hoping the authorities would give up searching for him. Here he killed another man and served most of his life in prison. Finally getting out of jail in the 1930s, at the age of eighty, he returned to Foots Creek to look for his buried treasure. There had been many changes over the years and the old man was not able to locate a madrone tree with a saddle horn in its fork.

Many believe this story and continue to look for the lost gold.

Letter in the Art Taylor file, Southern Oregon Historical Society library.

Lost Cabin Mystery – 1886

One of the legends of the Klamath area is about the Lost Cabin Mine. On August 4, 1886, two men set out to try to find it. The men were Charles Burns, a painter, and Nathan Fubbard, a barber. Fubbard had been a prospector and had searched for the mine for years.

Miner's cabin
SOURCE: Display at the Curry County Museum

The two men never returned to Linkville (Klamath Falls) and it wasn't until almost three years later that their fate was known. A gentleman had been grazing cattle in the Diamond Lake vicinity and came across their camp in a dense wilderness. The two men were found near each other, each clothed and wrapped in a blanket. With them was all the equipment they were known to be carrying with the exception of a Colt revolver, the horses and saddles.

A diary was found in the pocket of one of the men. It was badly weathered but in it was an account of their trip, including the fact that they nearly drowned in the Umpqua River on August 21, 1886. That was the last legible entry but later entries had been made.

There was no suggestion of a struggle. Two rifles stood against a tree and there was ammunition, so it didn't seem likely that the men had starved. The conclusion most people came to was that the men had eaten something poisonous, probably mushrooms.

Ashland *Tidings* (Excerpts, Vol 4)

Red Blanket Mine – 1897

ED SCHIEFFELIN WAS A man with prospecting in his blood. He was not content with striking it rich one time, so he continued to search for a second strike. He found it, but this is another lost mine story.

Ed's father had gold fever and instilled it in all three of his sons. By the time Ed was a young man he had prospected all over Northern California and Oregon, with no great success. Leaving his family, who had settled in the Jacksonville area, he went out on his own. Eventually he struck it rich and founded Tombstone, Arizona.

It wasn't the riches that Schieffelin wanted, although he lived it up for several years. Not content enjoying his wealth, Ed came back to Oregon and began prospecting. In the spring of 1897 he set out for Douglas County. He found a deserted cabin in the hills above Days Creek and moved in, giving his hired man, Charlie Warren, time off to go see his family.

The man who stabled Schieffelin's horses was expecting him to come back for supplies. When he didn't, he informed the sheriff. The two men found Ed, face down, on the floor of his cabin. He had been sitting at the table breaking ore when he died. The last entry in his diary read, "Struck it rich again, by God!" The sheriff wrapped him in a blue blanket and buried him nearby.

When Charlie Warren, the hired man, returned; he told the sheriff that Schieffelin had two blankets, the blue one he was buried in and a red one that he always took out prospecting with him. The conclusion was, that where they found the red blanket, they would find the site of Schieffelin's digging. The ore in the cabin assayed out at $2,000 per ton and was well worth looking for.

Charlie and the sheriff never found the red blanket or the mine and neither have hundreds of other hopeful prospectors.

Southern Oregon Historical Society *Sentinel*, January, 1983

Umpqua Indian Mine – 1896

OCCASIONALLY THE NORTH Umpqua Indians would come to trade using gold nuggets. They also wore them as forms of decoration. This was in the late 1890s, at a time when the tribe was rapidly fading away. One of the last members was a man named Meshe who had a wife named Nance. The two were being continually asked where they got their gold nuggets. Nance admitted that she had been to a mine with her mother when she was a child. She planned to take some white men to the mine but they got her husband, Meshe, drunk and made fun of him. This made Nance angry and she refused to show the men the location.

The only thing the men had been able to learn, was that the mine was "Two horses sweat from Old Man Rock." Another Umpqua woman had described the place as a mine in a "deep dark canyon (where it was) all the same as night." Still another Indian named Pedro, claimed he knew where the mine was and sold some white men a map. Several expeditions have gone in search of the mine but all have failed to find it.

Land of the North Umpqua, Bakken

Old Frenchy Mine – 1863

Two Frenchmen were very secretive about the location of their rich placer mine. It was reported that the mine yielded $50,000 in less than a year. The two traveled back trails, twisting and turning and doubling back in order to hide the route to the mine.

The winter of 1863–1864, they went to Portland and San Francisco and spent all their money. They returned by way of the Klamath Indian Reservation and hired a woman to act as their cook.

A few months later, the Indian woman arrived back at her reservation, saying that the men had abused her. Her brother and friends were able to find the cabin and shoot the two Frenchmen before they could fire back. The brother declared the site "bad medicine," forbidding anyone to return or to take anything back with them. But he was not able to stop the talk.

Attempts were made to get the Indians to guide men to the lost mine. As long as the brother lived, his friends were afraid to break their promise. He died in 1924, outliving all the others.

Many have searched, but none have found what is called the "Old Frenchy Mine."

Lost Mines and Treasures, Hult

Gold in a Lead Pipe 1925

In 1925, two young boys watched their father pour $2,000 worth of gold coins in a lead pipe. It was the family's lifetime savings. Next the father soldered both ends of the pipe shut and went out the door carrying it. He was back within twenty minutes empty handed.

Years passed and the father became an old man and died, never having said where he hid the lead pipe. By this time the value of the $2,000 in gold was worth about $80,000 and goodness knows what it would bring today.

Naturally the two sons hunted for the pipe. They looked in every nook and cranny of the outbuildings. They looked for hollow trees and fence posts but they didn't find the lead pipe.

The story spread and professional treasure hunters brought metal detectors to search for the pipe. So far nothing has been found. Figuring that the father knew ahead of time where he planned to hide the family savings, the radius of a ten minute walk from the front door of the house is a big area.

If you want to try your hand at treasure hunting, all we can tell you is that the farm was eight miles up Cow Creek out of Riddle, Oregon, near Iron Mountain Creek.

Pioneer Days in the South Umpqua Valley, 1976

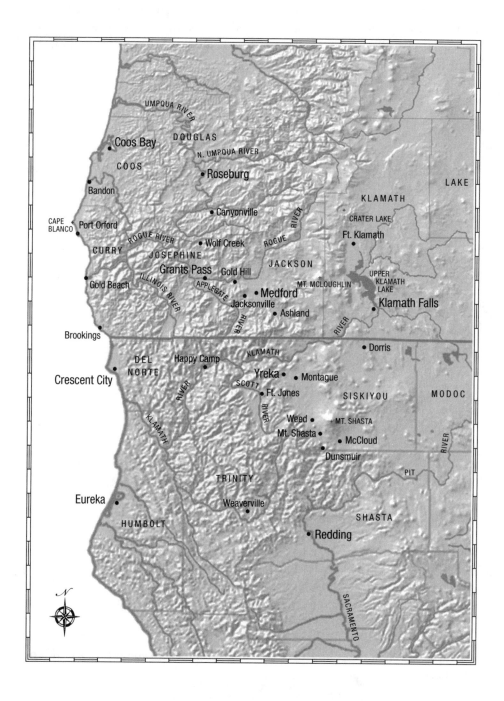

❦

CHAPTER 8

GOVERNMENT

Oregon – 1765

MAJOR ROBERT ROGERS petitioned King George III to explore in search of a northwest passage. He proposed to go from the Great Lakes to the upper Mississippi and on to the river the Indians called "Ouragon." There is no known Indian word called Ouragon, but Rogers' mention of it, in 1765, is the first recorded use of the name.

The first use of the name "Oregon" with the spelling we presently use, came in 1778 in a publication called *Carver's Travels* and referred to Oregon as "the river in the west." In fact, all early references were to the river and only later to the country drained by the river. The explorers Vancouver, Lewis and Clark failed to use the name at all.

The first settlers in Oregon were the missionaries. In 1836 Dr. Marcus Whitman, with his bride and other missionaries, brought the first wagon to Boise, Idaho. In the spring, they brought it as far as Walla Walla, Washington but then they had to remake it into a two wheel cart to go the rest of the way.

When the Hudson Bay Company was trying to make Oregon territory British, Whitman and a companion walked back over the mountains and on to Washington D.C. in an attempt to convince the government that Oregon was worth saving. On his return trip, Whitman guided a train of 875 pioneers to the new land.

Josephine County Historical Highlights I, Hill

California – 1854

IN 1848 THE POPULATION in all of California was only 6,000 non-Indians. A rough census taken in 1852, after gold was discovered, was 269,000, almost all male miners.

Five million dollars in gold was thought to have been taken from the diggings the first year. But was this gold coming from California or Oregon? In the rough mountains the men had no idea where the state line went.

In June 1854, a surveying party went out to decide who could claim the disputed area. It turned out that most of it belonged in Oregon Territory. Places like Sailor's Diggins and Althouse had been sure they were in the state of California only to find they were in Oregon Territory. Up to this time they had felt free to vote in both states while refusing to pay taxes in either.

Old California, White

Curry County – 1855

IN JULY 1853, 12 men settled in the valley of the Chetco river in southern Coos (now Curry) County. The Indian tribe living there consisted of about 350 people, many of whom had never seen a white man. They made no complaint about the settlement. One of the white men, A.F. Miller located at the river mouth and kept a ferry and public house. As the first winter approached most of the Indian men left camp to go up river following the salmon and collecting acorns.

One evening several tough men were visiting at Miller's tavern and decided for no apparent reason, to burn down the Indian camp. In doing so, they also killed three Indians. From then on the fighting between white and Indian was continuous.

Pioneer History of Coos and Curry Counties Oregon, Dodge

Curry County Courthouse hanging. Note gallows in background.
SOURCE: Curry County Historical Society

Josephine County – 1856

JOSEPHINE ROLLINS WAS the daughter of the man who first discovered gold in the area. In her honor he named a nearby creek Josephine Creek. In 1851 Josephine seems to have been the first white woman living in that part of the state. Josephine County split off from Jackson County January 22, 1856. By that time, Josephine Rollins had married and gone on to California but the new county took its name from Josephine Creek.

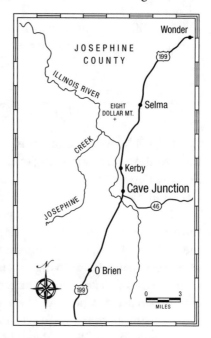

The mining town of Waldo was the first seat of government for Josephine County. Later the legislature moved the county line to include Grants Pass, which then became the county seat. Grants Pass had developed as one of the towns along the transportation route between Jacksonville and Crescent City. Its later growth was largely due to the Southern Pacific Railroad coming through on its route between Portland and Sacramento.

Oregon Geographic Names, McArthur

IN 1865 RESIDENTS petitioned to have a post office established at "Grant," Oregon. The request was turned down with the explanation that the name might be confused with Grant County, Oregon. As a result the name was changed to "Grants Pass."

Still not content with the name of Grants Pass, in 1883 an effort was made to rename the town "Sugar Pine City." This was defeated but another movement in 1893 wanted the name to be "Stanford."

110 Years With Josephine, Sutton

Dorris Bridge

PRESLEY DORRIS RODE down the Pit River Valley in May 1870. He and his friend were looking for grazing land for their cattle and thought they had found the perfect spot. Great fields of tall grass grew everywhere. Dorris located a claim near Pit River and went back to bring his cattle to the new range. There was no way to cross the river so he constructed a crude bridge. It was the only crossing for miles in either direction so others began using it and calling it Dorris Bridge.

Friends and family moved into the area, forming a small settlement which also became known as Dorris Bridge. Travel picked up and there was need for an inn and hotel. Attempts were made to grow vegetables but they were invariably lost to frost. Potatoes did well and cattle thrived.

The Pit Indians, living nearby, were destitute. The new settlers made friends with them and gave them food and clothing. The Indians, in return, helped with haying and were consistently grateful and did not steal from their new friends.

When Modoc County was formed, Dorris Bridge changed its name to Alturas and became the county seat.

The Modoc Country, Laird

Modoc County – 1874

UNTIL 1874 MODOC County was part of Siskiyou County. It is made up of about three million acres sprawling over northeastern California. With its history of fighting between whites and Indians it was known to the immigrants as "The Dark and Bloody Ground" or just "Bloody Ground."

The forming of the county was a great help to the settlers who had had to travel as much as 500 miles round trip to transact county business. Even though they were isolated, the settlers wanted to vote. In the presidential election of 1864 every male over 21 living in Surprise Valley voted. It was necessary to carry the returns to Yreka, a very dangerous trip. No one wanted to go, so the men cut cards to decide who would have to make the trip. C.T. Sharp was the loser and the others thought it a good selection as it was known that Sharp was the only man to vote for the "Black Republican" Abe Lincoln.

One newspaper, in the 1930s dubbed Modoc County, the "County California Forgot."

Annals of Modoc, Brown

Klamath County – 1874

AN ACT OF THE STATE legislature created Klamath County, Oregon on October 17, 1874. It was annexed from Lake County. Linkville (Klamath Falls), virtually the only town in the new county, was named the county seat. In 1892 the name Linkville was changed to Klamath Falls. The only other establishment of any size was the Klamath Indian Agency which had been created in 1866.

The name, Klamath was first used by Peter Skene Ogden, the Hudson Bay trapper and explorer. He spelled the name C-l-a-m-i-n-i-t-t. The origin of the word is not understood but soon after Ogden's time the Indians were also calling the area Klamath. Eventually the Indians themselves were referred to as Klamath Indians. Their original name, Auksni, meant "people of the lakes."

Klamath *Echoes,* 1967; *Oregon Geographic Names,* McArthur

Medford Firsts

THE PLAN FOR MEDFORD was laid out in December 1883. The town had an interesting number of "firsts."

- The first Medford post office consisted of a cigar box kept in the store of J.S. Howard.
- The first dance in Medford was an impromptu all night affair to celebrate the laying of a wood floor in this same Howard's store.
- The first ordinance passed punished disorderly conduct, riots and disturbances.
- The first carriage bridge was built over Bear Creek in 1887 but it washed away and had to be rebuilt after the hard winter of 1889–1890. Until that time only a foot bridge existed and when the water was low enough, the ford was used.
- The first school classes were taught in 1883 and functioned in a one-room school building.
- In 1884 the first circus came to town.
- The first hotel, the Torrey House, stood on the corner of Riverside and Main.
- The first brick building was a one-story, two room building started in 1884. One room became a saloon and the other a public hall for meetings, dances, etc.
- A.S. Davis built the first and only flouring mill in town in 1889.
- The first recorded use of an irrigation ditch was in 1862.
- J.S. Stewart was the first commercial orchardist, his business commencing in 1885. In 1890 he shipped the first carload of fruit to leave the valley.
- The first civic club, the Ladies Aid Society, started in 1884. Nearly all the ladies belonged.
- 1903 marked the first use of electricity.
- Dr. Roland Pryce was the first doctor to open an office, in 1888.
- The first wedding took place on July 31, 1884 between Lewis Doren and Ida Caldwell.
- The Medford Bank, the first bank, opened on January 20, 1899.
- Most important of all, the railroad first came to Medford in 1884.

Founding of Medford, Snedicor; Jackson County Weather Bureau

Shasta Register – 1892

WHEN A MAN REGISTERED to vote in California, he was required to list any identifying characteristics . Here are some of the interesting statistics for 1892:

- Shasta County had 376 men over six feet tall. Frank Cornaz of Burney Valley was the tallest at six feet, five inches. Only one man stood under five feet tall.

- Sixteen men were blind in one eye, while two were completely blind. One man had lost his left leg and two had lost their right leg. Sixteen limped. Only two males had lost an arm.
- Twenty-seven men had tattoos, 15 had moles, 13 had warts, and six had "other facial blemishes."
- Three registered voters were cross eyed. Three more had had their noses smashed.
- Unfortunately, women didn't have the vote. It might be interesting to know their distinguishing characteristics.

Shasta *Courier,* December 17, 1892

Census Machinery – 1889

THE 1890 CENSUS was to utilize the most modern methods. Census counting would make use of the recent development in electricity. The census collector was to call at each home with a printed blank. The answers to questions were to be written in the usual way. These answers were punched into a card by an operator using a machine that looked like a typewriter. The cards were about six and a half inches by three inches and where the hole was punched in the card indicated an answer to one of the questions. As many as 250 answers could be placed on one card. There were more possible answers to census questions but since some were contradictory, their space could be used by the answer to another question. For instance, a person could only be one of the following: Black, Asian, Hispanic or Caucasian.

When punched, the cards were taken, one at a time, and placed on a machine. When the lever was lowered, a series of pins were brought onto the surface of the card. Where a hole was punched, the pin dropped into contact with a mercury cup beneath, thus completing an electrical circuit. This counted the answers. After the counting, another electrical device sorted the cards according to groups or states.

The census machine was really very ingenious but still required a great deal of manual labor.

Ashland *Tidings* Excerpts, Vol 4

Divorce Statistics – 1891

ONE USUALLY THINKS that a hundred years ago, divorce was a rare thing. Such was not the case. At the meeting of the Oregon State Bar Association a summary of all the Oregon county reports showed that for the entire state, in the year 1891:

2,110 marriages occurred
615 divorce suits were instigated
458 divorces were granted
Of the remaining: 9 were denied

33 withdrawn
6 were closed due to the death of one of the partners.

Of the original 615 who filed for divorce:

317 had been married in Oregon
430 suits were filed by the wives
185 suits were filed by the husbands.

The average length of these marriages was nine years and three months.
There were 747 minor children living in the family at the time these suits were filed.

As much as these statistics tell us, they raise many more questions. Was this number in line with the national average? Were there any predominant reasons for the breakup of the marriages? What were the grounds for divorce in Oregon at this time? What ages were the husband and wife? Was this the first marriage for the parties? How many remarried? Who retained the children? If it was the wife, did the husband supply support?

Ashland *Tidings*

Andrew Carnegie Libraries – early 1900s

ANDREW CARNEGIE THOUGHT of himself as a scientific philanthropist. He made many gifts in his lifetime, but his greatest gift was the funding of libraries in small town America.

The Carnegie Library Commission was founded to handle financing these libraries. Any town who wished a grant wrote a request. The Commission acknowledged the request and sent back the criteria for receiving financing. These included the city supplying the site for the building and approving taxes sufficient to cover the cost of books and maintenance of the library. When these rules were met, the commission granted the funds on a basis of $2 per capita. Thus a town with a population of 10,000, and compliance with the other requirements, was awarded $20,000 for a library. Medford was one of those who built a "Carnegie library." Grants Pass declined, however, saying they did not want to raise taxes.

Andrew Carnegie enjoyed being involved with the buildings he endowed. The commission offered plans in the "Carnegie Classical" style to any who wanted to use them. Over the door would be some representation of rays of light and the motto, "Let There Be Light."

When it came to statuary, Carnegie wrote to the commission that he strongly urged that figures be shown draped and not nude. As he put it, "I do hope nothing in a gallery or hall will ever give offense to the simplest man or woman."

Andrew Carnegie

Ashland Carnegie library
SOURCE: Southern Oregon Historical Society, photo no. 12479

Fire Department – 1912

FIRES WERE A COMMON occurrence in early towns where almost all the buildings were made of wood and even the sidewalks were wood boards. Once a fire started the bucket brigades and later volunteer firemen had a hard time keeping it confined. Medford was no exception and it lost many old landmarks to fire.

In August 1886 Medford ordered fire equipment. It consisted of three dozen pails, two good ladders and hooks and 200 feet of manila rope.

On February 21, 1912 the Medford City Council proposed an ordinance providing for a paid fire department. Six men were to be on duty at the fire house. It was argued that this was necessary since the city had purchased an 'auto truck'. After getting the alarm, it was estimated that the new auto truck left the barn and set out for the fire so quickly the volunteers couldn't run fast enough to catch up and climb on board. This had not been a problem with the old horse drawn fire wagon. The Council approved the change.

Two of the horses that had pulled the old pump wagon were named Gold Bug and Danny. When the two horses grew older, they were transferred to the Water Department and given the job of pulling the sprinkler wagon which helped control the dust on the dirt streets. Gold Bug and Danny never forgot their training and when the fire whistle blew they would take off for the fire as fast as they could with the bouncing water wagon. The driver would be left running behind trying to catch up.

Southern Oregon Historical Society *Sentinel,* November 1986; *Founding Medford,* Snedicor
Medford Mail *Tribune,* February 21 , 1912

Abigail Jane Scott Duniway – 1912

IN 1869, WYOMING was the first state in the union to grant women the right to vote. Colorado soon followed with Idaho and Utah adopting suffrage in 1896. It wasn't until 1912 that Oregon joined the bandwagon. Even so, it was eight years before the U.S. Congress moved for national suffrage. On November 30, 1912, Abigail Duniway became the first registered woman voter in Oregon and the first to cast a vote. She had worked for over 40 years to make this dream come true.

In 1871 Abigail had begun the publication of the the *New Northwest*, a weekly journal dedicated to equal suffrage. She helped organize the Oregon Equal Suffrage Association. Through their efforts a bill to amend the state constitution and allow women to vote was brought before the legislature every two years from 1906 until its passage in 1912.

Abigail Scott Duniway was married to a man who supported her independence. She traveled throughout the state and came to Jacksonville in July 1879, lecturing in the area for a week. Jacksonville was not friendly. Audiences threw eggs at her and she was burned in effigy. Almost all the men and a surprisingly large number of women were against her. Sam and Huldah Colver, of Phoenix, were noted as broad minded people and supported her efforts. They took Abigail into their home.

It wasn't until August 20, 1920 that the 19th amendment was passed, giving women in all the states the right to vote.

Southern Oregon Historical Society *Sentinel*, November 1990; *Early Days of Phoenix*, Helms
Ladies Were Not Expected, Morrison

Women's First Vote

TWO DAYS AFTER OREGON women were given the vote, an important city election took place in Grants Pass. A new mayor and city council were to be elected. The state took intense interest. Everyone wondered how many women would register and how they would vote.

During the fight for women's suffrage, one of the arguments used in opposing its passage was that women didn't want the vote. The Grants Pass election decisively proved this wrong. The ladies were there early and late and they were ALL there. They cast fully half of the 1,600 ballots that were recorded.

The administration of Robert Smith as mayor was given a strong endorsement. He was returned to office, having received almost as many votes as his two opponents combined.

Rogue River *Courier*, (Grants Pass) December 2, 1912

City hall and fire station, Grants Pass
SOURCE: Kerbyville Museum

Election Day 1914

IN THE ELECTIONS OF 1914, Oregon women could vote on the state level but not on the national level. Some wanted to take part in the election process in any way they could.

Mrs. Thomas and Ida Grimes were two of the five members of the 1914 election board in Klamath Falls. The day dawned in a holiday mood. Sitting at the voting place one could see old friends, chat and knit. Lunch time was especially festive. The polls closed at noon and again at dinner time as the ladies picked up their ballot boxes and went off to some restaurant to dine. The county paid for these meals. As further compensation for the day's work, workers were allowed to take home the bottle of ink and the steel pens that had been used. After voting closed, the tired women had to count the votes and straighten out any errors that had been made.

Not all people were in favor of Oregon letting women vote. Those who exercised their power heard whispering behind their back. It was said that only coarse or hard women pursued their right to vote at the polls.

Klamath *Herald-News*, November 6, 1960 "Election Board Customs," King

Family Non-support – 1914

OREGON WAS AN EARLY leader in the rights of women. On January 2, 1914, a decision was made to take action in the problem of family non-support. It was announced that with the beginning of work on the Pacific Highway, Route 99, Jackson County authorities would wage a war against husbands who were too lazy to work in order to support their families. Under the stringent Non-support Act a man could be tried and, if convicted, he would be put to work on the new highway and his pay check turned over to his wife.

By this date it was not uncommon for a woman to work outside the home although jobs were generally limited to teaching, domestic work, clerking or nursing. None of these paid as well as men's jobs so the advantages of marrying and being supported by a husband must have been attractive.

Medford Mail *Tribune*, January 3, 1914

State of Jefferson – 1941

NORTHERN CALIFORNIA AND Southern Oregon complained bitterly that their needs, especially for roads, were ignored by their state legislators and the federal government. The result was a drive to establish the "State of Jefferson."

The participants were Siskiyou, Modoc and Del Norte counties in California and Curry County in Oregon. Mayor Gable of Port Orford led the movement. His intent was only to draw attention to the area's problems, but the declaration for a new state soon attracted serious followers as well.

One of the first acts by the group was to barricade Route 99, the main north-south road. Motorists were stopped by huge signs stating that they were entering the State of Jefferson. They were given a copy of the proclamation of independence stating that the area intended to secede on every Thursday until further notice.

The threat of World War II and the need for war materials was front page news in every paper. The State of Jefferson supporters pointed out to the motorists that just west of the roadway lay the greatest copper belt in the west, but that it was inaccessible due to poor roads. Copper was bringing 14¢ a pound so millions of dollars were buried in the ground. Manganese and chrome were found in the area also.

Lassen County joined the group but Siskiyou County kept faith with California. Modoc County thought the secession efforts were getting too serious and pulled out, but Trinity County joined up.

On December 7, 1941 the Japanese bombed Pearl Harbor. The next day an announcement was made that stated, "In view of the national emergency, the acting officers of the provisional territory of Jefferson here and now discontinue any and all activities."

San Francisco *Chronicle* quoted in "Notebook" 917.95, Medford Library

CHAPTER 9

NATIVE AMERICANS

Coos Indians

THE COOS INDIANS made four seasonal trips a year. The first was up the North Fork of the Coos River to catch eels and trout. The second trip was to Ten Mile Creek when the salmon ran. The fourth trip was to Whiskey Run for camas roots, but our story is about the third trip which was to Cape Arago for seafood.

Everyone went on these trips and each person was assigned a job. At Cape Arago, a great hole was dug in the sand and the bottom was lined with a deep layer of smooth rocks until the floor was even. On top of the rocks, a big fire was built using drift wood. It burned day and night heating the rocks. When the rocks were sufficiently hot, the fire was raked out of the hole. Bundles of wet seaweed were placed in the hole.

While this was going on, others had been cleaning and washing shell fish. These were put on top of the seaweed. Another layer of wet seaweed was put on top of the shellfish and sand piled high over that. Skins were laid over the sand to keep the steam in. Periodically water was added around the edges.

After a sufficient time, the pit was opened and the meat taken out of the shells. The bits of seafood were strung on thin sticks and hung over a fire to dry and smoke. The resulting dried seafood was stored all winter in baskets hanging in the Indians' quarters.

A Century of Coos and Curry County, Peterson and Powers

Umpqua Indians

IN 1780 THE UMPQUA and three other tribes in the area numbered 3,200 people. This was before the smallpox epidemic. Their numbers were decimated by the disease. The standard Umpqua cure for almost any ailment was the sweat bath. For this they would build either a skin covered pit or dig a deep pit in the ground and cover it. Heated rocks were placed on the floor and cold water poured over

Kitty Gensow, Yurok woman
SOURCE: Del Norte County Historical Society

them. A patient would be placed in such a hut and the opening closed, leaving the patient to sweat. The treatment was finished off with a dip in the icy water of the Umpqua River. This may have had a placebo effect but was not a good treatment for smallpox. Possibly because of it, many died who might not otherwise.

By the time Oregon became a territory the number of Umpqua Indians was estimated to be only 200. They occupied an area around Winchester and Diamond Lake in Oregon. The government sent troops to clear out the tribe in 1856. They were forced to march to a reservation at Grande Ronde.

Land of the North Umpqua, Bakken

Umpqua Thanksgiving

SAMUEL FLOWERS WAS honored with an invitation to an Umpqua Indian Thanksgiving Ceremony. Here is how he reported it:

"All the men sat in a large circle on the grass with a tall pine tree in the middle. Everyone remained with their heads bowed for some time until the head man rose, looked at the sky and began a prayer. 'Oh, bright sun, Oh noble sun, father of all living!' He continued praising the sun for rising daily, for giving light, for melting the snow and sending rain. He thanked the sun for making the leaves grow and the fruit mature and for sending the salmon up the river.

"Then the chief spoke to the earth, 'Oh, earth, mother of all living!' He praised the earth for feeding the grass which in turn fed the elk and the deer and for the wild fruits and berries.

"Next the head man called out to the wild fowl, the deer, bear and elk and the fish. He told them to thank the earth and the sun. He commanded the trees and rocks to pray to the sun. Then he exhorted his people to honor the sun and earth as the mother and father of all living things.

"Lastly, the chief asked the earth and sun to bring good to his people and keep them from harm.

"When this was done, the chief drew an arrow and slashed his bare chest bringing blood. This was to show his sincerity and devotion."

Oregon Historical Quarterly, December 1960

Modoc Tribe

THE MODOC INDIANS were thought to have once been a much larger and more powerful tribe. There seems to be reason to believe that in the 1830s there was a tremendous storm that wiped out over half of their number. The Modocs themselves believed this and had the following legend to explain their decrease in numbers.

The Modoc women had gathered "kamas" and "woca" roots for the winter. Because the tribes around them raided and stole their food, it was the custom to hide their stores in the sagebrush and rocks. So far the other tribes had never found their stored food.

Snow fell only lightly in this region but one winter there was a terrible storm which continued until there was seven feet of snow on the ground. The Modocs could not go out to their caches, nor could they identify them in the deep snow. The snow continued. The strongest men were sent out to find the hidden food but they returned weak and empty handed.

The Indians ate anything they could. Deer and antelope skins were cooked and eaten. Their pet dogs were killed and eaten. When all was gone the people began to die and those left were too weak to hunt. Only one village of Indians was saved. Near Tule Lake a large band of antelope came down from the hills. They,

Unidentified Native American, Shasta County
SOURCE: Fort Jones Museum

too, were searching for food. They were caught in the floating ice on the lake and the Indians were able to get the drowned animals and distribute them among the tribe.

When spring came it was found that at least half the Modoc population had died.

The Modoc Country, Laird; *Copper Paladin*, Palmberg

Takelma Indians

By 1850, WHEN the pioneers began to settle the Rogue River Valley, the Takelma Indians numbered only about 500 people. Perhaps because fish were plentiful, the Takelma hadn't developed their hunting skills to a high degree. Their bows were only accurate up to fifty yards. This was a problem when it became necessary to defend themselves against the whites.

Here are some Takelma beliefs.

- To stop thunder one should pinch a dog's tail until he barks.
- When a man hiccups, he has lied.
- Take the seeds of the wild peony, chew them to a pulp and put the pulp in your horses mouth just before he is going to be in a race. He will always win.
- Make a tea of Jimson weed. Wash the horse with the tea. This will keep him from straying.

- Desert rue and citrus plant were used to dye willow for making baskets. Do not carry one of these baskets on horseback. The horse will swell.
- Myths were never told to children in the summertime as it would make the days grow shorter.
- The screech of owls forecasts good.
- Hummingbirds were messengers of evil medicine.
- Prayers were offered to the Snow God to drive elk to the hunters.
- If a black striped snake crossed one's path unmolested, a relative would die.
- The cry of the blue jay indicated someone would be killed by an arrow.

The Takelma and Their Athapascan Neighbors, (U of O Anthropology paper #37);
History of Jackson County, Tucker;
History of Jackson County, Medford *Mail Tribune,* March 3, 1979

Takelma New Moon Charm

THE TAKELMA FELT A connection between everyday life and the spirit world. Here is a charm they said when the new moon appeared.

"May I prosper, may I stay alive yet awhile,
Even if people say to me; 'Would that he die.'
May I do just as thou dost, may I rise again.
Even when many evil beings devour thee,
when frogs eat thee up, still dost thou rise again.
In time to come may I do just like thee!"

The Takelma and the Athapascan Neighbors (U of O Anthology paper #37);
Southern Oregon Historical Society *Sentinel,* January 1985

First Indian Trouble, Rogue Valley – 1837

PHIL L. EDWARDS WROTE in his diary, "In this region, as in the rest of the United States, the white man has been the original aggressor." He was speaking of the Rogue Valley whites and the native Indians.

Edwards was a member of an expedition sent to California to bring back cattle. Under Ewing Young, they had sailed to Mexico and purchased 730 head of cattle. The route they followed north was roughly the same as that of Route 99 and Interstate 5 today. After making it over the Siskiyou Mountains, they stopped on the banks of the Klamath River to rest. Two young Indians approached the camp peaceably. For no apparent reason they were shot and killed. The two men responsible for the shooting claimed it was in retaliation for an Indian killing in another area. This killing had no connection with the Rogue River Indians.

Fearing trouble, Young and his 15 drovers moved the cattle on through the valley. The Indians sniped at them all along the way and a battle occurred at Rocky Point near Gold Hill, Oregon. None of Young's men was killed and they arrived in the Willamette Valley with 630 head of cattle.

A History of the Rogue River Valley, Pioneer Period; Gilmore

Fremont and the Modocs – 1846

JOHN FREMONT FIRST CAME into the Northern California area as a surveyor but he commanded a large force of soldiers.

In 1845 the Rogue Indians attacked Fremont's troops. When Fremont returned to the Klamath Lake area the following year, he was set on revenge. He had a large cavalcade with him which Kit Carson led. The Modocs were hidden in the tule near the mouth of Williamson River bent on harassing the soldiers. When Carson and his men appeared, they attacked.

What followed was a slaughter. Kit Carson and the advancing column outnumbered the Indians. Carson's men drove the Indians out of their hiding places and killed all they could find. There was a village nearby, used while the Indians fished. All was destroyed and the Indians who couldn't escape were killed. Most of these were women and children.

Whether these were Modoc or Klamath Indians is unclear, but they were not the Rogue Indians who had caused John Fremont and Kit Carson trouble the year before.

The slaughter greatly jeopardized chances of achieving a peaceful settlement between the whites and Indians east of the mountains.

Copper Paladin; Palmberg.

Captain Crosby's Retaliation – 1846

ANGERED BY FREMONT'S 1846 massacre, the Pit River neighbors, not always friends of the Modoc Indians, began waylaying and killing everyone from the wagon trains that came through their land. In Yreka, James Crosby called for volunteers to retaliate. Sixty-five men answered and Crosby became captain. Even among regular Army, the volunteers were notorious for their blood-thirsty attitude.

After leaving Yreka, they camped for the night and were visited by friendly Modocs. Later in the night a band of Pitt River Indians crept up to the camp and attacked them as dawn broke. Captain Crosby and his men were able to fight the Indians off with little damage. From now on they felt empowered to kill any Indian they saw.

That afternoon, Hot Springs Modocs innocently approached them. Eleven were immediately killed but three got away to warn other nearby Indians, who went into hiding.

Not far from Tule Lake another group of Modocs, who had not heard of the treachery, approached Crosby's encampment. Again all were fired upon and only a few escaped. The white men collected the scalps and proudly rode back to Yreka. While cheered by many, the sight of white men collecting Indian scalps sobered and alienated others.

Copper Paladin; Palmberg

Soldier's Sympathy – 1853

THE FOLLOWING ANONYMOUS letter first appeared in the Salem *Oregon States-man* in 1853. It was during the Rogue River Indian war. This soldier had a hard time justifying the white man's actions.

"A few years since the whole valley was theirs alone. No white man's foot had ever trod it. They believed it theirs forever. But the gold digger came with his pan and his pick and shovel and hundreds followed. And they saw in astonishment their streams muddied, towns built, their valley fenced and taken. And where their squaws dug camus and their children were wont to gambol, they saw dug and plowed. And their own food, sown by the hand of nature, rooted out forever and the ground it occupied appropriated to the rearing of vegetables for the white man. Perhaps no malice yet entered the Indian breast. But when he was weary of hunting in mountains without success and was hungry and approached the white man's tent for bread, where instead of bread he received curses and kicks, ye treaty kicking men, ye Indian exterminators, think of these things."

Talking on Paper, Applegate and O'Donnell

Treaty of Table Rock – 1853

A FEW MILES NORTH of Medford are the two Table Rocks. They have been landmarks since the earliest times.

From their first contact with the Hudson Bay fur traders, the Rogue River Indians feared the white trappers would kill their food animals. They retaliated by being "roguish." Every mule train taking supplies to California encountered skirmishes with the Indians as they came through the valley. For this reason the Southern Oregon area was the last in the state to be settled.

Gold was discovered in Jacksonville in 1852 and the undisciplined miners provoked the Indians further. The miners were quickly followed by settlers who selected sections of land scattered around the Jacksonville - Table Rock area. Seeing their land being taken over, the Indians did all they could to harass the settlers. Finally troops, led by Joseph Lane, were sent to quell them. On September 10, 1853 eleven white men met with the Rogue River Indians at the foot of Table Rock and signed a treaty that was to hold for two years.

Early Days in Phoenix, Helms

Andrew Smith, Rogue Indian – 1855

BY THE TIME the early settlers came to the Rogue Valley the situation with the Indians had deteriorated to a point where tensions between Indians and whites were high. Andrew Smith's mother was a Rogue River Indian and his father was Major General Andrew J. Smith.

Siskiyou County Native Americans
SOURCE: Fort Jones Museum

Smith was born in 1854, near Table Mountain in Southern Oregon. When the Rogue River Indians surrendered in the fall of 1855, he was taken, with his mother and her tribe, to the Grand Ronde Reservation. From there, under his father's orders, he was taken by a Captain Miller to live in the Willamette Valley. In 1861 Smith's father become a major general in the Civil War.

When he was nearly grown, Andrew Smith got a job in a traveling store. One day a man started talking to him and asked if Smith knew his father and mother. He knew very little because his father had wanted him brought up as a white. The man offered to find out what he could.

As a result of this conversation, Andrew Smith learned who his father was and that his mother was still at the Grand Ronde Reservation. For twenty years she had tried to find his whereabouts. Smith went to find his mother.

"My mother was old and bent and wrinkled and poor," Smith reported. "Finally in 1876 I gave up my work and went back to the reservation and took an allotment of land, farmed and took care of my mother."

Voices of the Oregon Territory, Lockley

Wintu Women

THE WINTUS LIVED IN north central California, in an area with present day Redding as its center. They were peaceful people who treated their women with equality. They lived a very simple life with no elaborate costumes, dances or ceremonial rituals such as the surrounding Indians had. Instead of celebrating the coming of age of the young men, their major ceremony was the adolescent girl's initiation dance. In preparation for this, the girl had to spend five days without sleep. During this time she ate only acorn soup and would shake her deer foot rattle to ward off evil spirits. At the end of the five days there was a dance to which her family invited the neighboring tribes.

In Wintu villages a girl had an equal opportunity to become the shaman after receiving a "calling." Many boys and girls might think they had this calling but they were further tested at a village dance. At this time the spirits would enter the body of the chosen one, striking the person unconscious. After this choice was made, the candidate went through years of vigorous training. Having fulfilled the requirements, a woman shaman received the same reverence as her male counterpart.

Unfortunately the peaceful Wintus have disappeared, either dying from whites' diseases and killings or intermarrying until they have become unrecognizable as a separate tribe.

The Wintu Indians of California, Knudtson

Fort Ter-Waw, Klamath River – 1855

IN NOVEMBER 1855 the United States government established an Indian reservation on the Klamath River. It gave the tribes one mile of river frontage on both sides of the Klamath River and extended twenty miles back.

Fort Ter-Waw was built six miles upstream from the mouth of the Klamath where the soldiers could keep an eye on the Indians. The name "Ter-Waw" was Indian for "nice place." The soil was rich and vegetable gardens were planted. A sawmill was set up to make the lumber for the camp. By 1861 the fort was a flourishing community but things were to change.

That winter it rained and rained. Roads where washed out and the gardens disappeared under flood waters. As the waters continued to rise, twenty buildings were swept away leaving only three officer's quarters. These went a few days later. Meanwhile all the improvements at the Indian reservation went downstream.

As the waters receded, all sorts of debris lined the river banks, some of it reclaimable. But that was the end of Camp Ter-Waw. With the water down, the men were marched out to take up new quarters north of Crescent City.

The Lower Klamath Country, McBeth

John Beeson – 1856

JOHN BEESON WAS known as an eccentric. One of his "eccentricities" was defending and befriending the Indians.

By 1856 many whites automatically believed the Indians guilty no matter what charges were laid against them. John Beeson stood up for them. In May 1854 there was an "Indignation Meeting." As a result of that meeting, Beeson was run out of his home town under the protection of a military guard. After years in the east lecturing in behalf of Indians, he drifted back. Here he again wrote and spoke in defense of the Indian.

What led a man like John Beeson to take such an unpopular stand? He was an energetic man of strong convictions. Brought up a Methodist, he turned away from sectarian religions. He delved into all sorts of ideas that were unpopular at the time and, in his enthusiasm, tried to inform his conservative neighbors in Southern Oregon. The rights of Indians was only one of his crusades. "The Prevention of Inherited Evil" was another topic he lectured on. He finally became an ardent Spiritualist and tried to promote these beliefs.

Beeson never gained a personal following but he was well known and attracted other free thinkers. The majority of people simply thought of him as a strange, eccentric man and often as a nuisance. He is buried in Talent, Oregon.

Religion as an Influence in Life and Thought, Farnham

Chief John, Umpqua – 1856

CHIEF JOHN WAS the last great Umpqua Indian chief. The Umpqua vigorously resented the white men taking over their land. Both sides resorted to violence. Finally, the majority of the Indians agreed to a truce. On May 26, 1856 they were supposed to assemble and surrender their arms to Lt. Colonel Roger Buchanan. Chief John refused to comply. In these words, he addressed Buchanan and the others:

> "You are a great chief, so am I. This is my country; I was here when these trees were very small, not higher than my head. My heart is sick with fighting but I want to live in my country. If the white men are willing, I will go back to Deer Creek and live among them as I used to. They can visit my camp and I will visit theirs but I will not lay down my arms and go to the reservation, I will fight."

The chief strode out of the meeting.

A company of soldiers had been stationed nearby expecting trouble. At eleven the following morning the Indians attacked. The fight continued for a month when the Indians were forced to surrender.

On July 19, those remaining were taken to the Yaquina Reservation. Even here Chief John would not give up. He led a revolt which only resulted in his being taken to Alcatraz prison along with his son.

Umpqua Valley Oregon and Its Pioneers, Minter

Captain Jack, Modoc – 1864

ON OCTOBER 14, 1864, the Modoc Indians signed the Council Grove Treaty giving up all their lands. They were to go to live on the Klamath Reservation with the Klamath and Yahooskin and Paiute. Captain Jack signed this treaty reluctantly and later refused to stay on the reservation.

It was the whites who gave the Modoc chief the name "Captain Jack." To the Indians he was "Kientpoos." It is said that in his young years he spoke out for peace with the whites, even against his father, Chief Modocus. His father died when he was sixteen and he assumed the position of chief.

All chroniclers agree that Captain Jack looked the part of a leader and was extremely intelligent. One of his good friends was a Yreka lawyer, Elijah Steele. Captain Jack visited Steele often and learned much about the white men's ways. He tried for years to be friendly with the settlers but as their numbers increased he realized they were not going to leave. They were fencing the land and limiting access to traditional water supplies. Captain Jack protested and, in return, the settlers began pressuring the government to put the Indians on reservations.

For years Captain Jack's wish was for a compromise reservation where his band could live in the Tule Lake–Lost River area. However, the land was choice fertile ground and coveted by the whites.

After the treaty of 1864 Captain Jack and his band went to the Klamath Reservation.

Copper Paladin, Palmberg

Tule Lake Lava Beds

TO THE WHITE SOLDIERS, the Tule Lake lava beds were Hell. To the Lava Bed Modoc Indians it was part of their way of life. It was no accident that Captain Jack and his loyal band of followers decided on the lava beds as the site of their last holdout against life on a reservation. Tule Lake was the lowest depression in the area and the Modocs made their winter camp near where Lost River entered Tule Lake. It was this isolation that had left them relatively undisturbed for many years.

The lava beds were desolate and rugged. While the surface appeared randomly strewn with huge lava boulders, underneath were tunnels that could be traveled for thousands of feet. In the volcanic period that shaped the mountains, underground vents opened and rivers of lava made their way to the surface. As it flowed toward the Tule Lake basin, the upper, exposed surface cooled and hardened while the lava kept flowing underneath. As these tubes of lava emptied they left underground tunnels that often branched and rebranched. In places great caverns were created. In some, cold winds caused ice to form.

The Indians knew this area well. It is little wonder it took a large number of white soldiers to oust Captain Jack's small band from the lava beds.

Copper Paladin, Palmberg; *Ancient Tribes of the Klamath Country*, Howe

Rain Rock, Fort Jones

IN 1948, WORKMEN repairing a county road ten miles south of the Oregon border in California, unearthed a two ton rock. It was an Indian "rain rock."

Before white men came, when rain was needed, the Indians would chip a shallow conical pit in the rock to produce wind and rain. However, the storms were so severe during the winter of 1889–1890, the Indians buried their rock and never used it again.

Word of the find quickly got out. The rock was moved to the Fort Jones Museum.

It was thought that all that was needed to bring on rain was to pour some water over the rock. If sunshine was desired, the rock was covered with a tarp. Soon requests began coming in. Among them, the Oroville Chamber of Commerce asked that the rock be covered for their centennial celebration. At the time Jersey Joe Wolcott was challenging Joe Louis for the heavy weight boxing title, the bout was rained out two days in a row. It was found that the tarp had come off the rain rock. When it was restored, a telegram was sent to Yankee Stadium saying it would be clear weather. The fight went off that night as scheduled.

Pioneer Press, January 1985; Record *Searchlight*, January 15, 1985
Sacramento *Bee*, October, 27, 1951; *Siskiyou Pioneer Notebook*, Part IX

Rain Rock
SOURCE: Fort Jones Museum

Citizenship for Indians

EVEN BEFORE THE Revolutionary War, the description of who was a "native" was controversial. The general agreement was that anyone born "within the allegiance" or "under the Republic" qualified. After the United States won independence, these "natives" were automatically U.S. citizens. But they did not include Indians.

Indian tribes had always been considered sovereign political communities, similar to foreign nations. The Indians' allegiance was to their tribe. The government negotiated treaties with these tribes. Occasionally such treaties established ways for the people to become citizens.

Many individual Indians merged into the white population, some by marriage, others simply through time.

Even the Civil War failed to answer the Indian problem. On June 13, 1866, when the fourteenth amendment to the constitution was approved by congress it did not include Indians.

It wasn't until 1924 that Indians were granted citizenship but still allowed to be members of sovereign Indian tribes. The Bureau of Indian Affairs remained the governing agency for Native Americans on reservations but tribal councils also had jurisdiction.

History of United States Citizenship

CHAPTER 10

MINORITIES

Chinese Miners, California

IN THE BEGINNING, the California miners welcomed the Chinese miner who worked hard for low pay. But the miners soon changed their attitude when the number of Chinese increased and they began to operate their own mines.

The first act against foreign miners came in 1850, but it was aimed at Mexicans and South Americans.

In 1852 a law was enacted requiring a monthly fee from all Asians. Next came a charge of $50 for every person landing on U.S. shores who was ineligible for citizenship. This included all Chinese laborers. In 1870 it was ruled that no one carrying merchandise on poles could walk on the sidewalk.

Chinese miners usually lived together in cramped quarters, so a law was passed that every adult had to have 500 cubic feet of living space. This is roughly an area eight feet long by eight feet wide by eight feet high, a luxury by the standards of any mining camp.

Chinese men wore their hair in a queue, a sort of long braid. Now a California law said that if an Asian was arrested, he would have his queue cut to no more than one inch. This was severe punishment. Chinese men could not return to China without wearing a queue because of religious beliefs and Chinese law.

The final blow was an ordinance saying that anyone carrying laundry had to use a horse and wagon or buy an expensive license.

As if this were not enough, it became illegal for a ship to carry more than fifteen Chinese passengers. A violator was charge $100 per passenger.

In spite of the difficulties, Chinese miners still wanted to come to California. On November 17, 1880 the Exclusion Act forbid any foreign laborers entry into the state. It did allow tourists, students, merchants and teachers, but even these had to register.

Siskiyou *Pioneer*, 1989

Jacksonville – 1856-1857

THE MARYSVILLE, CALIFORNIA newspaper of September 1856 reported that, "The Chinese are going to Jacksonville from Yreka to avoid the foreign miner's tax imposed in California." Known as "John Chinaman" or the "Celestials," the Chinese miners had quietly filtered into Jacksonville until suddenly their number became an issue. The Chinese miner had moved north on foot, wearing native dress and with a pole across his shoulders carrying about 50 pounds of provisions, tools and clothing in two bundles, one tied to each end of the pole.

The majority of Chinese had crossed the Pacific on credit tickets. That is to say, merchants in San Francisco paid their fare and the Chinese workers owed this money back to the merchant. Generally they worked under Chinese bosses and would be hired as a group with the boss in charge. They were poor men, often from Canton, who came with the hope of taking money home so they could live out their lives. It was this intention that caused much of the irritation with the other inhabitants. The Chinese had no desire to be assimilated into the American culture. Their curious standards and customs made people think that they were an inferior race. The argument was also made that they added nothing to the area in which they lived. As a result, they were always discriminated against.

In 1862, when there were about 300 Chinese in Jacksonville, a poll tax was declared on Chinese, African–Americans and "Kanakans" (Hawaiians). The $5 tax went to the county.

In spite of discrimination, the number of Chinese in Jackson County peaked in 1870 at about 650 which represented about one in every eight men. By the turn of the century most had left, presumably returning to China.

The Chinese in the Rogue River Valley, Handbury

Chinese Miners Oregon – 1858

NEITHER OREGON NOR CALIFORNIA has a very good record when it comes to racial prejudice.

Chinese miners lived clustered together in one area. They kept to themselves, worked hard and were willing to do the most unpleasant kinds of work. When they got into trouble it was almost always with another Chinese. On March 1, 1858 legislation went into effect in Oregon saying that no native of China could mine gold, trade or buy goods, chattels or any property whatsoever, for the purpose of maintaining a livelihood in Oregon Territory. Chinese miners were not allowed to locate claims, but as gold played out, other miners were glad to sell to the Chinese. With stubborn determination the Asian miners worked long, backbreaking hours on already worked mines and made good money.

Another law passed in 1859 taxed every Chinese $2 a month. If he was a storekeeper he was taxed $50. Undaunted, the Chinese dominated mining in the 1880s.

Very few Chinese women ever came to the mining towns. It is true that the Chinese miner sent his money back home and left little behind to show that he

MASS MEETING.

A Mass Meeting of the citizens of this place and vicinity will be held at Darby's Hall, on Sunday, Jan. 31, at 2 o'clock P. M., to devise some lawful means of ridding Crescent City of Chinese.

R. W. Miller, R. G. Knox, L. F. Coburn and others will address the meeting.

All are invited to attend.

Notice posted in Crescent City
SOURCE: Del Norte County Historical Society

had ever been in the area but you can still see occasional stone walls, irrigation ditches and wells.

The Chinese in the Rogue Valley, Handbury

Chinese Customs

AS THE CHINESE NUMBERS increased, some people claimed that they mixed brass and copper filings with the gold dust they sold. Others said they robbed sluice boxes.

Angry white miners threatened to cut off the queue of an erring Chinese or to whip him. The worst punishment was to threaten to turn over the man to the Indians, whom the Chinese feared. They were not allowed to testify in court. They were usually harassed and over charged by storekeepers. The custom of sending their countrymen's bones back to China annoyed many. Every Chinese miner had made arrangements to be buried back in the place of his birth. It was said that sometimes cases and coffins of bones made up the major cargo of steamers going back to China.

After gold mining petered out, the Chinese stayed to work on the railroads. Others became servants, laundry men and gardeners.

By the mid 1880s, "Chinese must go;" became the slogan and grew to such a pitch that most areas ran them out.

Shasta County *Centennial Edition*

Chinese Laundry – 1851

AN OCCASIONAL CLEAN shirt was a luxury a miner was willing to pay big money for.

Living in a mining town, a wife who wanted to make money, often took in laundry. She made good money. Even men who didn't mind being ridiculed went into the laundry business in competition with women. When the Chinese began to filter in, they captured the trade. A Mrs. Bates tells us of their mode of ironing:

> "After the articles are dry, they take them to their houses to iron. They starch each article, even to sheets and pillow slips. Their mode of ironing is entirely different from anything I ever before saw. They have a copper vessel, shaped like a saucepan and large enough to hold about two quarts of coal. They fill it with burning coal... and shove it back and forth over the articles.

To keep the articles evenly moist there was a dish of water standing beside them. The ironer would put his mouth down to it and draw in the water. As he pushed the copper iron he would blow the water out of his mouth in a fine spray.

"They iron very smoothly, and the clothes have a beautiful polish."

They Saw the Elephant, Levy

Gin Lin – 1853

FEW CHINESE INTEGRATED into the communities in which they worked. In fact, they were called "sojourners" because they only intended to live in the area long enough to earn money to take home.

Gin Lin was a "Boss," meaning that he controlled groups of Chinese laborers who he farmed out to mine owners. A boss also had exclusive rights to sell supplies to his group of miners. The employer gave the miner's salary to Gin Lin and he would subtract the debts the men had incurred for their transportation to this country and for their living expenses. He would give the men the small remainder.

Gin Lin lived in the Jacksonville–Applegate area for 30 years and was so successful he was able to buy and operate his own hydraulic mining operation near Palmer Creek.

Legend has it that Gin Lin deposited a total of two million dollars in several banks. He had his own carriage and drove around in style. He never became a citizen but owned 200 acres of land. While the citizens might fear and dislike the Asian workers, Gin Lin was given their respect and some even thought of him as a friend.

Like almost all the Chinese, Gin Lin eventually took his money and went back to China in 1894.

Southern Oregon Historical Society *Sentinels*, April 1983, December 1987

Lan Kee

LAN KEE, MINER, was luckier than most. His story starts back in China where he owned a small plot of ground, with a wife, children and two parents to support. No matter how hard he worked, it was too much for his small plot to provide.

One day a "boss" came and offered him the opportunity he needed. For a $50 debt he could go to the gold fields of California and make his fortune. Gladly Lan Kee signed on, but the trip more than doubled his debt to the "boss" as he had to pay for food and water. This was in 1850 and the men were told the California gold fields were played out. They were shipped to Oregon. This was another expense. Finally Lan Kee arrived in Jacksonville owing $200 but eager to work and pay off his debt.

Gin Lin was the boss overseeing new arrivals. He put the men to work digging ditches and reworking old claims. Lan Kee put away every penny he could and was able to be free of debt at the end of a year. Now, with two others he bought a claim of his own. When the previous owners tried to take back the claim, the court ruled in Lan Kee's favor, a most unusual occurrence. One of Lan's partners was killed by men angered at the court ruling.

Meticulously, the two remaining men worked their claim. It lead back into a rocky hillside with a rift in the rock. Finally the day came when they dug into the crevice and broke through to a vein of gold. They were rich.

Lan Kee worked his claim to the end but he was still thrifty and he only allowed himself an occasional glass of rice wine and the purchase of a beautiful gold chain. The rest of his wealth he took back to his family in China.

Southern Oregon Historical Society *Sentinel*, April 1993

Chinese Cook

CHINESE MINERS HAD been working the tailings of former gold mines for years. Some found it paid better to work in the white men's homes. Clarissa Birdseye hired a Chinese man to cook. He was named Yung Sam. She had to teach him everything and he had little knowledge of English. After he learned such things as biscuits, pancakes and fried potatoes, she thought she would try to teach Yung Sam to make a shoo-fly-pie.

Shoo-fly-pies take several eggs. Clarissa always broke an egg in a sauce dish to check that it was fresh and had no developing chick. She showed Yung Sam how to do this. Egg one, two and three were fine and she put each in the mixing bowl as she went. Egg number four was bad and Clarissa casually threw it out the open window and cracked another egg.

Yung Sam became a good cook and made many shoo-fly-pies but every time he made one he threw the fourth egg out the window. That was the way he had been taught.

Interview with Nita Birdseye

Hawaiian Laborers – 1850s

KANAKAS, OWYHEES, BLUE MEN, were all names given to the Hawaiian laborers who appeared on the west coast as early as 1788.

The English were one of the first to stop at the Hawaiian Islands, known at that time as the Sandwich Islands. They needed water and supplies but they soon started replacing sailors with the native men who were hard working and reliable. The Hudson Bay Company also used the islanders for lumbermen, blacksmiths, farmers and builders.

The Hawaiian laborer began to appear in our area as the gold fields opened. They found themselves in conflict with the other miners because they preferred to dive in the rivers to get at the gold rather than use conventional methods.

Some Hawaiians worked their own mines but the majority were hired by other miners. Unlike the Asians, with whom they were often grouped, they wanted to stay in this country and be assimilated. There were some who intermarried with the Indians and lost their racial distinction. Gradually others returned to their islands and by 1900 very few remained.

There is little visual evidence left of the Kanakas' era but they were important to the merchant ships and to the Hudson Bay Company. They had built shelters and provided food for the early missionaries. They had worked the gold fields and provided labor for early businesses.

Minority Without a Champion, Duncan

The Slavery Issue

SLAVERY WAS AN ISSUE in Oregon beginning with the first Provisional Legislature. The compromise the government decided on was not to allow slavery in the territory but neither to allow free men of color to live here. They added the following:

> "In all cases where slaves have been or shall hereafter be brought into Oregon, the owners of such slaves shall have three years to remove them out of the country. Such slaves will be free at the end of said three years if the owner does not remove them.
>
> "If a free Negro or mulatto comes to Oregon, he or she must leave the country within two years if they are males or three years if they are females, after reaching their 18th birthday or if over 18 after entering Oregon"

If a former slave refused to leave, he or she would be given between 20 and 39 lashes. These were to be inflicted by the county constable. Later this was changed and the penalty was simply to remove them from the territory.

Oregon Oddities, WPA

China Town, Happy Camp, California
SOURCE: Fort Jones Museum

George Bush

OREGON HAD ITS OWN George Bush, who was one of the first African–Americans to bring his family across the plains. He was an intelligent and wealthy man. His black father had married his Irish mother. He himself married a white woman and they had five children by the time they immigrated to the west.

Bush was fleeing prejudice, but in 1844 prejudice was everywhere. He vowed that though he wanted to live in Oregon he would move to Washington or California if he found that men of color did not have free rights in Oregon. That very year Oregon had passed its first exclusion law. Southern Oregon was largely pro-slavery. Exclusion was accomplished by forbidding blacks to own property or vote. Neither could they go into business. Intermarriage was also forbidden. These laws stayed in effect until 1870 when a civil rights bill was passed.

Needless to say, George Bush took his family and left Oregon to settle in Washington.

A Peculiar Paradise, A History of Blacks in Oregon 1788–1940, McLagan

Alois Kalina of Malin – 1911

A COLONY OF BOHEMIANS settled on the north shores of Tule Lake when it was being drained for farm land. They called their town Malin.

Alois Kalina opened the town's first mercantile store. Every so often he would have to go to Merrill or Klamath Falls for supplies. Klamath Falls had more to offer but it was farther and took three days to come and go. In summer he would be attacked by clouds of mosquitoes that rose from the boggy edges of the lake.

Even more frustrating was getting down to open and close 17 gates going and 17 gates returning to Malin. Merrill was only thirty miles away and the trip could be made in a day or two. So when he didn't need as much, that was where he went.

During the winter of 1911 the snow and mud was the worst Kalina had ever seen. He was returning from a buying trip with 25 sacks of sugar weighing 100 pounds each. In one spot he bogged down and had to unload the sugar, one sack at a time and take it a quarter mile where he stacked it. Then he returned to dig the wagon out of the mud and pull it to the stack of sugar. He now had to reload 25 bags each weighing 100 pounds.

Any profit Alois Kalina made on his sugar was hard earned.

Klamath *Echoes*, #8

KKK

SOUTHERN OREGON WAS settled by many Confederate sympathizers just before, during and after the Civil War. The racism against the blacks continued into the 1920s in the form of the Klu Klux Klan.

The Klan promoted "pure Americanism," protection of pure womanhood, free speech, a free press, temperance, free public schools, restricted immigration, white supremacy, law and order. This resulted in anti-Catholicism and anti-Semitism.

The base of the Oregon Klan was in Jackson County and the early 1920s was the height of their popularity and political strength. They boasted 1,000 members, politicians, capitalists and churchmen. Because there were so few blacks in the area, they directed their hatred against Catholics. They were able to enact a compulsory school bill which forced parents to send their children to public schools and closed the Catholic schools.

On March 19, 1922 the Medford Klu Klux Klan kidnapped J.H. Hale, drove him out of town, placed a noose around his neck and threatened him. This was not the first time such a thing had happened. The Klan was interested in intimidating Hale and others rather than killing them. On this occasion, when the Klan threatened Hale, he outwitted his capturers by pretending to have a heart attack. The affair got much publicity which rallied public support and created a backlash of sentiment. As a result, the governor issued a proclamation declaring that no one could appear on the streets in unlawful disguise.

The KKK never again regained its full strength and by 1924 it had lost its power and its members.

Southern Oregon Historical Society *Sentinels*, September 1983 and December 1993;
Great Moments in Oregon History; Medford's First Century, Medford *Mail Tribune*

CHAPTER 11

LAW & ORDER

Sailor Jim – 1857

JULY 16, 1857 WAS THE scheduled date to hang Sailor Jim in Yreka. Jim had been convicted of killing John Burke earlier that same year. He was also known to have killed several Indians and was generally well known around the county as an unsavory character.

The hanging was to take place on the east edge of town. The scaffold was erected. The hook and ladder company and the hangman were on hand along with the sheriff and Sailor Jim. The Siskiyou Hook and Ladder Company led Jim to the scaffold, the noose was placed around his neck and the trap sprung. Jim jerked at the end of the rope and dropped to the ground, the noose having slipped off his neck. He was helped back onto the scaffold and as the noose was being replaced, Jim demanded of the sheriff, "For God sakes, don't do that again!"

All went well this second time and Sailor Jim was laid to rest.

Siskiyou Pioneer, 1993

Dr. Cabaniss Duel

DR. CABANISS WAS a true hero of the Modoc Indian war. At the time of our story he was a Siskiyou County physician at the County Hospital. David Colton was part owner of Yreka's newspaper, the *Union.*

The two men represented politically opposite points of view. When David Colton editorialized that Dr. Cabaniss was not doing his job properly at the hospital, it was politics, but Dr. Cabaniss took exception to it and replied in Yreka's other paper, the *Chronicle.* The result was that a representative of editor Colton called upon Dr. Cabaniss challenging him to a duel. The challenge was accepted.

Keys to old Del Norte jail
SOURCE: Kerbyville Museum

The rules of dueling said the doctor could choose the weapon. He chose the United States Yaeger rifle, at forty paces.

It was unconstitutional to duel in California, so a spot was decided on forty miles away, just over the line in Oregon. On the night of February 8, 1858 some fifty or sixty people left Yreka for Coles Station to be at the site in time for the morning duel. The weather was crisp with a light snow on the ground. Several attempts were made to reconcile the two men but all had failed. Finally both agreed to let a mediation board decide. At last Colton agreed to withdraw his challenge and Dr. Cabaniss also agreed.

Thus the duel was averted. Neither man ever referred to the affair again.

Saddle Bags in Siskiyou, Jones

Black Bart – 1881

WHEN THE STAGECOACHES began carrying gold for Wells Fargo, the era of holdup men began. None were more colorful than Black Bart.

Most holdups were conducted as the horses pulled slowly up the long slopes. On August 31, 1881 Black Bart robbed a stage southbound for Yreka on Anderson grade. It was 2 a.m. Over a period of eight years he had made 28 successful holdups. He wore socks over his boots to disguise his footprints, and a flour sack over his head. He carried a rifle and propped others behind rocks to give the impression that he was not alone.

Bart got his nickname, the Poet, because he usually left behind a mocking verse propped on top of the Wells Fargo box he had emptied. Lawmen looked everywhere and reward posters were placed in local towns. Finally Black Bart slipped up. A handkerchief was found at the site of one of his holdups. The laundry mark lead to a well dressed, mild appearing man, Charles E. Boles, who posed as a wealthy mining man.

When law officers went to arrest Boles, they found a suitcase with a disassembled shotgun but no shells. The ever polite Boles told them that he never owned any ammunition because he didn't want anyone to get hurt.

The Mythical State of Jefferson, Sutton; Southern Oregon Historical Society *Sentinel*, Dec. 1983

Illegal Cigars – 1873

IF THE EARLY CHINESE couldn't earn money one way, they would try another.

In January of 1873, the Assistant Assessor of the Internal Revenue Service made a raid on some Chinese houses. They were looking for cigars that were being made and sold without the proper tax being paid. Sure enough, they caught one man actually in the process of making a cigar and immediately seized his fifteen pounds of leaf tobacco and the few cigars that had already been made.

In another house the assessor removed a piece of matting on the floor and discovered a trap door. This disclosed a cellar stairs, at the bottom of which were boxes containing over 1,800 cigars. When the Chinese found they were discovered, they tried to bribe the law man. He refused.

Crescent City *Courier*, January 16, 1873

Punch Boards

WILLIAM SHADRACH HAD A mercantile business on the lower Klamath River. One day a man came in and sold him a punch board. A punch board had small round holes with a slip of paper folded inside. For 10¢ a customer got to punch out one hole. The paper inside would announce whether they were a winner or not. In this case the prizes were to be money. Like all gambling games, the money coming in was to be more than the money going out. Shadrach decided to try this on his customers. Shortly after he had bought the board, a stranger came into the store. He bought ten punches and won a total of $44. Shadrach quickly realized no punch board should pay out that kind of money. Putting two and two together, he knew he had been had. The seller of the punch board and the winner of the money were in this together.

Shadrach went in search of the men and when he found them he drew his gun and demanded his money back. Before the confrontation was over, Shadrach was shot in the shoulder and the customer who had won the money was dead—a pretty high price to pay for $44 in winnings.

Siskiyou *Pioneer*, 1964

Station Robbery – 1884

THE MEDFORD *Mail Tribune* reported that on the Monday before they went to press, a masked man entered the Medford railroad station and with his gun cocked, demanded the agent give him the contents of the safe.

No one was near enough to come to railroad agent Cunningham's aid so he gave the man the $680 in gold and silver coins that were in the safe. The man left.

Cunningham told the police his story and a detective was called in. The detective became puzzled as he worked on the robbery and kept coming back to Cunningham to review the incident. Something sounded wrong. Under renewed questioning, Cunningham confessed. There had been no armed robber. Instead, he had taken the money and concocted the story. He led the detective to a point 50 yards from the station where he dug up the remainder of the stolen money. He had already spent $100.

Cunningham never came to trial. His father rescued him, paid back the money and the charges were dropped.

Southern Oregon Historical Society *Sentinel*, 1987

Dunsmuir "601" – 1892

AN ASHLAND NEWS item read:

"The railroad town of Dunsmuir in Siskiyou County had been infested with a crowd of tin horn gamblers, pimps and other disreputable characters until Tuesday night."

This called for a clean-up by the town's "601," a group of vigilantes. Signs were posted early Tuesday morning, warning the "undesirables" to leave by 7 p.m., "by order of the 601." Several left by the southbound train. As night fell the 601 gathered and about 10:30 p.m. 30 to 40 masked men marched down Main Street. Going into the saloons, they picked up three men and invited them to leave town.

If this was the end of the story we might condone the act, but by now the mob spirit prevailed and the 601 marched into Chinatown driving all the Chinese out. Unlike the gamblers and pimps, the Chinese came back the next day, only to find their homes broken into and their belongings looted. This was condemned by the people generally but no action was taken against the men responsible for the looting.

Ashland *Tidings*, October 7, 1892

Execution of Frank Smith – 1899

AN EXECUTION WAS big news in 1899 and the fate of murderer Frank Lawrence Smith was well publicized.

Hanging Melson
SOURCE: Kerbyville Museum

Smith had been convicted of killing Peter Nelson while the two rode in a Southern Pacific Railroad boxcar. He then threw Nelson's body out of the train.

The days of quick "justice" were past. The crime Smith was accused of took place in February, 1898. What with appeals and legal business, the hanging was to take place over a year later in Jacksonville, Oregon. A special enclosure was built next to the jail. The area was large enough to accommodate 150 people. Some were there in a legal capacity but the majority were invited guests.

Frank Smith, meanwhile, was cheerful and full of confidence that Gov. Geer would commute his sentence to life in prison. According to reports Smith sang songs, ate heartily and joked with the guards. The newspapers kept the public informed of every development.

Less than twenty-four hours before the scheduled hanging, no word had come from the governor. At last the truth hit Frank Smith and he broke down. Still declaring his innocence, he wept. The sheriff, however, encouraged Smith to "die like a man."

At two o'clock in the morning a telegraph message came. Gov. Geer had commuted Smith's sentence to life in prison. The 150 guests, invited to the hanging, had to find some other entertainment for that day.

Ashland *Tidings,* May 22, 25, 29, 1899 (Excerpts)

Nearly Hanged – 1900

ABOUT THE YEAR 1900, two men got into a fight in Callahan, California. One of them whipped out a knife and went after the first man. The other customers in the saloon overpowered the assailant and tied him up.

So far this could be the start of any story but from here on it takes a strange turn. It was decided to take the knife wielder out to the bridge over the East Fork of the Scott River and hang him. The mob marched out, tied one end of the rope to the bridge railing and tied the other end around the man's neck. The man was bound hand and foot and placed on the top of the superstructure of the bridge. The victim was pushed off the bridge but splashed into the water unharmed. The rope was too long. He was pulled out, the rope shortened and a second try was made. Again the murderer fell unharmed.

By now the men were ready for another drink so they left the tied man and went off to the saloon. When they returned, their man had disappeared and was never seen again.

Along Our History's Trail, Hayden

Con Men

CON MEN THRIVED EVERYWHERE, especially in the early west. Some of them were very ingenious. Farmers bartered their produce and few of them had any coin money. Here is how con men took advantage of this.

It was customary for anyone traveling to stop at a farmhouse and ask for a meal, or they might stay overnight, the farmer putting up the man's horse and the wife feeding him dinner and breakfast. The usual charge was 25¢ for a meal and 50¢ for an overnight stay. The traveling con man would plunk down a $50 gold piece to pay, knowing that no farmer would have change for $50. The traveler would go away free saying, "When I come by this way again, I'll pay you."

Oregon Folks, Lockley

De Autremont Brothers – 1923

WE TEND TO GLAMORIZE wild west stagecoach and train robberies. The De Autremont brothers caused excitement, but what they did was far from glamorous.

The Southern Pacific "Gold Special" was southbound for San Francisco on Thursday, October 11, 1923. At 12:40 p.m. the train was emerging from tunnel #13 in the Siskiyou mountains, just south of Ashland. Here the three De Autremont brothers jumped on board. They were twenty-three year old twins, Ray and Roy, and their 19 year old brother, Hugh.

The brakeman, engineer and fireman were shot and killed. The three armed men then dynamited the mail car, killing the mail clerk. As it turned out, the

Kerbyville's first jail
SOURCE: Larry McLane

$40,000 they thought was aboard was not even in the shipment and the bandits fled empty handed.

Newspapers across the country took up the story and photographs of the three brothers were circulated widely. Almost three years later Hugh was identified as being in the Army and stationed in the Philippines. He was arrested, returned to the U.S. and put in Alcatraz prison. About a month later, his two brothers were picked up in Ohio where they went under the name "Goodwin." Ray had married a 16 year old girl, had a son, and was expecting another child.

What became of the brothers? Hugh was tried and the jury took only an hour and twenty-four minutes to declare him guilty of murder and recommend life imprisonment. When Ray and Roy heard the outcome of Hugh's trial, they were prevailed upon to plead guilty for which they, too, were given life sentences.

Hugh was paroled in January 1951. He was 55 and had served 31 years. Less than three months later he died of cancer.

Roy and Ray shared a cell for years but Roy was finally declared mentally incompetent and moved to the Oregon State Hospital. He died in 1983 in a nursing home.

Ray was paroled in 1961 after 34 years. He made a good adjustment to his freedom, gladly giving autographs and enjoying being a celebrity. He died in 1984.

Medford *Mail Tribune*, October 1923; *Oregon's Great Train Holdup*, Webber

Kidnapping of Charles F. Urschel – 1933

In July, 1933 Charles F. Urschel of Oklahoma was kidnapped. He was taken to Texas and the kidnappers demanded $200,000 in ransom. Urschel was a millionaire who had made his money in the oil fields. The $200,000 was paid.

Fifteen people were convicted of the kidnapping but still the Federal agents could not account for all the ransom money. They quietly watched for the money to surface. It finally did—in Southern Oregon. Alvin H. Scott came under suspicion. Ransom money was found in a bank deposit he made, but still the agents waited. On November 2, 1934 Scott was driving up to Portland when his car swerved off the highway going at high speed. He was just north of Roseburg and was taken to the hospital there with a brain concussion. Police found $1,360 from Urschel's ransom in the car.

Scott's housekeeper, a Mrs. Hurtienne, was with him in the car. She was also arrested.

The search moved to the Scott home in Medford. The home had originally been squalid but had been re-roofed, added onto, painted and had a new car in the garage. It was thought Scott would have received $50,000 as his cut in the kidnapping. Agents began digging and uncovered most of the money, buried in fruit jars.

Before all was over, Mrs. Hustienne's sister, the sister's son and the son's wife were also arrested.

Medford *Mail Tribune*, November 8 & 11, 1934

Last Lynching – 1935

Lynching is something we tend to relate to the early days of the wild west. Surprisingly, the last lynching in the west occurred on August 3, 1935. C.L. Johnson was the confessed killer of Chief of Police Jack Daw of Dunsmuir. Siskiyou County residents were outraged. This was not the first time a police officer had been shot to death. The legal process was slow and often murderers were not caught or were given light sentences. Some of the citizens decided Johnson was not going to have a chance to get away with his deed.

Late at night a group of men approached the Yreka jail where Johnson was held. They got hold of him and took him out the old wagon road that went to Fort Jones. About two miles west of Yreka they hanged him. It was 2 in the morning.

This was the last time in Siskiyou County a wild west mob took the law into their own hands and got away with it.

Siskiyou *Pioneer*, 1965

CHAPTER 12

COAST

Cape Blanco – 1603

A SPANISH SEA CAPTAIN, Martin de Aguilar, sighted a point of land on January 19, 1603. He named the point Cape Blanco de Aguilar, but for many years it was called Cape Orford. Now known simply as Cape Blanco, the point is the westernmost tip of land in Oregon.

The lighthouse at Cape Blanco is the oldest in Oregon having been in use since 1870. A white conical tower, it rises 255 feet above the water and can be seen 22 miles at sea. Before the lighthouse was built, Louis Knapp, proprietor of a hotel in Port Orford, used to burn an oil lamp all night in a window facing the sea. Feeble as it was, the mariners were grateful for its light.

During World War II, the Cape Blanco lighthouse grounds were used as headquarters for the Coast Guard Beach Patrol Detachment. It was their duty to watch for signs of a possible Japanese invasion. The beaches were patrolled 24 hours a day, alert for a crisis that fortunately never materialized.

Oregon's Seacoast Lighthouses, Gibbs

Klamath City – 1850

THE SHIP *Cameo* sailed up the west coast expecting to start a settlement at Trinidad Bay. When they arrived they found they were too late. Someone had already taken possession of the site. The group, lead by a man named Ehernberg, went back to the mouth of the Klamath River where they anchored on April 16, 1850. They made soundings and found that there was 20 feet of water at low tide. This looked like a good harbor and there was a site where a city could be laid out. They had already discovered that there was gold in the black sand nearby.

Streets and town lots were laid out and the site became Klamath City. Twenty houses went up almost overnight. The frames had been put together before sailing. An iron house had been brought and was set up. This was to act as a fort in case of Indian attack.

Troubles began almost immediately. Relations with the Indians were difficult. No possible trail across the mountains could be found. But most important, the harbor, which had looked so promising, was protected by a river bar that proved too treacherous to be crossed safely.

Less than one year after its optimistic beginning, Klamath City was abandoned. The houses were taken down and sent elsewhere, and the iron house was returned to San Francisco.

Lower Klamath Country, McBeth

Umpqua Lighthouse – 1851

JOSEPH LANE, THE FIRST Territorial Governor of Oregon, used his influence in Washington to get appropriations for a lighthouse at the mouth of the Umpqua River. The river bar was treacherous. Silt drifting down the river over the years had deposited a wide stretch of shoals and sandbars. This, combined with unreliable wind, caused trouble for the early sailing vessels. Many wrecked while looking for the channel.

In 1851 Congress appropriated $15,000 for construction of a lighthouse. An additional $10,000 was added a few years later. Construction started in 1855 but was hampered by the Indians. Tools, clothing and materials disappeared daily. This eventually erupted into violence. Finally, with a guard on watch day and night, they were able to continue, and the light was turned on in 1857. It was the first lighthouse on the Oregon coast.

Unfortunately, the story doesn't end here. Shortly after its completion, the flooded Umpqua river undermined the new lighthouse tower and it toppled over.

For thirty years the Umpqua went without a light. Wrecks continued. Finally in 1888 Congress appropriated $50,000 for the purchase of a site for a new lighthouse. After many setbacks and more appropriations, the lighthouse was completed on August 30, 1892. Offices and dwellings were finished by January of the following year but service didn't begin until 1894.

In the 1960s the Coast Guard placed the Umpqua light on automatic beacon. It is still in use.

Land of the Umpqua, Beckham

Crescent City – 1854

THE FIRST VISITOR to the Crescent City area was the schooner *Paragon*. In 1850 she entered the Crescent City harbor and was wrecked.

The following year prospectors came through the area but despite its many assets, no one settled there until spring of 1852 when a town was laid out. About this time, Ida Pfeiffer visited Crescent City. She was traveling alone around the world. Here is part of her impression:

> "I was astonished at the good and fluent speeches that I heard, especially as many of the speakers looked like sailors and miners, and had on red flannel shirts and jackets. . . . The fair sex appeared in quite simple domestic looking dresses of printed cotton."

By the fall of 1853 the steamer *Columbia* made regular trips bringing freight and passengers to Crescent City. The following spring brought a surge of growth. The mines nearby were beginning to attract miners, with an average yield of $5 to $15 a day. With money available there was a demand for supplies and workers.

On June 10, 1854 the first issue of the Crescent City *Herald* was published. Mail delivery improved to the point that a delivery was made every two weeks during good weather and once a month when the weather was bad. In August, the first ship built here was launched. A plank and turnpike road was surveyed connecting the city to Yreka.

When Klamath County was divided, Crescent City became the seat of government for Del Norte County.

Del Norte County, Bledsoe; *Lower Klamath Country*, McBeth
A Lady's Second Trip Around the World, Pfeiffer

Whale Island – 1855

WHALE ISLAND, IN Crescent City Harbor, is about a two acre island made largely of rock. In 1855 a company formed calling themselves the Crescent City Whaling Company. They established works for "trying out" or rendering the whale blubber on Whale Island.

The only part of the whale used commercially was the blubber, or thick layer of fat just under the skin. When a whale was killed, a so called "bomb" would be fired into the body which would explode inside the whale, causing it to inflate enough to be towed to the Island. Here it was tied to a dock. Men would stand on the whale, skinning it and removing thick strips of blubber. This was "tried out" or heated, to melt out the oil. The hump back whales most commonly caught, would give as much as 35 barrels of oil, each barrel being 31½ gallons. The oil was much in demand, mostly for whale oil lamps.

By August 1860 the Crescent City *Herald* reported that Whale Island was no longer occupied for whaling and that four men had taken it over and were trolling for "red" fish. They were able to catch large quantities of them, as many as 400 to 800 fish per day. These they sold on the San Francisco market.

Del Norte Historical Society

Coos Bay Shipbuilding – 1856

UNTIL ABOUT 1910, the major connection between the Coos Bay area and the outside world was by ship. The earliest and most important shipbuilder was Asa Meade Simpson. He built a lumber mill in 1856 and next door, started building ships to move the finished lumber to ports up and down the Oregon Coast. His first ship was a brig or brigantine, christened *Blanco*.

Simpson's was not the only shipyard near Coos Bay but it produced the most ships over the next 50 years. On an average, it took seven months to complete a vessel.

Incoming ships brought food and merchandise and took out coal, lumber, agricultural products and salmon, both canned and salted.

People used ships to take them from one place to another. Except for travel on the sandy beaches, roads didn't begin to improve until 1910. By then the automobile had taken everyone's fancy and better roads were demanded.

The Coos Bay Region, Doughit

Shipbuilding: launching the Daisy, Bandon, Oregon, 1908 (by Moore Mill)
SOURCE: Coquille River Museum, Bandon Historical Society

Side Wheel Steamer *America* – 1855

IT WAS SUNDAY, June 24, 1855 when the side-wheel steamship *America* anchored in Crescent City. On board were 123 men of the 21st U.S. Infantry. The sea was calm and it was a fine June day. The ship would be at anchor only long enough to unload.

When the freight and mail had been taken off, it was noticed that there was an unusual amount of smoke and steam coming out all over the ship. Quickly fire broke out. The crew and infantrymen worked frantically to put it out. Meanwhile, small boats left shore and surrounded the *America* ready to help in any way they could. The soldiers who weren't needed to fight the fire were taken to the beach. The ship was run aground about 150 yards from shore.

In spite of all efforts, the smoke was so dense the firefighters couldn't get close enough to fight the blaze itself. Finally the call came to abandon ship. By morning, all that remained was a smoky ruin.

What caused the fire? The ship was almost new and thought to be the finest in the Northern Pacific. It is possible that spontaneous combustion may have occurred in the coal bunkers.

History of Del Norte, Bledsoe

Fourth of July

AT ONE TIME, celebrating the Fourth of July was a greater event than Christmas. In Crescent City three brass cannons boomed out as the sun came up. These were cannon from the wrecked steamer *America* that had been placed on Battery Point. Nearby was a stout pole set in the ground. It had wooden pins sticking out at intervals, forming a rough spiral of steps which led to a lantern that was fixed on the top. This was kept lit to act as a light house.

For the fourth of July, a procession was formed and marched through the streets. A detachment of the U.S. Infantry marched as did the Hook and Ladder Company and important individuals. In most towns, the main feature would be a float with Miss Liberty on it. The reigning beauty would be dressed in white with bunting draped all over a hay rack.

At noontime everyone collected at a vacant lot and spread cloths for a sumptuous picnic dinner. After visiting around and perhaps a baseball game, people congregated to hear the Fourth of July speeches. The people of Canyon City still tell the story of the time John Luce got up to read the Declaration of Independence. He read about half of the United States Constitution before someone pulled his coat tail and turned to the page with the Declaration on it.

Oregon Oddities, WPA; *History of Del Norte*, Bledsoe

Cape Arago Lighthouse – 1866

A LIGHTHOUSE WAS BUILT at the mouth of the Coquille River at Cape Arago. Because of the cost of the Civil War, Congress only appropriated $15,000 for the construction. This was only enough to build an iron tower with a light on top. The lard oil lamps were first lit in November 1866.

Known for years as the Cape Gregory Light, it sat on an island about 300 feet from shore. The light keeper had to use a small boat to go to and from the mainland until 1876, when a footbridge was built. The bridge caused problems right from the start. The spot was known for its high winds. They were so strong they could knock a man down. Damage was always occurring, either to the bridge, the keeper's dwelling or the light itself. The high seas were undermining the tip of land and the lighthouse was in jeopardy. Seamen complained the light and foghorn were too weak.

In 1908, a new lighthouse was built. It had a bright light and powerful fog horn. But this did not end the problems. Erosion continued and a third lighthouse had to be built in 1933. This had a 44 foot tower using the lenses from the previous tower but electrifying them.

Through all these years, the old iron tower remained standing until it was blasted down in 1937.

Oregon's Seacoast Lighthouses, Gibbs

Coos Bay Transportation

IN THE EARLY DAYS, along the coast, the only way to get from one place to another was by boat. These might be canoes, rafts, or flat bottomed boats. Between 1860 and 1880, if you wanted to go to Coquille from Coos Bay, you took a steamer up Isthmus Slough to a railroad hand car. This would take you over a hill. Here you boarded another steamer to take you down Beaver Slough to Coquille. One of these little steamers was called the *Mud Hen.* She ran up and down Beaver Slough between the hand car and Coquille. She was only 23 feet long and just narrow enough to fit the stream.

At night, beaver would build dams across the stream. In the morning, members of the crew would have to wade in front of the boat, kicking out the dams so that the steamer could get through.

Life and Legends in the Coos Bay Area, Coover

Canning Salmon

THE FIRST COMMERCIAL fishing on the Klamath River began in 1876. These first fisheries salted the majority of the fish. Some they lightly cured. The rest was marketed fresh. Very little canning was done before 1900. It was a problem getting the supplies in for canning and the canned product out again to market.

Canning salmon
SOURCE: Del Norte County Historical Society

The Occident and Orient Commercial Company was located at the mouth of the Smith River. The fish were netted here. Each seine gang was made up of 10 to 15 men. A boat would take a large seine to the middle of the river near its mouth. A second boat would take one end and go to the beach upstream. Gradually the men would haul in the net, trapping the fish. Small fish could swim out of the net. About 1,000 fish were caught each time the net was drawn. They weighed between five and sixty pounds each.

Commercial fishermen delivered their catch right to the fish house. The fish splitter cut off the heads, cut off the seven fins, split the fish open, cleaning out the insides, and finished by cutting off the tail and shoving the fish in water. The entire process took only ten strokes.

The scaler got the fish next. He scaled the fish under running water and set them so the excess water would drain off. Next they were cut into pieces a little shorter than the length of the can and the pieces put into boxes for the stuffing table. Women filled the cans which were then capped and sealed in the soldering room. Here a small furnace was set on the floor, and on top of the stove there was a groove filled with melted solder. A can would be placed on an inclining board where it rolled across the furnace with the bottom edge passing through the hot solder. Men inspected the cans and stopped any vent holes. Now the cans were ready to be lowered into the cooking kettle where they were covered with boiling water for five and a half hours. Out of the cooking kettle, the cans were dipped into a lye bath to remove any grease. When cool, they were dipped in a varnish solution to keep the cans from rusting. Now they were ready for labeling. In 1880, 7,000 cases of canned fish went to the San Francisco market.

After 1908 canning machines were rented for the season from the American Can Company. These machines were able to cap 32 cans a minute and did away with spoilage due to leaking.

Del Norte Historical Society Museum; *History of Del Norte*, Bledsoe

Rogue River Cannon – 1882

THE TOWN OF ELLENBURG had a new cannon. It seemed to have been designed for the deck of a ship. It was 57 inches long and weighed an estimated 1,300 pounds. It came from Mexico and tradition had it that it had been used in Maximilian's time.

The cannon was placed on a rock on the north side of the mouth of the Rogue River. It was normally fired only on the fourth of July. This continued until 1903 when there was an accident.

It is told that George Cook and some other young men were given the job of firing the cannon. None of them had any experience with it. The cannon had been sitting out in the weather for the 20 years it was in Port Orford and goodness knows how long before that. The first two firings went all right but not the third. It was speculated that the barrel had deep rust spots that held embers from the previous firings. These were not properly cleaned out when Cook put in the wadding and started to ram it down. Whatever the cause, the gun blew up, killing George Cook.

After this mishap, the gun was dismounted and never fired again.

Curry County *Echoes*, March 1985

Steamer *Alaskan*

ON A MAY NIGHT IN 1889, the steamer *Alaskan* made its way south. Nearing Cape Blanco, the winds picked up and the seas increased. They were 18 miles off shore when the ship began to leak. The men tried to caulk the seams in the hull with bedding. Meanwhile, Captain Howes was trying to keep the ship heading into the wind. Rolling and pitching, the boat began to break up. Waves came over the deck, taking with them most of the upper rigging. Down below, the pumps were not keeping up with the water that was seeping in.

For another 12 hours the ship labored. The crew took to the four lifeboats leaving the captain and nine crew members aboard in hopes that a nearby ship had seen their distress rockets and might still come to their aid.

For another day, the ship remained afloat. As it sank and broke in two, the men leaped free of the whirlpool caused by the sinking vessel. Clinging to pieces of wreckage, the men floated for a day and a half before the tub *Vigilant* found them. Thirty-one men had died, many from exposure.

Captain Howe, a sailor since the age of twelve, was one of the survivors.

Oregon's Seacoast Lighthouses, Gibbs

S.S. Bawnmore – 1895

ON THE NIGHT of August 27, 1895 the steam ship *Bawnmore* became lost in the fog. It was off shore from the emerging town of Lakeport in Curry County, Oregon. Imagine the surprise of the town surveyor the next morning when he arrived on the beach to see the grounded ship some 700 feet from shore. Through his pocket telescope he could see that an anchor had been dropped but the ship seemed unable to pull itself off.

The surveyor improvised a sign from a flat, weathered piece of driftwood and using a charred piece of wood, wrote, "Will Send Help." The ship tooted its whistle in answer and the surveyor ran back to his campsite where he mounted his horse, rode to the nearby town of Denmark and told the postmaster. He then continued on to the Bandon Lifesaving Station for help.

The crew of the ship was saved and over a period of several weeks cargo was brought ashore. Among the cargo were several bulls who got loose. Trolley cars were another part of the inventory but there were no rails so the cars were used for buildings.

When most of the cargo was taken off, the ship caught fire and sank. A huge beach sale took place to get rid of the salvage.

Oregon's Seacoast Lighthouses, Gibbs

Lakeport, Oregon – 1910

TEN MILES NORTH of Port Orford, just inside the beach, is a blue lake, known as Floras Lake. Real estate promoters from Spokane, Washington looked at this 25 square mile lake and envisioned a thriving vacation town. They called it Pacific City but it soon took on the name Lakeport.

The 80 mile coastline of Curry County had no bay or port. The town's promoters were able to convince people that all they had to do was dig a short canal through the sandbar to connect the lake with the ocean and they would have a snug harbor. Almost immediately a sawmill went up to provide the wood needed for building. Merchants arrived, doctors, lawyers and a dentist. The Floras Lake *Banner* began printing and a post office opened to serve the 400 residents. Lakeport was the largest town in Curry County.

The first idea for making Lake Floras a harbor began as early as the 1890s but nothing came of it. What happened to Lakeport in 1910 should have been obvious. It was discovered that the lake was higher than the ocean. Any channel they dug would drain the lake. As soon as this fact was known, people began moving out of town.

The sinking of the *Czarina*, 1910. Note the sailors clinging to the rigging.
SOURCE: Curry County Historical Society

Weeds have taken over the site of this promising town and nothing more is to be seen of it.

Lakeport, Ghost Town of the South Oregon Coast, Webber

Sinking of the *Czarina* – 1910

ON THE MORNING of January 12, 1910, the ship *Czarina* left what is now Coos Bay, loaded with coal and lumber. It was bound for San Francisco. As the ship approached the bar, conditions were poor. The ocean was rising in large swells. Observers at the Lifesaving Station wondered why the captain would even try to make the crossing. The vessel was soon in trouble as the keel hit the reef near the south spit. Sounding the whistle, the men at the station launched their surfboats and called in the tug *Astoria*. Seas were too high to approach the distressed *Czarina*. By dawn the next day only the funnel and the ship's masts were above water. The crew and one passenger were clinging to the rigging. The cargo of lumber had broken free, tossed by the waves. The floating wood had wrecked the lifeboats.

Attempts were made to shoot a line to the *Czarina* but they all fell short. Other ships stood by to help, but the seas never calmed. One by one the exhausted men dropped to their deaths in the water. The First Engineer was able to lash himself to a plank which drifted toward shore. Those watching pulled the man to safety. He was the only survivor, though efforts went on throughout the second night in hopes that someone else might be found.

Battery Point Lighthouse, Gold Beach, California
PHOTO: Carol Barrett

The disaster was followed by accusations of cowardice on the part of the captain of the Lifesaving Service. It was doubtful, even if he had risked the lives of his men, that anyone from the *Czarina* could have been saved.

Oregon's Seacoast Lighthouses, Gibbs with Webber

Steam Ship *Elizabeth* – 1922

IT WOULD HAVE BEEN hard for the early people of Bandon, Oregon to imagine existence without the steam ship *Elizabeth*. In fact, some people thought the town should be renamed Elizabeth Town.

Affectionately known as "Lizzie," the vessel was built in San Francisco and immediately began bringing merchandise to Bandon. On the return trip they would load lumber, cheese and milk. Passengers were always welcome. There was room for 27 first class passengers and six in steerage. They paid $10 to make the trip which took 40 hours. But it was the merchandise on which Bandon depended.

Even though they lost money in the early days and again during the depression years, the company kept the ship on schedule.

On July 27, 1922 the Elizabeth completed its 600th round trip between San Francisco and Bandon but its days were numbered. In 1927 the ship was sold and used to transport lumber between Crescent City and San Francisco. In 1942 it was wrecked on a reef off Mazatlán, Mexico.

Coquille River Museum, Bandon, Oregon

OUR DARLINGS

WILLE C.	LEAH M.
DIED	DIED
OCT 15, 1890	OCT 21, 1890
AGED	AGED
6 YRS. 4 MO.	5 YRS. 3 MO.
20 DAS.	12 DAS.

CHILDREN OF
DR. J.W. & TILLIE ROBINSON

PHOTO: Carol Barrett

CHAPTER 13

INTERESTING PEOPLE

Jacksonville Doctors – 1878

IN EARLY OREGON, the only place for formal medical training was the Medical Department of the University of Willamette in Salem. In June 1878, Ella Ford received a degree from the medical school as did her sister. They were among the first women to graduate. Upon graduation, Ella married Dr. James W. Robinson, a member of her class.

James went to Jacksonville to begin his practice. He described the town:

"When I arrived.... on a lovely Sunday evening, I felt I had found my paradise. The church bells were ringing as we entered the old mining town...It was the center of business in Southern Oregon...so I found a fair field for my work. Dr. Parsons of Ashland was the only other graduate M.D. in the county."

James and Ella opened their practices immediately with Ella advertising that she gave special attention to diseases of women and obstetrical care.

Unfortunately Dr. Ella Ford-Robinson had tuberculosis and in a few months became seriously ill. She returned to Salem where it was hoped the climate would help her. In July, less then nine months after her wedding, she died. Her husband was inconsolable and left Jacksonville for awhile but finally returned to his practice.

In 1882, Dr. Robinson married Matilda (Tillie) Miller. They had two children, a son Willie Cecil, and a daughter Mary Leah. Both died in the diphtheria epidemic of 1890. A third child, Regina Dorland was born. Tragedy struck yet again. At age 25, the gifted Dorland committed suicide.

An Honorable History, Atwood; Southern Oregon Historical Society *Sentinel*, February 1985

David Linn

DAVID LINN WAS a man of great ability, great ingenuity and great imagination. He had been brought up in the carpenter trade. When he decided to come west in 1850 he brought all the tools he could pack. He worked in the Humbug Creek and Yreka Flats area and did quite well for himself. When he heard of gold near Table Rock City, he immediately headed there and became one of the founding fathers of Jacksonville, Oregon.

Instead of mining, Linn set up a carpentry shop, made sluice boxes for miners and constructed cabins and sheds. He even made wooden water pumps. He soon added simple furniture to his line and always there was a demand for coffins. As the town grew, so did business. He built a two story building on the main street and behind it a factory with a steam engine and boiler room. He employed twelve to fifteen men and was responsible for building many homes and stores in Jacksonville. Next, he purchased a stand of pine trees to furnish his own lumber.

Linn took his saw mill over the mountains and constructed Fort Klamath. He also built a boat in sections. In 1869 he and a party of men took it to Crater Lake, carefully lowered it and reassembled it by the water. The party circled the lake and were probably the first to visit Wizard Island.

In September 1888, fire broke out at Linn's factory, burning it to the ground. Linn never rebuilt but continued in the furniture business until he was 77 years old.

Southern Oregon Historical Society *Sentinel,* August 1986

Joaquin Miller – 1860s

ONE OF THE MOST flamboyant characters in the west was Joaquin Miller, "Poet of the Sierras." Miller's home town was Eugene, but he lived for a time in Jacksonville, and in 1856 arrived in California working as a miner and cook on McAdams Creek in the Humbug camps of the Klamath River. In his pocket he kept a book in which he jotted down verses. The majority of his poems were drawn from this mining background. The poems became highly popular in the mining camps. However he didn't become really famous until his trip to the English stage. Dressed in buckskins and sombrero he sat on a bearskin rug and spouted ungrammatical couplets. When not on stage he wore boots and the red flannel shirts he had worn during his Scott Valley days. He was a startling figure on the London streets.

Always dramatic, Miller also wrote plays which are now nearly forgotten but were hits in his day. His melodrama, *Mexico* headlined in New York in 1878. One of his major plays, *The Danites* was a fictional story of a group of Mormons avenging the death of their leader, Joseph Smith. Another entitled, *Forty-nine* presented gold rush characters and scenes. Both were performed extensively in this country and abroad.

In 1872, Miller returned to Pittsburg, on the Pit River, to get his daughter, Carrie. Several men who had known him recognized him as Meiner Miller, a man who was arrested and indicted in 1859 for stealing a horse owned by Thomas Bass.

Stories were being written about Joaquin Miller, glorifying his early life. In spite of offers of financial reward, his early friends kept quiet about the unsavory aspects of Miller's past. As one man put it,

"We thought that if Joaquin Miller could start out in poverty from amid the mountain solitude of Shasta, and raise himself to eminence by the force and brilliancy of his genius, we would not hasten to engage in throwing stones at him, but would even excise him for taking a little romantic ride on Bass' horse."

Miller adopted San Francisco as his home but he is remembered as "The Poet of the Sierras."

Trouping in the Oregon Country, Ernst; Fort Jones Historical Brochure;
From listener Joe Mazzini

Minnie Myrtle

IN THE EARLY 1860s everyone read poetry. Minnie Myrtle was able to get several poems printed in newspapers, one of which was in Eugene.

At this time Joaquin Miller was a poet of growing importance. He was earning his living editing the *Democratic Register*. He was attracted by Minnie's poems and began a correspondence with her. Encouraged by her responses, Miller rode over to Port Orford to see Minnie. He found her a tall, dark and striking looking woman, cheerful and full of warmth. He arrived on a Thursday night and the two were married the following Sunday. The passion was not to last. As Joaquin Miller's fame grew, he left to travel all over the world and the two were divorced. Minnie and their two daughters stayed in Port Orford.

Here is the last verse of Minnie Mrytle's most famous poem. It will give you an idea of what people liked in the 1860s and 1870s.

> To the splendid grave they have laid him,
> Where the tropical drowsiness floats,
> Where a bird in the plumage of Eros,
> Is tolling his funeral notes.
> I will come, sometimes with the shadows,
> I will hush the wild notes of the bird;
> And then in the listening silence
> The voice of my heart shall be heard.

Minnie Myrtle died in 1884 and is buried next to Joaquin Miller.

Curry County *Echoes,* May 1993

Bret Harte – 1857

BORN IN 1836, Bret Harte was 18 when he went west to be with his mother and stepfather. For a few months he worked for Wells Fargo Express on stage lines in Trinity, Siskiyou and Humboldt counties. He may have mined some but little is known about his first three years in California. He must have absorbed all he saw because he used these people and these settings for his later stories.

1857 found Harte working and writing for the *Northern Californian,* a weekly newspaper in Arcata. He was run out of town in 1869 when he took the side of the Indians in the Mad River Indian Massacre.

San Francisco was Harte's next stop, where he worked on the newspaper, *The Golden Era.* His international fame as an author is connected with the success of Anton Roman, who published the *Overland Monthly.* Hart became editor and wrote a monthly column named "Etc." plus poems and stories. Harte quickly found himself a world wide celebrity.

In 1871, Bret Harte left California and never returned. He went to Boston where his fame brought him celebrity status for a short while, but his popularity waned and never returned.

Harte died in 1902. He is remembered for his nostalgic short stories set in the gold country of Northern California.

Western Writer Series #5, Morrow; *Saddle Bags in Siskiyou,* Jones

Judge Hanna – 1872

WHEN HE WAS JUST eighteen years old, Hiero Kennedy Hanna came west in search of gold. He mined for ten years with moderate success. All this time he had been carrying around a few law books hoping that someday he could study law. While mining near Waldo, Oregon he began studying the books seriously. He made friends with a young lawyer who lent him further reading material. Soon Hanna found himself arbitrating miner's disagreements. In 1870, before he had even finished his studies, he was elected justice of the peace for Waldo. Almost immediately he became district attorney for all of Josephine, Jackson, Klamath and Lake counties. Only after this appointment was Hanna admitted to the bar in 1872. He was already considered one of the best legal brains in the state.

Setting up practice in Jacksonville, Hanna became circuit judge in 1880. He retired 30 years later at the age of 78. Judge Hanna died six months later, one of the most highly thought of men in Southern Oregon.

Southern Oregon Historical Society *Sentinel,* April 1987

George Sightman – 1873

GEORGE SIGHTMAN WAS a real entrepreneur in California gold mining history. He was forty-five years old when he began mining with a pick, shovel and rocker at Blue Gulch in the mountains of northern California. He did well and saved his money. When he realized the demand for lumber in the new mining towns, he became a sawmill owner and operator. Eventually he owned at least three mills and several water rights. In 1873 Sightman bought what was left of Cecilville, a once active mining town. He became the bartender, storekeeper, postmaster and hotel manager. With one other helper, he did all the work, gradually bringing the town back to life.

In the fall, Sightman dried apples and made apple cider which he sold in his store. He had a method of fermenting the cider until it was potent and had no trouble selling it.

All merchants bought and traded in gold. Sightman was no exception. A scale was kept on the counter to weigh the gold brought in. Never one for exactness, Sightman spilled a little every time he measured a weight. Two miners, seeing this happen, asked if they could clean the counter and have the soil on the floor under the scale. When they were through panning, they were $200 richer.

The practice of giving unlimited credit finally bankrupted George Sightman but he had had a good life.

Siskiyou *Pioneer,* 1957

Aaron Rose and Roseburg

THE TOWN OF DEER CREEK was built on the South Umpqua River where Deer Creek enters. We know it today as Roseburg.

Aaron Rose, a merchant, settled here in 1851. He and his wife, Sarah, had come to the valley via the Applegate Trail. Rose purchased a squatter's claim and built his home, opening it as a tavern. He also built a store, butcher shop and horse sales business. He was so successful, he talked the government into moving to Deer Creek from Winchester, which was just a few miles north. He offered them three acres of land and $1,000 toward a building. Before he was through, he had also given land for a school and several churches. He encouraged and invested in many businesses.

Well respected, Rose was elected to the Territorial Legislature. The town was named Roseburgh in 1857. The spelling was changed to Roseburg in 1894.

During the Indian wars, Roseburg acted as the headquarters for the Northern Battalion of Oregon Volunteers. This brought recognition and business. It also became the terminus of the Coos Bay Wagon Road. The California & Oregon Railroad ran into financial difficulties on its way from Portland and stopped in Roseburg. For ten years, this was the terminus. When it did go on, Roseburg still remained a division point.

Aaron Rose married four times, leaving several children when he died on March 11, 1899, a very successful man.

Land of the Umpqua, Beckham; *Oregon Geographic Names,* McArthur

President Hayes in Yreka – 1880

PRESIDENT AND MRS. Rutherford B. Hayes toured the west coast in 1880. The trip was said to be for recreation and observation. The railroad had crossed the country but the line between Portland and San Francisco was not complete. From Sacramento north the presidential party traveled by stage coach. On September

Aaron Rose
SOURCE: Douglas County Museum of History and Natural History

26th they reached Yreka. It was a Sunday and the town was decked out with flags and a "Welcome" sign.

At five o'clock the president's carriages appeared. The band burst into "The Star Spangled Banner" and the reception committee greeted the president and his wife. With him was General Sherman. It had been planned that when the party reached the hotel, President Hayes would greet the many residents and make a short speech. However, both he and General Sherman refused. It was Sunday and for either of them to make a speech on a Sunday would not be considered proper. The local judge made his speech greeting the presidential party to which the President gave his thanks.

The following day, the party left for Jacksonville.

Siskiyou *Pioneer,* 1969

President Hayes in Jacksonville

HEADING FOR JACKSONVILLE, the presidential party stopped at Little Shasta. In Jacksonville, the U.S. Hotel was not yet finished but that didn't deter Madame Holt, the owner and proprietor. She had been in the business for 20 years and had served other famous people.

When the great day came, the president made a speech from the balcony and then retired to the new hall. The chandeliers shown down on a large crowd of invited guests. They were wined and dined like royalty. The president and his wife expressed their appreciation.

The next morning the town turned out to cheer the visitors as they boarded their coaches. Madame Holt was there to present her bill to the president's secretary. He was aghast. Each member of the party had been charged $15 for room and board. The secretary reluctantly paid the bill with the reported remark, "My dear Madame, we wished only to stay the night, not to buy the hotel."

The next stop for the party was in what is now Sunny Valley. Knowing the president was coming, a farm house had been enlarged and turned into Harkness Inn. They stayed there overnight and went on.

Southern Oregon Historical Society *Sentinel,* January 1983; Siskiyou *Pioneer,* 1988

President Hayes in Canyonville

THE PRESIDENTIAL PARTY reached Canyonville September 29th. The town had been preparing for days. Children were let out of school to wait for the stage and cheer their president. The Concord stage pulled in, drawn by six matched gray horses. Promptly at noon the party was ushered to the Overland Hotel for dinner. The citizens had provided the food and their best china, silver and table linens.

The party went on to Myrtle Creek where Hayes made a speech before embarking for Roseburg.

Pioneer Days in the South Umpqua Valley, August 1971; *Land of the Umpqua,* Beckham; *110 Years With Josephine,* Sutton

Grave Creek stage station where President Hayes' party stopped.
SOURCE: Larry McLane

President Hayes in Roseburg

ROSEBURG HAD KNOWN for months that the president was coming. They had no hotel large enough or elegant enough to house his entire party. The President, Mrs. Hayes and three others spent the night at the beautiful home of William Willis. Here a dinner party was put on at which the women were beautifully gowned and the men wore uniforms. After dinner, a mass meeting was held in front of the hotel where the rest of the party were staying. Fortunately the weather was fine as there was no room large enough for the gathering. The president and others spoke from the balcony of the hotel to the crowd below.

Selected ladies had gathered at the Willis home for a reception in honor of Lucy Hayes. She and her hostess got along very well and Mrs. Hayes invited Mrs. Willis to board the train and make the trip to Portland with them the next day. This she did.

The train left very early in the morning and stopped at Oakland for breakfast. Here, as elsewhere, the president smiled and waved from the back platform of the train.

With Her Own Wings, Smith

Marshfield *Sun* – 1891

JUSE ALLEN LUSE published the first issue of the weekly Marshfield *Sun* in early 1891. Newspapers had a tremendous influence on their community and the editor had complete control over what was written. Luse was no exception. He edited the *Sun* for 50 years. He wrote the copy, set the type and printed the paper. In his first issue he clashed with the police concerning a Chinese opium joint that was running "full blast" and being patronized by white people, young and old.

The *Sun* began as a Populist Party newspaper, appealing to the interests of farmers and workers who were suffering from the depression of the 1890's. It took a strong stand against monopolies and most taxes. As Populism died out, the paper supported the Republican Party and Luse, in his editorials, became more and more conservative. Throughout, it was a newsy frontier town paper.

Luse finally had to retire. He issued the last edition of the *Sun* in June 1944.

The Coos Bay Region, Doughit

Theodore Roosevelt

THE NEXT PRESIDENT, after Rutherford Hayes, to visit this part of the country was Theodore Roosevelt in 1903. In Grants Pass, two bands and a huge crowd turned out for his arrival. Unfortunately, the train engineer forgot to stop.

Roosevelt also spent five minutes in Roseburg. It was 2:30 in the morning and he was asleep in his comfortable Pullman coach.

Land of the Umpqua, Beckham

Sam Colver – 1891

SAM COLVER WAS the first resident in Phoenix, Oregon. He built a home and solid fortifications to which the local residents fled during the many Indian threats of the early 1850s. He was a man universally liked and it was only natural that he became the leader to whom people turned. He filled that position until his strange death in February 1891.

One day Colver left his home to go on business to Klamath Falls. When he failed to return, a party went to search for him. He was never found but his horse was discovered on the shores of Klamath Lake. It was presumed that Colver either drowned trying to cross the lake or froze to death.

Colver had always been interested in spiritualism and on the night it was presumed he died, his wife, Huldah, was sitting in their living room. She heard his distinctive knock on the front door but when she went to answer, no one was there.

Early Days in Phoenix, Helms

Jack London

JACK LONDON WAS a superstar in the early 1900s. Naturally flamboyant, he found his name in the papers for barroom fights, notorious love affairs and his adventurous past. But there was another side of London. He loved the wild outdoors and hated the destruction of the land that he saw in his native California.

Jack London
SOURCE: Larry McLane

He bought some misused, overgrazed land in Sonoma Valley California and tried to reclaim it. The story of this project, and his belief in man's relationship with the land, was used in his book *The Valley of the Moon*. While he was writing the book, he lived in Wolf Creek. One of his favorite spots was a mountain peak nearby which was named London Peak. This was only one of several summers London spent in the Rogue River Valley.

Jack London died at age 40, before his project was completed. Few read his books now but London Peak is a lasting reminder of this colorful man.

From listener Larry King, Wolf Creek

Jack London at Crater Lake – 1911

JACK LONDON WAS at the height of his career when he traveled with his wife and a Japanese servant from San Francisco to Crater Lake. Their route took them right up the trail Interstate 5 roughly follows today. He stopped at Medford and stayed at the famous Nash Hotel.

Since his conversion to socialism, London had worked to promote its ideal. While in Medford he spoke before a large audience about his socialistic convictions. His speeches were full of colorful tales, drawn from the hard, fast life he led.

London loved to travel and considered himself an authority on the world's most beautiful places. After seeing Crater Lake, he declared it far above anything he had ever seen or expected to see in the future saying, "Crater Lake is the greatest asset in Southern Oregon."

Jack London, who is still considered one of America's great writers, died five years after this visit.

Southern Oregon Historical Society *Sentinel,* July 1980

Wilbur Dodge

WILBUR DODGE WAS a character who lived near Trinity Center in the 1920s. He wore ragged clothes, long hair and a scraggly beard. He carried a six-shooter on his hip and an alarm clock tied around his neck. He was respectfully call "Mr. Dodge" by everyone, perhaps due to stories like this one.

Two men were sitting on the bench in front of a store. Their two dogs were curled up under the bench. Along came Wilbur Dodge. One of the dogs jumped

First airplane to Grants Pass. Barnstormers.
SOURCE: Larry McLane

out and bit the man on the calf of his leg. Without a moments hesitation Dodge drew his six-shooter and shot the dog. He then faced the two men and asked, "Is there any argument gentlemen?"

There was none.

Along Our History's Trail, Hayden

Charles Lindbergh – 1927

CHARLES AUGUSTUS LINDBERGH was 25 years old when he barnstormed in the Rogue River Valley in September 1927. He had made his historic non-stop flight across the Atlantic May 21 of that same year. He returned to the area shortly after his first visit, for a week of fishing on the Upper Rogue. Even there he was not able to entirely get away from his fawning public.

Lindbergh was the darling of the United States until he made a speech in September 1941 in Des Moine, Iowa. He is quoted as having said, "The British, the Jewish and the Roosevelt administration" are trying to draw the United States into World War II. He went on to say that the Jewish groups should oppose the prospect of war instead of "agitating" for it.

This speech sparked charges that Lindbergh was anti-semitic. This he denied but he would not withdraw his statement. It was already known that he strongly opposed our country becoming militarily involved in the war with Germany.

Lindbergh never again regained his earlier popularity.

Medford *Mail Tribune; History of Jackson County,* Tucker

Zane Grey – 1927

ZANE GREY WAS a passionate, but not very skillful, fisherman. He made many fishing visits on the Rogue River. His greatest thrill was to ride down river through the wild white water. This persuaded him to buy property at Winkle Bar upstream from Marial, where he built a fishing cabin. It was accessible only by trail or river boat. Nevertheless Grey always arrived with family and friends plus secretaries, a cook and a cameraman.

Zane Grey was born in 1872. He received a degree in dentistry from the University of Pennsylvania and practiced for several years. He was thirty and newly married before he became a serious writer. His first stories were historical novels. It was the fishing that got him started writing westerns. He traveled from one fishing spot to another and would write a story with the local history as a background.

Grey was already well established as a major writer when he built his Winkle Bar cabin. He wrote a number of stories centered on the Rogue Valley. He describes the area in detail and his love of the wild country rings true.

When Savage Rapids Dam was built, Grey became disillusioned with the Rogue River. Later he fished the North Umpqua River but never publicized it as he had the Rogue.

Rogue River Communities, Selected Writings; A Guide to Oregon South Coast History, Doughit
Southern Oregon Historical Society *Sentinel,* November 1992

Zane Grey

WHEN ZANE GREY built his cabin on Winkle Bar, he was not popular with his neighbors.

He was a good athlete and a rugged man, but was said to be shy. Whatever the reason, he made no effort to be friendly. One story is told about two boys who took their boats upriver to help Grey move. They worked all day and were never given even a thank-you.

Even if he was not liked, the people knew Grey was a celebrity and made the most of it. One time when he arrived by train in Grants Pass, he had to wait for transportation. His impressive fishing equipment was stacked on the platform. A native came up bragging, "That is some fishing equipment, but it's not as good as what Zane Grey had. I spent one summer with Grey and his equipment was the best."

Grey answered him, cutting him down to size, "I never saw you before. Just where did you and I fish that summer?"

George Morey, Gold Beach

Jesse Winburn – 1920

JESSE WINBURN WAS an eccentric millionaire philanthropist who made his start by promoting advertising on streetcars and buses. He arrived in Ashland in 1920 promising to put its name on the map. He formed the Ashland Development

Company and decided to buy the Ashland Hotel and the bottling plant for Lithia water. He bought a cabin up Ashland Creek and here his troubles started. The creek was the water supply for the town but he insisted on dumping garbage into it and allowing his livestock free access to the stream. The town objected. They didn't even want him to fish in their drinking water but he continued to do so.

After about two years, Winburn became disenchanted with Ashland. Everyone had their hand out for money and he believed the Ashland Development Company he founded was swindling people. He withdrew his support, sold his house and left town.

Winburn had done much for Ashland. He had improved and modernized the hospital, financed the finishing of the women's club house, built a road to Mount Ashland and brought swans to the pond in Lithia Park.

History of Jackson County, Mail Tribune, May 12, 1979

John B. Gruelle – 1923

THE BOOK *Raggedy Ann and Andy and the Camel With the Wrinkled Knees* was published in August, 1923. It had been written while Johnny Gruelle, the originator of Raggedy Ann, was living in Ashland. An outstanding artist, journalist, humanist, nature lover, spiritualist and cartoonist, Gruelle was going through the most creative period of his life.

The doll Raggedy Ann had been patented in 1915. Gruelle was a prolific story teller and when asked how the idea started he often told varying accounts. His wife, however, stated that an old rag doll of his grandmother's was found in the attic. Their daughter took a fancy to it so Gruelle painted a new face on the doll and used shoe buttons for the eyes. They named the doll Raggedy Ann. He took to telling his daughter stories about the adventures the doll had. It wasn't until 1918 that Gruelle submitted the first manuscript of these stories. The family made dolls to put on display for the promotion of the new book and both the book and the doll were an immediate success.

The Gruelle family only lived in the Ashland area a year and a half before they moved back to Connecticut. Johnny died of a heart attack in 1938. He was only 57 years old.

The Last Great Company, (Southern Oregon Historical Society)

William Randolph Hearst

MONTAGUE, CALIFORNIA had an airport. It was also known as a place for good hunting and fishing. Such notables as Herbert Hoover and Babe Ruth flew there for fishing vacations. William Randolph Hearst was another who flew to Montague on a regular basis. One of his five large homes was in nearby McCloud. He would lavishly entertain his Hollywood friends. Sometimes he even sent a train car load of bicycles for his guests to use.

Weekends when he was in McCloud, Hearst hired Peterson's Band to play for dances. The band was made up of seven local people including Leah Reichman on the piano. Hearst paid them each $15. Leah remembers how he would go off to bed at midnight while Marian Davies stayed up dancing with everyone. Often they played until dawn always ending with "Goodnight Sweetheart."

Interview with Leah Reichman

Alfred Hitchcock

HOW ARE ALFRED HITCHCOCK and the Peter Britt Music Festival in Jacksonville connected?

The Peter Britt committee wanted to interest Alfred Hitchcock in making a guest appearance at the festival. Should he accept, it would give them great free advertising. When they were able to reach Hitchcock by phone, he claimed to be pining for a vacation on the Rogue River. He even nostalgically remembered eating Newton apples from Oregon when he was a youth in London. His father was a green grocer and had imported the apples for his store. This was enough to inspire the committee to send Hitchcock a box of Newton apples as a further incentive. The gift was not as strange as it might seem as Peter Britt is credited with planting the first apple trees in the Rogue River Valley.

Apparently Alfred Hitchcock was not impressed enough to make the desired appearance, although he politely cited prior movie commitments as the reason he had to decline the offer.

Medford Mail Tribune, *April 13, 1965*

Crater Lake Movies – 1950s

THE DRAMATIC SCENERY at Crater Lake attracted Hollywood stars and film producers. Clark Gable had come to the Rogue River fishing several times. About 1939 he brought Carole Lombard to Crater Lake Lodge for a vacation. Carole loved it and reportedly danced with all the employees. This did not sit well with Gable who swore at her and finally went off to their room without her.

About the same time, the movie *Sun Down* was filmed at the lake level requiring a seaplane to move all the equipment. The action was supposed to be taking place in Africa where a gun smuggling ring was operating.

In the fifties, *Canyon Passage* was filmed in Jacksonville but the crew moved to Crater Lake to shoot a scene with the Indians riding over the rim and attacking a wagon train moving along the rim road. For those old enough to remember the names, the film starred Ward Bond, Loretta Young, Brian Donlevy and Dan Daily.

Smith Brothers Chronological History of Crater Lake

Chapter 14

Business

Lone Ranch Borax Mine – 1860s

IN THE 1860s there was great hope of money being made from borax in southern Curry County, Oregon. In 1857 John Cresswell took up a homestead near the mouth of Lone Ranch Creek. He raised cattle and sheep. Trees from the nearby hills furnished all the wood he needed for building. What intrigued him was the white chalky outcropping along the creek. Housewives polished their silver with it and others used it for chalk. Finally someone sent off a sample to be analyzed. It was found to be borate of lime. The mineral is hard while underground but when exposed to water and air it crumbles and becomes a powder.

It wasn't until 1890 that commercial possibilities were explored and development of the mine began. Tunnels were dug in from the bay, only a few feet above high water. The mined borax had to be stored, then loaded on small boats which took it out to large barges. These were loaded and sailed to a San Francisco refinery.

Mining was dangerous and difficult. The operation only lasted two years. The mining site went back to being sheep pasture and the tunnels started to fill in. After the December 7, 1941 Japanese raid on Pearl Harbor, the Coast Guard dynamited the remaining tunnels for fear the Japanese might hide in them if there was an invasion.

Curry County Historical Society Monthly Bulletin, April 1974

Telephone and Telegraph – 1878

ON DECEMBER 8, 1878 the first long distance telephone call in the region was made. Yreka called Jacksonville, a distance of 60 miles. Songs were sung and responded to from both ends of the telephone wire. It seemed like quite a novelty. The only useful purpose people could foresee would be in an emergency.

SOURCE: Ruth Minear Alborn

It was five years before Dr. Elijah Pickel installed the first telephone line in Medford. It was between his home and his office which was located in one of the first brick buildings erected in town. Apparently it worked well because he extended the line to the home and drugstore of his friend George Haskin.

In 1896 the Pacific Telephone and Telegraph inaugurated Medford service with 16 subscribers. During the first four years, a single switchboard was all that was needed. It was located in the drug store with Mr. Haskin and his assistant handling phone service between customers.

As the line extended service to Jacksonville and other nearby communities, a larger switchboard came into use and with it the switchboard operator who held a very special place in the life of this, or any, community.

Founding of Medford, Snedicor; Scott Valley Bank Calendar

Klamath Telephones – 1904

WHEN JOHN HESSIG was 12 years old, and going to school in Hornbrook, California, he made friends with the lady who sent telegrams from Henley. Noting his interest, she taught young John all she knew. John got enthused about the telegraph and as soon as school was out he strung a mile of wire from his house to a resort at Beswick. He telegraphed news to the resort and taught others how to send and receive messages.

In 1902 Alexander Bell's patent expired on parts of his telephone. Hessig immediately sent off for two telephones and installed them at the ends of his mile long wire. He gathered baling wire and barbed wire to string line to a neighbor's ranch, thereby installing the first telephone in Klamath County.

Next Hessig connected up with the Bessick station and began taking business calls. Meanwhile, his father had moved to Fort Klamath and thought it would be nice to be able to talk to his sons. As soon as it became known that such a line was going to be constructed, demand grew. The Klamath Indian Agency was one of those wanting service. Hessig agreed to provide it if each Indian male would furnish three days work. With careful organization the line was put up in 30 days.

By May 1904 the lines were incorporated under the name Klamath Telephone and Telegraph Company. What began as a school boy's interest had developed into a lifetime career.

Klamath *Echoes*, 1975

Thomas Edison – 1888

IT WAS ON October 21, 1879 that Thomas Edison invented a workable electric light in his lab in Menlo Park, New Jersey. No one could have foreseen the effect of this invention on life around the world.

The idea of electric power reached our area quickly. In 1888, Ashland formed the Ashland Electric Power and Light Company and built a primitive hydroelectric plant on Ashland Creek. They soon had one light burning in the plaza area.

James Quinn of Yreka made a trip to San Francisco and returned determined to be the first one to bring electricity to his town. He met with little success promoting electricity, but he was finally able to build a plant on the Shasta River, five miles from Yreka. The plant went into operation in 1892, generating 1,100 volts which were transmitted to Yreka. Service was offered from sundown to midnight and from 4 a.m. to sunup. The number of electric lamps a customer could have was limited and rates varied depending on the use of the lighting.

Quinn did not attempt to expand his operation but other small plants appeared in Northern California by the end of the century. Very few residents had electric lights—and only a few public buildings. A hotel might boast one light in its lobby and others in the dining room, kitchen and barroom but none in the bedrooms. Underground mines wanted lighting but they had to be located near a town as electricity did not extend into rural areas.

After the turn of the century, electrical operations expanded rapidly. Even so, years went by before it was used as a power source rather than just as a device for lighting.

Medford *Mail Tribune*, October 21, 1991
The History of Electrical Development in Northern California and Southern Oregon

Kappler Pool Hall, serving Etna Lager Beer
SOURCE: Paul and Leah Reichman

Etna Brewery – 1875

FOR 50 YEARS the Kappler Brewery was a successful business in Etna, California. The brewery won first prize for its beer at the 1915 Panama Exposition in San Francisco. Charles Kappler had come to Yreka from France where he was a brewer by trade. He bought the P.A. Hearststrand brewery about three miles from present day Yreka. He moved it to Etna Mills four years later.

In 1875 a fire destroyed the Kappler Brewery. Rather than giving up, Kappler built a new and larger operation. The bottling works were in a nearby basement. Kappler had several teams of four to six horses and wagons for delivering the beer in Northern California and Southern Oregon. Where horses and wagon couldn't go, mules carried ten or fifteen gallon kegs to outlying areas.

The brewery created a market for local farmers' hops and barley. When the hop picking season began it was a festive occasion. Traveling shows timed their arrival to entertain the pickers in the evenings.

The brewery was successful right up to the passage of the 18th Amendment, when Prohibition closed it down.

Siskiyou *Pioneer*, 1956

Weed

ABNER E. WEED was looking for a place to build a sawmill. Thirteen years after the railroad went through, he chose the present site of Weed, California because the railroad was there and provided easy transportation to other areas. Besides the mill, a company store was built. Then boarding and bunk houses for the men; a machine shop and a few homes were added. The business was so successful, a box factory was built. Later, Weed went into the sash and door business. Gradually the town grew, adding a depot, churches and a school.

The Weed Mercantile Company Store grew into a large business and was typical of other company stores in the early 1900s. It contained all kinds of dry goods, clothing, a tailor, groceries, a butcher shop, the Weed post office and a Wells Fargo office.

Unlike many company towns, Weed has survived many changes and still is an active place today.

Siskiyou *Pioneer*, 1967

Christmas – 1893

THE VERY FIRST electrically lit Christmas tree in the region was in Yreka in 1893. Yreka had installed an electric light plant two years before. Henry Schultz was a tin smith and electrician by trade. He, his wife and baby lived in a converted store with large windows. Schultz decided to make an electrically lighted tree in honor of his son's first birthday.

The first step was to fasten the main feeder line to the base of a four foot fir tree and lead it up the tree trunk. Off this line, wires ran along each branch. On the wires were small white porcelain sockets screwed to a metal clip adapted from the standard Christmas tree candle holders. The little lights were clear.

The tree was decorated with spun glass, paper and strings of cranberries and popcorn. Through the glass windows, adults as well as children looked enviously at the beautiful lighted Christmas tree.

Siskiyou *Pioneer*, 1969

Denny Bar Stores – 1896

IN 1866 TOM AND JOE DENNY built a store with wide iron doors at Callahan's Ranch. It was called Denny Brothers. The store was so successful they wanted more money to expand so they approached their brother Albert. Gold had been discovered in the upper Trinity River area in the 1880s and the town of New River City was established to serve the area. Albert sold his ranch and opened a Denny's store there.

There was a Parker Denny Company in Etna and a store now called Denny and Bar Company in Callahan and Gazelle. In 1896 they reorganized these stores as Denny, Bar and Parker Company and branched out to a total of eight locations. Finally known as the Denny Bar Stores, they were the first real chain stores in the country. At first supplies were delivered by mule train but in 1896 roads were sufficiently improved to accommodate freight wagons. They did a thriving business supplying mines and were the first dealers in Studebaker cars (sometimes known by owners as E-M-F cars for "Every Morning Fixit").

Denny Bar store, Fort Jones, California
SOURCE: Fort Jones Museum

After years in business, the Denny Bar stores were unable to compete with mail order retailers. They closed one store after another during the depression and never went back into business.

Siskiyou *Pioneers*, 1964 and 1967; *Trinity County Historic Sites*, Trinity County Historical Society; Mt. Shasta *Herald*, January 12, 1978

Coal Mines, Coos Bay

AT ONE TIME there were 72 coal mines in the vicinity of Coos Bay. Many of these were situated along Isthmus Slough, which emptied into the bay.

The dictionary says a "slough" is an area of soft, muddy ground; a swamp or swamp like region. This presented problems for transporting the coal. In a 55 acre area around the slough, about 250,000 tons of coal were mined until the mid 1920s. Coal was transported by rail to wharves and loaded on ships, which took it to markets up and down the coast. In its heyday coal caused towns to be built, short railroads to be laid and large sums of money to be invested in Coos County.

While coal had always been in use, fuel oil and gas greatly diminished the demand for coal. The Coos County coal was no longer considered of high enough grade to be marketable. The mines slowly closed.

Much coal was taken out of the mines along Isthmus Slough, but much more remains.

A Guide to the South Oregon Coast History, Doughit

Box Factory

THE REGION'S FARMS and orchards created a great demand for wooden boxes to ship fruit and vegetables. Factories were scattered throughout the State of Jefferson. The Algoma Lumber Company was just such a factory in Montague, California. It employed 100 men. The company owned timber in the area which came to Montague by train. Horse drawn wagons moved the timber to the box mill. The clear wood was cut to make sash and door stock.

When the boxes were made, the name of the shipper was printed on the box end and the slats. Oranges and lemons were the most common. Apples and dried fruit boxes were also needed. Fires were always a big danger and in July, 1927 a big fire demolished the box factory. It was determined that this one was started by a flare thrown from a train. It had bounced into the open doorway and ignited the sawdust. The Southern Pacific Railroad had to pay $89,000 in damages.

Siskiyou *Pioneer,* 1980

Drummers

"I REMEMBER THE DRUMMERS," Leah Reichman tells us. "They were salesmen who came on the railroad. They had these gorgeous suitcases, huge suitcases full of all kinds of goodies that they showed." Leah's uncle owned the General Store in Montague. She always tried to be there when the drummers came. "Oh, the dolls and the silks and the wonderful yardage. A big part of the Shock's store was into yardage and thread and pattern books."

Merchants would order things to be delivered later. The drummer usually stayed the night at the Montague Hotel. In the morning he would take the train to the next place to show his wares.

Interview with Leah Reichman

Bulb Industry, Brookings

TONY OLSEN LIVED in the Brookings, Oregon area and ran an unsuccessful chicken ranch. In 1922 he found someone who would buy his chickens and he gratefully looked around for another way to make a living. He bought some gladiolus bulbs and planted them. He was so successful, the next year he branched out into several kinds of lilies, daffodils and hyacinths. His neighbors thought he was crazy. They reasoned that anything that couldn't be eaten, could not be profitable. They were proved wrong and many went in for bulb growing themselves.

The Brookings-Harbor area is ideally suited for growing bulbs. The ocean makes for mild winter weather. The summer fogs that frustrate vacationers, protects plants from the hot sun. Most important, at the time the industry was beginning, land was cheap along the coast.

Algoma Box Factory, Montague, California, 1908
SOURCE: Paul and Leah Reichman

Traditionally bulbs had been imported from Japan and Holland. During World War II, with those sources cut off, the bulb industry boomed even with the shortage of labor.

A Brief History of the Brookings-Harbor Flower Farmers, Southern Oregon College paper.

Gladiolus

IN 1927 JOSEPHINE COUNTY had 43 acres of gladiolus bulbs. The next year there were an estimated 350 acres. The bulb industry peaked at a total of over 1,200 acres. It was an important part of the agricultural economy.

In 1936 the idea of a Glad Show came into being. The whole Grants Pass district got behind the idea and made it a huge affair. Prizes were given for the best new variety, the tallest spike and for artistic displays.

It just so happened that Shirley Temple and her family were on a vacation trip in Josephine County and came to the Glad Show. Shirley became the main attraction. The Grants Pass *Courier* kindly posed her pictures so as to hide the fact that she had just lost her first tooth. One of the loveliest pink gladiolus was named the Shirley Temple.

The Glad Show was interrupted by the war but was revived again in 1947. In 1953 the show was combined with the County Fair and the gladioluses lost their importance. Gradually the Glad Show passed into history.

Josephine County Historical Highlights II, Hill

Gladiolus farmer
SOURCE: Kerbyville Museum

Shasta Dam

IN AUGUST 1938, the first bulldozer began clearing for the Shasta dam on the Sacramento River. There were great expectations that this was the answer to the need for irrigation water for the San Joaquin Valley and it would forever prevent flood damage. It was hoped the 35 mile long lake created by the dam would attract tourists. Who could be against such a spectacular manmade wonder? There were many. Most important were the residents of Kennett.

Kennett was situated in a steep canyon. It was originally built as a brake testing station for trains going over the mountains. In the early 1900s a combination of copper and gold ore was found nearby and the town suddenly boomed. With it came all the color, wild living and problems of a mining town. The mine was so rich the production of gold paid for everything and the copper was clear profit. During World War I copper prices skyrocketed and the town with it.

When the Armistice was signed, the bottom fell out and the mine struggled but finally closed.

All that was left of Kennett were a few diehard residents of the copper market who tried to save their town, and fought having Shasta Dam built.

Shasta County *Centennial Edition; The Sacramento, River of Gold*, Julian Dana

Hartman Syndicate

WAS THE HARTMAN Syndicate legitimate or was it just a money making scam?

It was known that there was a deposit of oilbearing shale east of Ashland. Mr. H.W. Hartman came to town with an incredible idea. He had a model of a retort that he demonstrated, showing that by putting in shale, one could produce oil. Crowds of people watched his demonstrations and believed. The retort worked by heating the crushed oil bearing shale and distilling off the vapor which condensed in copper tubing. Oil ran out the end of the retort.

Hartman formed a corporation called the Hartman Syndicate Incorporated. Capital stock was set at $3. Shares in the company were sold at $10 each, many to local residents. The Syndicate leased the public land and work began. The workmen were paid by further shares of stock being issued. The Ashland Iron Works began to build the 250 ton retort.

When all was ready, local businessmen came to watch as the guests of Mr. Hartman. The kerosene burners were ignited and a gasoline engine revolved the disks. Crushed oil shale was loaded. But here, the stories vary. One report stated that the highest expectations were exceeded and the process produced over 1,200 gallons of oil from 6,000 tons of shale. Then the motor idled. After corrections and several unsuccessful trials, Hartman announced he was going back to New York to look into refinancing.

On March 4, 1925 Hartman sent a telegram saying:

"Have arranged finances to take care of all our obligations. One half to be paid in 30 days, the balance in 60 days. Am sending a man to Ashland the first of the month to put the plant in operation."

As it turned out, the Syndicate had gone broke. Hartman disappeared.

Southern Oregon Historical Society *Sentinel*, July 1980; Medford *Mail Tribune*, August 22, 1965; *The Oil Venture at Shale City* (Term Paper, Wayne Breeze, 1961)

Shale City

WHEN THE HARTMAN SYNDICATE leased 2,680 acres for oil extraction, they started by cutting a road through to the shale beds. They built a sawmill, school, store, cookhouse, shops and homes. The town was named Shale City. It was to house the workers who were to run the oil processing plant. Those who worked on the building project were again paid in stock rather than money.

Shale City retort
SOURCE: Rogue River National Forest, Historic Photograph Collection

In April 1924 Hartman and his wife moved to Shale City. When financial troubles began, they disappeared. The other residents of Shale City were left on their own. They decided to run the lumber mill and to cut firewood in order to work off some of their debts. They still believed in the oil producing shale and when the syndicate was reorganized as "Pacific Lumber and Shaleries Inc." many were still willing to work rebuilding while being paid in still more stock. After two years rebuilding the retort, it melted when it was fired up. Gone were the life savings of many investors and workers.

What happened to Shale City? A few people lived on in the cabins that had been built but the town gradually rotted away.

Southern Oregon Historical Society *Sentinel,* July 1980; Medford *Mail Tribune,* August 22, 1965

Shale Oil

WHAT PRODUCED THE oil shale that is found east of Ashland?

The rock deposit was laid down in an era when the elevation was lower and when the temperatures were higher. The deposited shale was the result of an ancient lake. Organic material, which was not oxidized, was buried in the lake slowly over a long period of time. There are fossils in the shale of plant leaves that only grew in tropical or sub-tropical climates. During the time they were forming, there were violent volcanic eruptions, producing great amounts of lava and ash.

According to tests done by the United States Bureau of Mines in the 1950s, there are an estimated 37 gallons of oil per ton of shale. This is very high grade shale. However, the total amount of shale, by today's standards, is too small to make mining profitable. The estimated 150,000 barrels of oil at Shale City, or 600,000 gallons, remain for some future entrepreneur to find a new way of extraction.

Diane Parry, BLM geologist

West Coast Air Transport – 1927

THE WEST COAST Air Transport Company was organized in Portland in 1927. When they began scheduled flights, in 1928, they stopped twice on the route between Portland and San Francisco. They began by offering one round trip a day, except Sundays, between Portland and San Francisco. Montague was a noontime stop. As the plane approached Montague it would circle the hotel and the pilot would gun his motor in spurts. This was a signal giving the number of passengers. The hotel kitchen would quickly prepare the required number of lunches and deliver them out to the airport. The passengers had already been flying two hours and twenty minutes. They stretched their legs, drank coffee and ate while the plane refueled. Then on again for a 3:30 arrival in San Francisco, five and a half hours after their Portland departure.

When the airline was bought by Pacific Air Transport, the refueling site moved to Medford. Here the airport was often foggy in the winter months. At other times, the unpaved runway was too soft and wet for landing. There being no radio contact, the pilot would circle the field to see how conditions looked. If he couldn't land, he would go on to Montague and make his stop there. For years United Airlines used the Montague airport as an alternate landing site for their mail planes when the Medford Airport was fogged in.

Siskiyou *Pioneer*, 1980

United Airlines

VERN C. GORST WAS interested in transportation and established auto stage and bus lines in several areas including Coos County. This grew into airmail service and later, into United Airlines.

Gorst, a man with curiosity and self confidence, had always been interested in airplanes. He had taught himself to fly and believed in the future of aviation. He founded Pacific Air Transport and received a contract to carry mail from San Francisco to British Columbia.

There were four original lines that carried Air Mail in the United States: Pacific Air Transport, Boeing Air Transport, Varney Air Lines and National Air Trans-

Biplane stopping in Montague, California
SOURCE: Paul and Leah Reichman

port. Gorst suggested that the four companies join together. The government quickly approved the merger and United Air Lines was formed and inaugurated in June, 1931. Hereafter Gorst was known as the "Grandad of United Air Lines."

The Post Office Department considered United Air Lines a monopoly and canceled all mail contracts. They substituted Army pilots and planes to carry the airmail. However, this caused great losses in both planes and people's lives. United Airlines continued to fly as a passenger carrier. Eventually they again bid on mail contracts and got most of the runs back.

The west coast is still serviced by United Airlines, in part because of a far-sighted man named Vern Centennial Gorst.

Listener Dow Beckham Sr.

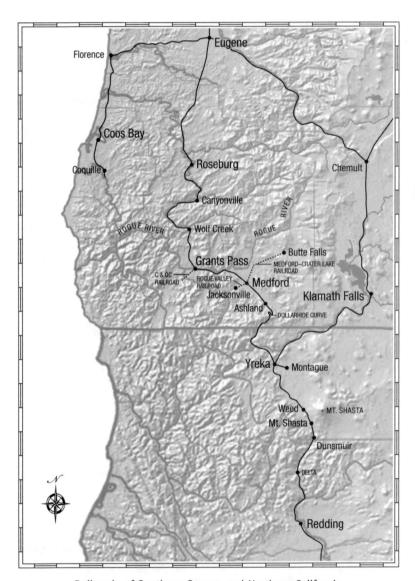

Railroads of Southern Oregon and Northern California

❦

CHAPTER 15

THE RAILROADS

Coos County Railroad

COOS COUNTY, OREGON had one of the most unusual railroads you are likely to hear about. Indians, with straps over their foreheads, pulled the train cars up the rails on the first railroad constructed in Coos County. It was only two and a half miles long and connected the head of Beaver Slough overland to the Isthmus inlet. In laying the track, logs were used for a road bed and strap iron for rails. Before the track was laid, Indians had been required to carry everything. Pulling the train cars was considered a great improvement.

Even when a locomotive was bought for the line, it sometimes lacked the power to push the train over the summit. In this case, passengers were asked to get out and help.

This line carried freight, passengers and logs for many years.

Oregon Oddities, WPA

Standard Time

IMAGINE THE CONFUSION if everyone determined what time it was by looking at the sun and deciding for themselves. Originally, every locality in North America set its own time by the sun. It made little difference to most people as few owned clocks or watches.

When the railroads began connecting distant points, estimating time became a problem. In an effort to standardize, each railroad company would determine its own railroad time. Trouble with this system developed because of the growing number of small railroads. By 1883 over 100 different railroad times existed. Finally, the railroad companies got together and established one standard time for all to follow. They divided up the United States into zones according to the meridian of longitude.

During World War I, daylight savings time was instigated as a means of conserving energy. After the war, the law was repealed and not reinstated until World War II when it was employed on a year around basis. After the war, standard time was used for the winter months only.

World Book Encyclopedia, Vol 18

Train between Delta and Redding – 1884

THE OPENING OF a section of rail track on the Southern Pacific would be a major event in the history of any town that was to be the terminus. When the train steamed north from Redding to the town of Delta, California on August 30, 1884, it was of particular interest. The trip up was 39 miles long and followed the beautiful Sacramento River. The track had gained altitude but still the formidable Siskiyou Mountains loomed ahead with no easy way across. Delta was to be the end of the line for some time. The town had been created here by the railroad. A site of 20 blocks was laid out. Corner lots cost $150 and inside lots were either $75 or $100. For several years it was a bustling town of great importance.

On the other side of the mountains the southbound track had stopped at Ashland. One hundred twenty-six miles stood between the two towns. It was the last link in the railroad loop that was to encircle the United States.

To go by stage from the train station in Delta to the train station in Ashland took about 24 hours. Fifteen dollars, fifty cents was collected for the bumpy ride over the mountains. The passengers declared the scenery "simply grand." Food along the way was always plentiful but simple. Even so, the traveler arrived tired and stiff.

Delta still exists but you will have to look at the small print on your map to find it.

My House was a Concord Wagon, Boggs

First Train to Montague – 1887

IT WAS GOING TO BE a big day in Montague. The first train was coming to town. Everyone for miles around was excited. Four of the older Soule children were going to go. The two little girls set off in the spring wagon wearing black mourning dresses because of the recent death of their grandmother. Even in black, they looked smart with their elegant hats. One brother drove the wagon and another rode his horse with their cousin. They met other cousins on the way. Brother George was the only one experienced with trains. He had gone to New Orleans to school so he acted as escort.

Montague was not much to look at. Construction had only begun. The depot, saloon, one eating place, a store and stable were all that had been finished. The main event of the day was the auctioning off of town lots. About 1,000 people had gathered to watch and to buy. Many came on the train as it pulled into town.

Climbing the mountains: Dollarhide trestle on the Siskiyou grade
SOURCE: Paul and Leah Reichman Collection

At four p.m., the nine cousins boarded the train to ride to the end of the line. The highlight of the outing was dinner in the palace diner. They all ordered oysters both raw and fried. The fried oysters went over well but it was reported that some of the raw ones went out the window.

The gala train ride only went to the Klamath River but it made an exciting trip for people who lived an isolated life around Mount Shasta.

Siskiyou *Pioneer*, 1988

Golden Spike in Ashland – 1887

A FEW FEET SOUTH of the Ashland, Oregon railroad station, on December 17, 1887, the "golden spike" was driven, completing a loop of train track around the entire United States. It had not been an easy task. The Oregon and California Railroad had built south from Portland in spite of financial difficulties and takeovers. The Californian and Oregon Railroad had come north from Redding. The last push over the Siskiyou Mountains had involved tremendous engineering skills. There were 16 tunnels and 100 miles of curves as the trains climbed to an elevation of 4,135 feet. The track crossed the Sacramento River 18 times.

On the great day when the golden spike was to be driven, the northern party arrived in Ashland at 10:30 in the morning and were greeted by a crowd of over 2,000. They waited throughout the day and into darkness for the southern train, which was having difficulties over the mountains. Finally at 4:45 in the afternoon, Charles Crocker drove the golden spike.

Now the train could make the trip from Portland to San Francisco in 39 hours.

Railroading in Southern Oregon, Webber; *Rogue Valley Communities, Selected Writings*

Hobo Story

HORNBROOK, CALIFORNIA was another stop off for hoboes traveling the freight trains. Bernice Pinkham remembers one time when a man knocked on their door asking for food.

"Dinner was the meal in the middle of the day. On this day mother had cooked a veal roast which she sat down in front of (father) to carve. 'What kind of meat is this?' he asked. When informed that it was veal he roared, 'Veal. I hate veal.'"

It was at this point the hobo knocked at the door wanting food. Bernice's father grabbed a paper bag, put the roast in it and added a loaf of bread. Needless to say the hobo was overwhelmed and must have shared it with other grateful hoboes down at the tracks.

Siskiyou Pioneer, 1992

Rogue Valley Railroad – 1891

JACKSONVILLE WAS THE seat of Jackson County when a proposal was made to build a train line from Portland to San Francisco. The city had every right to expect the tracks would be laid through their town. However, the railroad expected to be compensated in land to make it worth their while to route the line one way or another. This met with some opposition and wrangling among Jacksonville officials.

In the meantime, a group of businessmen offered the railroad good land at a site seven miles east of Jacksonville and the railroad accepted. Jacksonville was shocked and soon realized that they could not survive without a connection to the through north-south trains. Thus was born the Rogue Valley Railroad. It made its first run between Jacksonville and Medford on January 16, 1891.

The first run was a disaster. The tracks sank in the mud due to insufficient ballast. The engine, which had been borrowed for the occasion, tilted and turned over while the horrified crowd looked on. Once corrected, some freight was hauled over the lines but basically the Rogue Valley Railroad was for passengers. It was owned and run by the W.S. Barnum family. The one car took twenty minutes to transport passengers from Medford to Jacksonville at a cost of 25¢. Teenagers sometimes greased the track on the upgrade, where it passed the school. When this happened, passengers were enlisted to help wipe the tracks with gunny sacks.

With dwindling mining, and competition from the new town of Medford, Jacksonville shrank. So did the train business and the company finally folded in 1923.

Rogue Valley Communities, Selected Writings; Railroading in Southern Oregon, Webber

Medford–Crater Lake Railroad – 1905

CRATER LAKE WAS considered of prime tourist importance from earliest times. Medford wanted to take advantage of the possibilities. It was with this in mind that the Medford and Crater Lake Railroad was conceived. In April 1905 Mrs. A.A. Davis turned the first shovel of earth in the ground breaking ceremonies. The event warranted the closing of schools and businesses in Medford. But problems beset the enterprise from the start.

The line had begun buying right of way property as early as 1896. After the ground breaking they progressed only as far as clearing the land when they ran out of money. In 1907 the company was taken over by the Pacific and Eastern Railroad. Their goal was to build a line over the mountains to Bend and Pendleton, thus hooking up with the east–west lines. Only when that was done did they want to branch off to Crater Lake.

The first goal was Eagle Point. The idea of moving the town to a new site had been overridden and the line went right through the heart of town. A boost to the economy was immediate. Residents were hired and hotels filled with outside workers, many Hindu and Chinese. The next goal was the new town of Butte Falls which necessitated the building of many long and high trestles. This was reached in 1910. Passenger service to the Medford station, located in what is now Hawthorne Park, ran for several years but never proved profitable.

With the coming of WWII, the Pacific and Eastern Railroad only extended a little past Butte Falls. It was sold to lumber interests with Medco being the last to own the line. They continued hauling logs until 1959, when they closed the run. It was thought to be the last steam logging train still in use in the country.

Once maintenance stopped, it didn't take long for the trestles to begin to disintegrate. The small stations fell down or were moved. Rails were torn up and used for scrap. Like so many other small rail lines, nothing remains of those early hopes and dreams.

Southern Oregon Historical Society *Sentinel,* Jan–Feb 1992; *Country Folk,* Hegne; *Eagle Point Structures,* Barrett, Interior Department Overview

C and OC Railroad

HAVE YOU EVER HEARD of the C and OC Railroad? It ran 14½ miles.

The Southern Pacific Railroad ran through Grants Pass from Portland to Sacramento. The people of Grants Pass thought that what they needed now was a train track to the coast. The first leg of the line was to go from the Southern Pacific Station in Grants Pass to Williams Valley near Oregon Caves. Work began with a bridge across the Rogue River. With a great celebration, in April 1911, a small locomotive proudly steamed across the river to the end of the line, a distance of one mile. This was the end of the Grants Pass and Rogue River Railroad.

By 1913, the town of Grants Pass was again in the railroad business. Track was laid to Wilderville, a total of ten miles. Another big celebration took place. The train consisted of a 16 passenger gasoline coach with a baggage trailer. The original small engine was to be used for carrying freight.

Eastern investors became interested in the struggling railroad and the Twohy Brothers Company contracted to build the line to the coast. Thus was born the California and Oregon Coast Railroad. This called for a third and bigger celebration.

The Twohy Brothers built four and a half miles of track. A wood burning engine was added. Passenger service was brisk up and down the line. There were several stations but a person could flag the train and be picked up anywhere along the track. The new engine hauled sugar beets to the factory just outside of town, limerock from Marble Mountain and lumber to and from the mills.

Plans were always being made to extend the railroad to the coast but they all failed. On October 31, 1954 service was discontinued and the C and OC Railroad was no more.

Josephine County Historical Highlights I, Hill

Fanny and the C and OC RR

FANNY WAS A DOG. Just a plain dog with coal black hair.

Jack Hathaway was an engineer on the California and Oregon Coast Railroad. He befriended the dog and named her Fanny. He let her ride in the tender behind the engine. Everyone knew Fanny and waved as she barked happily when the train went up and down the line. When not traveling, Fanny would lie under the engine and growl possessively at anyone coming past.

One day Fanny was not in her usual place, so the train took off and left her behind. The engine stopped at Marble Mountain to take on water. The crew lounged around eating lunch when the tired, footsore dog came limping up the track, having followed them for twelve miles.

Fanny would never go across a trestle so she had come all that distance through the mountains following the track, but where the track went over bridges, she ran down and up the gullies and swam across the Rogue River.

Fanny never missed another train.

Josephine County Historical Highlights I, Hill

Gas-driven passenger car
SOURCE: Curry County Historical Society

Incline Railroad – 1914

THE KLAMATH *Evening Herald* announced, on November 14, 1914, that crews had begun to work on the grade for the Algoma Incline Railroad. It is one of the most unusual railroads in the area.

The problem was how to get logged trees out of the woods and down an 800 foot incline to the mill. The incline averaged between a 55% and 57% grade. The options were to build a rail line with five miles of switch-backs or to run the track straight down the hill. The railroad decided to do the latter.

To accomplish this project, a large double drum steam engine hoist was erected on top of the hill. Tracks were laid both up and down so that cables attached to the cars from the hoist engine would unwind from one drum while the opposite drum would rewind. In other words, an empty flat car would be pulled up to help balance while the full car was being lowered.

The cement bases for the hoist engine can still be seen at the top of the incline but a logging road has long since replaced the hoist system that worked the trains. Only the scar on the mountain side remains as evidence of this ingenious method of log transportation.

Klamath *Evening Herald*, Nov. 14, 1914; Klamath County Historical Society Newsletter, Summer 1990

Liberty Bell – 1915

THE PANAMA–PACIFIC International Exposition opened in San Francisco in February 1915. It celebrated the Panama Canal, which had opened the preceding August.

One of the great attractions of the Exposition was the Liberty Bell in the State of Pennsylvania building. It was the first time the bell was to be seen west of the Mississippi. To move to the exposition, from Philadelphia, it traveled in a specially built gondola train car. The bell was lighted and draped in red, white and blue. The train included seven cars for the convenience of guardsmen and dignitaries. The prized gondola was on the back. When the train reached the Northwest, nine other trains sponsored by eastern groups, joined the caravan. All traffic on the Southern Pacific lines was stopped for two days.

The train came through Roseburg late on the night of July 17, 1915. It arrived in Grants Pass at 2:10 the next morning. The late hour didn't deter thousands from coming to see the historic Liberty Bell in the ten minutes it remained in the station.

Medford was also allotted ten minutes. Here 5,000 turned out in the middle of the night. Ashland had 3,000 waiting to see the bell.

In Hornbrook, a delegation boarded to go the remainder of the way to San Francisco, where it arrived on July 17th.

Southern Oregon Historical Society *Sentinel*, Dec. 1987

64-Horse Freighter Team – 1924

EARLY RAILROAD CONSTRUCTION brought about some unusual situations. In 1924, there was need for a steam-shovel to be used in the construction of the Natron Cutoff high in the Cascades. The trouble was that the huge 30 ton shovel would have to be moved 12 miles from the end of the existing rail line to the site. Horses were available but they had only been trained to be used in small teams.

A local teamster name Hunsaker volunteered to take on the job if he could use the company teams and borrow more. He also insisted on his own driver. He planned to use 64 horses at one time. No one believed it was possible.

Hunsaker began by mounting the steam shovel on skids. The teams were finally hitched together. While a small crowd watched, the driver went around to every pair of horses and talked to each horse individually, calling it by name. Then he gave the word to pull. The horses responded and moved the steam shovel about 12–15 feet. The driver again went to every pair of horses and repeated his talk. Again the horses pulled on command and the steam shovel went a little further.

Repeating this process again and again each day for six days, the 30 ton steam shovel was moved 12 miles to the cut-off site. The impossible had been done.

Oregonian, Nov. 28, 1948; Klamath *Echoes*, #16

Southern Pacific loop and tunnel over the Siskiyous
SOURCE: Paul and Leah Reichman Collection

Railroad Sandhouse

WHEN DRY SAND WAS thrown into a locomotive fire box, the fire would burn soot free. Every railroad freight station stored sand in a large sandhouse. Next to the sand room was a smaller room where there was a fire box open at the top. Damp sand was shoveled onto a surrounding apron where it dried and was dumped.

Warm sandhouses were a mecca for hoboes in cold weather. Most railroad agents let transients stay unmolested. Only those who tried to make it their home for several nights were forced to leave.

Passenger Trains

FOUR DAILY PASSENGER trains once ran up and down the line between Portland and San Francisco. The pass over the Siskiyou Mountains, with its many turns and tunnels, was always a problem.

A new rail line was built, branching off the main line at Oakridge, Oregon and going southeast through Klamath Falls. It rejoined the main line north of Sacramento. While still requiring some tunnels and turn backs, the inclines were gentler. All together, it was a great improvement. Gradually the through passenger trains chose this route. The old pass over the summit was closed.

Passenger service continued from Ashland north to Portland for many years. The trip took 14 hours, stopping at every small town along the way. As one train went north, the other came south. Each was composed of a combination of mail car, baggage cars, coaches, a lunch car and a Pullman sleeper. The engine required a turn around in Ashland and in Portland. As the train moved south, cars were left at Salem, Albany, Eugene, Roseburg, Grants Pass and Medford. These would be picked up the next day.

One crew would work from Portland to Roseburg and another crew, from Roseburg to Ashland.

With more people driving automobiles, train usage dwindled. By 1955 Southern Pacific was losing money and discontinued passenger service.

Southern Oregon Heritage, Summer 1995

CHAPTER 16

EAST OF THE CASCADES

Linkville to Klamath Falls

GEORGE NURSE SOLD goods to the Army at Fort Klamath. He requested permission to establish a ferry at the mouth of Link River where it joined Lake Ewauna. He moved his goods to this new location and was the first settler. He soon laid out a town site and named the new town Linkville for Link River.

Later the ferry was replaced by a wooden bridge across the river. This bridge became an essential supply route during the time of the Modoc Wars. About 1884, the town experienced an influx of settlers and the newspaper, The Klamath County *Star,* began publication. All this was wiped out by a fire in 1889 and for a time the rebuilding of the town was in doubt. However, construction of the railroad continued north and made the town the supply center for a large area of Eastern Oregon.

SOURCE: Ruth Minear Alborn

With the rebuilding of the town, new pride developed. People began to feel that the name "Linkville" didn't produce the image they wished to present to the world. As one resident said, "Linkville is not nationally known." In 1892 the post office officially changed the name to Klamath Falls. At that time the population consisted of only about 450 men of eligible voting age.

Klamath *Echoes,* 1973 and 1975

Klamath Stove

A LINKVILLE MAN sold his cook stove to another man and let the buyer take the stove away before he received payment. Somewhat later, the two men met in a saloon. The seller confronted the buyer, wanting to know when he was going to get his money. The man responded that the stove was cracked and not worth a thing. To this, the first man said he wanted his stove or his money, one or the other. The threat only egged the buyer into saying he would throw the stove in the river before he would give it back and he certainly wasn't going to pay for it.

Being under the influence of drink, the man who sold the stove said, "I'll bet you $5 you wouldn't dare."

That was all the buyer needed. He hitched up his horse, went to his cabin and put the stove in the wagon. By the time he got back to Linkville there was quite a crowd waiting to see what would happen. The man drove his wagon onto the bridge and, being a strong man, he picked up the stove and threw it into Link River.

The seller not only was out the stove, it cost him another $5 to pay off his bet.

Oregon Oddities, WPA

Klamath River Ran Uphill – 1906

A STRONG WIND with gusts up to 30 miles an hour came from the south. Pushing the water northward, it dried up Link River. Residents say they walked across the channel without even getting their shoes wet.

Link River, which is now known as Klamath River, flows out of the south end of Upper Klamath Lake, past Klamath Falls and widens to become Lake Ewauna. It then narrows to become Klamath River again.

In November the waters of the river were probably at a low point. With the strong winds, the flow of the shallow river was held back for over 24 hours. The residents must have been thinking about Moses parting the Red Sea waters, but no further miracles seem to have occurred.

Now there is a dam at the mouth of Link River which did not exist on November 6, 1906 when this happened.

Klamath *Republican*, November 8, 1906

The Falls in Klamath Falls

POWER COMPANIES PUT in dams all over the west to provide electricity for growing communities. In the case of Klamath Falls, a canal or water tube was started at the outlet of Upper Klamath Lake and brought down both sides of Link River to Klamath Falls. There was a drop of 30 feet in elevation. The water was put through a turbine that made enough electricity to take care of the town. Later, the bypass on the side toward town was discontinued.

The dams that were put in didn't dry up Link River entirely but it dried up the Falls. The flow was further diminished when irrigation water was taken from Upper Klamath Lake. At the time it was built, the 200,000 acre irrigation system was the largest in the United States.

Netting fish, Klamath River
SOURCE: Paul and Leah Reichman

Link River doesn't look like much now but before the town was built its impassable rapids were impressive enough to add the name Falls to Klamath.

Interview with Cal Peyton

Klamath Castle – 1908

THEY SAY A MAN'S HOME is his castle and that is just what Captain Alex Nosler wanted. Whether or not he was a real sea going captain is in question. It was known that he even liked the title "Admiral." Be that as it may, he came to Klamath Falls with the idea of building an imposing home. He chose a hillside site on the shores of Klamath Lake, and began building in 1908. The house was to have four towers, an observatory and a burnished dome. He named his creation "Saint Cloud."

Nosler was a genius at wood working and his specialty was life sized figures with movable parts. These gradually filled the rooms of Saint Cloud, arranged in picturesque groupings. Word got about and people came to see the "Saint Cloud's Castle" for which the enterprising captain charged them 10¢ each. Several times a year a fancy dress ball was held. These were serious affairs with no drinking or revelry. Music was the finest Klamath Falls could offer and the suppers were lavish.

In the early 1920s Nosler disappears from record. People thought he had gone to Medford on a project but nothing more is known of this interesting and eccentric man. Nothing remains of his castle, either.

Pages From the Past, Drew

Snakes

THE AREA AROUND Klamath Falls was known to be snake paradise. Something about the many hot springs and small creeks that filtered into Link River and Lake Ewauna bred tadpoles, frogs and insects, all of which produced food for snakes.

As spring started to warm the earth, snakes would come out of their hiding places and congregate in huge piles. Some piles were reported to be 20 feet across and seven or eight feet high, draped over rock walls or on creek banks. There were all sorts of snakes bunched together, water snakes, blue racers and ordinary garden snakes, all considered harmless but unappealing.

Linkville had board sidewalks. Snakes liked to huddle under the walks and where the boards were separated they would stick their heads up. Men would come along in their boots and kick off the snake heads. When the summer heat came, this caused quite a problem as rotting snakes under the board sidewalks gave off a terrible stench. Finally a law was passed forbidding people to kill snakes in this manner.

Klamath *Echoes*, 1964

Snakes For Sale – 1900

A FIRM NEAR Rochester, Minnesota was starting a snake farm. Having heard of Klamath Falls' snake reputation, they contacted the postmaster and told him they would like to buy 3,000 pounds of live snakes. They agreed to pay 25¢ a pound for them.

J. H. Jardine took 700 snakes to Ashland, for shipment to Rochester. The trip was not without incident. The Klamath *Republican* reported:

"The express messenger on the train which conveyed Jardine's shipment of snakes north, reports that he was kept busy all the way from Ashland to Portland sweeping juvenile snakes from the car, and suggests that either the shipment ought to be made in tighter boxes or the produce should be of uniformly large size."

Unfortunately this suggestion was never acted on because no more orders came through for snakes. Other sources made a few inquiries but nothing came of the idea of selling snakes.

Klamath Falls *Herald*, January, 28, 1962

Frogs in Klamath Falls

IN THE SHALLOW LAKES around Klamath Falls there were many frogs. Every few years the frogs would migrate from Lake Ewauna north to Upper Klamath Lake, and their route took them through town. They went up Third and Fourth Street, across Main Street and hopped right through town. There were so many frogs the streets would get slick from traffic running over them. A noticeable smell hung over downtown.

These frogs were only a few inches long, too small to provide the delicacy of fried frogs legs.

Interview with Cal Peyton

Ewauna Box Factory – 1912

BY THE EARLY 1900s, California was already noted for its produce. The Ewauna Box Factory was ready to supply the boxes for shipping.

Ewauna is an Indian name given to the small lake south of Klamath Falls that is really only the widening of the Link River. When a box factory was built in 1912 on the shores of this lake, it was naturally called the Ewauna Box Factory. It made a significant impact on Klamath County.

Because of the advent of the railroad from Klamath Falls to California, many box factories were built in the county to supply the growing number of fruit and vegetable producers in California. Hundreds of logs floated in the lake awaiting their turn in one of the sawmills. When this first Ewauna factory burned down in 1917, it was rebuilt as a larger and more productive mill becoming the second largest box factory in the United States and the largest west of the Mississippi River. At its height of production, it covered a 53 acre site and was the largest employer in the area.

Klamath residents used the tag ends of boards from the factory to fuel their kitchen stoves. Because the ends came in any size and shape, they were called "block wood." Children loved block wood for making all sorts of creative toys.

History of Klamath Country, Lumbering in Klamath County

Fly Traps – 1919

KLAMATH FALLS WENT all out to beat the fly problem in 1919.

On April 17, 1919 the City Health Officer announced that all manure must be kept in carefully screened bins.

The manual training department of the High School was making fly traps for the city. They were to be placed in the rear of eating houses and other spots. A smaller version could be used in the home.

Even when screen doors were kept shut, farm homes accumulated a lot of flies. When things got too out of hand, the family would gather together and each member would be given a towel. Starting at the back bedroom, they would line up in a pattern to "herd" the flies toward the bedroom door, shaking their towels and driving them into the living room. The family would go through the rooms, shutting the doors behind them. The final drive was shooing the flies out the back door.

A mop up operation with fly swatters was carried out and for a while the hum of flies quieted.

Klamath *Evening Herald*, April, 18, 1919

Geothermal Heat

THERE IS HOT WATER along a big geological structure on the east side of the valley in which Klamath Falls is located. Two hundred degree water is available in spots along this line as far north as the Indian Agency and as far south as Olene. The water might be 40 feet down or it might be 1,000 feet down. The line runs right through the town of Klamath Falls.

People have been using geothermal heat in the Klamath Basin from the earliest days. One way to heat a home was to drill a hole to the available hot water. A loop of pipe was put down in the hot water. The top of the loop would connect to a heat exchanger similar to a car radiator. The pipe system would be filled with water and sealed tight. Working on the fact that heat rises and cold falls, the water inside the bottom of the pipe would heat and rise. The cold water in the pipe fell and, in turn, became heated. The water inside the pipe was constantly circulating. Meanwhile, the radiator was getting hot. In order to heat a home, a fan would blow air through the radiator and up into heating ducts that led to registers in the house.

Once installed, the only expense of running a geothermal heating system was the electricity to run the fan blowing the air through the radiator.

Interview with Cal Peyton

Hearse

LINKVILLE WAS THE CENTER for a vast cattle country. One man, who had become quite wealthy, ran cattle and was doing well but still hauled firewood 30 miles from his ranch into town to sell. On one of these trips he saw the local undertaker with a brand new beautiful hearse. It boasted a carved frame, plate glass sides and a door at the rear to accommodate the casket. There were four posts like a four poster bed. Each post was topped with a carved black plume. The horses had real black ostrich feathers on the bridles.

Nothing as elegant as this had come to the pioneer community before. The rancher took one look at this gorgeous vehicle and decided he had to have it right then and there. Arrangements were made and he mounted the driver's seat and rode off with the black plumes bobbing on the heads of the ponies.

The next time the rancher came to town, his wife was sitting inside the hearse while he was in the driver's seat.

It wasn't long before the hearse was seen again, the glass on the sides had been broken, and the inside was piled high with firewood to deliver to the man's customers in town.

Klamath Falls *Herald-News*, August 3, 1959

Main Street, Fort Klamath
SOURCE: Southern Oregon Historical Society, photo no. 16045

Klamath County Courthouse(s)

IN 1920 KLAMATH COUNTY had three courthouses.

Fritz Muntz, a German bachelor, settled in Bly, Oregon in 1875. Clinton Brown was a neighbor of his and kept bothering Muntz while he was building his irrigation ditch. In May, 1878, Muntz drew his gun to threaten Brown. Thinking to shoot over his head he accidentally shot Brown in the jugular vein. Muntz turned himself in at Fort Klamath where he posted $9,000 bond for his release. He then quietly left the country.

Suddenly finding themselves blessed with $9,000, Klamath County financed the building of the first Klamath County Courthouse.

The second courthouse was the Hot Springs courthouse on the hillside known as the Hot Springs residential section. It was of Greek design with columns on its south facade. It had been controversial ever since it was begun in 1910. Construction was stopped when only the exterior was finished.

The third courthouse stood on Main Street and was a large, three story structure of light pressed brick. It looked ready for use but so far had not been used for anything.

In 1920 the first courthouse was still the official courthouse. It had seen hard usage and was now weatherbeaten and ramshackle. An annex had been built to house two of the departments. Everyone agreed that it was inadequate, but couldn't agree which of the other two courthouses should be used.

It wasn't until 1926 that the matter was finally settled and the business of the county was moved to the courthouse on Main Street. This was damaged in the earthquake of 1993 and torn down. A new courthouse is under construction on the same site.

Klamath Echoes, #5, 1967

White Lake City – 1905

THE BOOM AND BUST story of White Lake City is typical of many land speculations. It was located two miles west of Merrill, Oregon, on the shores of White Lake. It took its name from the white alkali lake bed.

In June 1905, 40 acres of town sites were platted with proposed sites for two grocery stores, a hardware store, a butcher shop and a newspaper. The first building to go up was a two story office building from which the Oklahoma and Oregon Town Site Company sold lots for $15 each. Literature with pictures and glowing reports was circulated around the Midwest. The company foresaw a $12,000 profit in return for their small investment.

As soon as the lots were sold, the newspaper closed. The few businesses that had been started moved to Merrill, stranding the population of 200 who had actually built homes.

Today White Lake is dry and there are no signs of White Lake City.

Klamath Echoes, 1977

Straw, Tule Lake Basin Post Office

THE LAND RECLAIMED from draining Tule Lake lay partly in California and partly in Oregon. This caused many problems. It wasn't just the state line that was affected, the land that was in California was divided by the Siskiyou County and Modoc County line.

One of the problems was in acquiring a driver's license. If you lived in California and wanted a license, you were required to have a California post office address. There were no California post offices in the Tule Lake Basin area. Some enterprising individual found the solution. He nailed a mail box on a tree on the California side of the state line and created the fictitious town of "Straw." This was accepted by the authorities until a post office was opened at the new town of Tulelake. The Straw post office box was then taken down from the tree and the town of Straw, population 0, no longer existed.

Years of Harvest, Turner

Fairport – 1912

GOOSE LAKE IS situated half in Oregon and half in California just south of Lakeview, Oregon. It was a landmark along the Applegate Trail. In the early, wet years, it covered quite an area. The town of Fairport was located on the lake and was an early recreation spot where people picnicked, swam, boated, raced horses and played baseball.

The Nevada, California, Oregon Railroad built a line through this area and when gold was discovered nearby, Fairport was a busy place. A modern hotel was built on the shore of the lake with a dance pavilion extending out over the water. Most of the 28 guest rooms had their own bath with hot and cold running water. A pier led to rented boats, available for the good fishing. The name, Goose Lake, was changed to the more glamorous "Sunset Lake" but this too was temporary.

The hotel operated for about 10 years. "Sunset Lake" began to dry up and, once again, became Goose Lake. The gold mining in the east mountains played out and Fairport became a ghost town.

In 1930, the vacant Fairport Hotel burned to the ground.

Schminck Museum files

ᦒᦂᦒ

CHAPTER 17

ENTERTAINMENT

Siskiyou County Fair – 1859

FORT JONES HOSTED the first Siskiyou County Fair in October, 1859. It was sponsored by an organization with the intriguing name of Mining, Mechanical and Agricultural Society.

Fort Jones was competing with Yreka as the most important town in Siskiyou County. The fair was held there for another seven years. By that time the event had grown into a great tourist attraction, overwhelming small Fort Jones. Lodging was so scarce people slept in the livestock pavilion, fields and anywhere else they could find.

Yreka became the site of all the fairs after 1867. No special fairgrounds existed so the exhibits were held in tents and vacant buildings. This went on until the 1880's when several counties joined together to have a larger fair.

The Siskiyou County Fair resumed in Yreka in 1919 but it wasn't until 1925 that the old race track was purchased as the site of a permanent fairground. Even with its own buildings, the "Annual Fair" happened only intermittently because of the depression and World War II.

Once called the Paul Bunyan Jubilee, the fair is now known as the Siskiyou Golden Fair. It can still be found on the old race track site with several of the old buildings preserved.

Siskiyou Daily News, August 1992

Dan Rice Circus – 1860

THE DAN RICE CIRCUS toured Northern California in 1860. Rice was a one time jockey and had worked for P.T. Barnum. Of one thing we can be sure, he knew how to handle animals.

Special among Dan Rice's animals was Lord Byron, a pig. Lord Byron would appear wearing horn rimmed glasses and a necktie. He had been taught to play

Montague Brass Band, c. 1904
SOURCE: Paul and Leah Reichman

checkers and chess. Sitting in his own chair, he would stare at his opponent through his glasses while the game was played. And he usually won.

Lord Byron and a trained horse were also good at any mathematical problems. The pig answered with grunts and the horse by stamping his foot. Rice eventually admitted that he signaled the animals by clicking his fingernails the proper number of times. The sound was not audible to humans. But even with his methods explained, Dan Rice was an amazing animal trainer.

Along Our History's Trail, Hayden

Lewd Dancing – 1874

EARLY CHURCHES ALL seemed to agree that dancing was indecent and sinful. The Methodists didn't mince any words in their magazine, the *Methodist Advocate* of January 15, 1874:

"The exercise connected with any kind of dancing, where male and female are associated together as partners, tends naturally to lewdness and inordinate affection."

The Presbyterians referred to it as "Unscriptural."

The Baptists called it, "A great detriment to…growth in grace."

In 1852 Oregon newspapers were reporting complaints about the "shocking new dance called the waltz."

As late as 1914, English society leaders were boycotting the new Tango dance claiming it to be immodest and suggestive.

Religion As An Influence, Farnham

Theater in Marshfield

THEATRICAL TROOPERS CAME late to Marshfield (Coos Bay) Oregon. The local residents had managed their own entertainment in the form of concerts and plays. Grand masked balls were put on with people dressed in rented costumes sent up from San Francisco.

This section of the coast attracted a large number of Scandinavians and an active Swedish Singing Society formed. The group toured to nearby towns. Professional vocalists gave singing lessons and music was the center of social activity. These early productions were put on in Norman's Hall, which the Marshfield *Coast Mail* reported as having "undergone complete renovation." It occupied the room upstairs above the town's most elegant restaurant.

In 1889 the Marshfield Oddfellows Hall was built and quickly replaced Norman's Hall. Here political gatherings and dances took place. Major traveling companies began including Marshfield on the circuits. Groups such as the Wizard Oil Theatrical Company stopped by. Their productions were little more than extravagant medicine shows. They might rent the hall for a week and put on a series of dramas. Most entertainers began their careers in such troupes and many returned to them when those careers began to fade.

Trouping in Oregon Country, Ernst

Buffalo Bill, Medford – 1882

BUFFALO BILL'S FIRST Wild West Show took place in 1882. Twenty-two years later, he made an appearance in Medford. Pawnee Bill and Buffalo Bill combined to put on a single performance in an open field on the outskirts of town. A parade preceded the show with beautiful horses and carriages, a covered wagon drawn by oxen, a band and mounted cowboys and Indians. Featured in the show were his standard acts such as "The Battle of Summit Springs" and "An Attack on an Emigrant Train."

Cody received a royal welcome everywhere he went. One would think that, with such success, he would have retired a wealthy and happy man. This didn't prove to be. Although money came in, Buffalo Bill never knew how to handle it and speculated it all away. Thus he was forced to continue performing even though he longed to retire to his ranch in Montana. He died in Denver, Colorado in 1917 and 25,000 people attended his funeral.

Southern Oregon Historical Society *Sentinel,* March/April 1992

Buffalo Bill, Roseburg

BUFFALO BILL CODY was a true showman. He was tall, handsome and looked the way everyone believed a buffalo hunter should. His fame as a hunter and scout was justified and he cashed in on that fame to attract people to his shows. For 30 years he traveled across the country with a show that was a combination rodeo, circus and wild west drama.

The Buffalo Bill Show came to Roseburg. To add to the realism of his show, Cody had brought real Indian warriors, Rough Riders, Arabs, South American gauchos, German Cavalry and Russian Cossacks. The show was preceded by a parade through the downtown and out to the site of the performance. Tickets cost 50¢ for adults and 25¢ for children. This was a stiff price in 1850 but few people complained.

Southern Oregon Historical Society *Sentinel*, March/April 1992; *Umpqua Trapper*, 1975

Literary Societies – 1892

WINTERS SEEMED LONG in small communities. One of the ways to entertain people was to form Literary Societies. The one in Talent, Oregon was organized in November 1892. Officers were elected, songs were sung and recitations were performed. But the debate was the most exciting event of any evening. Subjects for debate might include, "Be it resolved that there is more pleasure in pursuit than in possession," or "Resolved that the horse is a more useful animal than the cow." The society would divide into two parts, one side arguing for the resolution and the other side arguing against. Everyone had a chance to put forth their views and a judge decided the winner.

Unidentified vocal quartet
SOURCE: Kerbyville Museum

The Talent Literary Society had an unscheduled, heated argument one meeting when a motion was made to assess each member 10¢ to cover the cost of certain necessary expenses. Some members vigorously opposed the motion as a reckless extravagance. They pointed out that times were hard and that the group ought to practice economy. One person even suggested it might be a temptation to the treasurer.

In this case, the opposition lost and henceforth each member had to pay dues of 10¢.

Talent *News*, Vol 1, #20

Broom Brigade – 1888

VICTORIAN FAMILIES WERE always looking for ways to keep their daughters on the straight and narrow path. The Women's Christian Temperance Union stood willing to help. They suggested that parents find someone with knowledge of military tactics, one who was "pure and noble." This noble character was to drill young women in unison marches. It was the beginning of the "Broom Brigade."

The idea spread quickly and became very popular. The participants followed the manual, *Broom Brigade Tactics* supplied by the WCTU, which also prompted the ladies to keep in mind that they were marching under the temperance banner. The manual described how to carry your broom and such positions as, "present brooms," "rest on brooms," and "fire kneeling."

Towns like Jacksonville, who had at least one brigade in 1888, would have them drill in parades and at local events. Competing drill teams started up with names such as, the "Scarf Team" and the "Fan Brigade."

As quickly as they had sprung up, the drill brigades disappeared about the turn of the century. Young women went on to other interests.

Southern Oregon Historical Society *Sentinel*, August 1982

Baseball

AS EARLY AS THE 1860s baseball clubs were forming throughout the Northern California, Southern Oregon region. Watching the games became a popular social outing. Sunday games were taboo. Those who watched or played on Sundays were given dire warnings about breaking the Sabbath.

In 1867 the Oregon State Fair included baseball as an attraction. Today's fans would find it hard to recognize the game. The score at the state fair was 92 to 25.

In 1903 the Southern Oregon Baseball League was formed, including Medford, Ashland, Jacksonville and Grants Pass. Semi-pro baseball came in the 1940s with the appearance of the Class D Far West League. It didn't last long but the desire for baseball never died and every few years another league would form.

In 1979 the Medford team became professional when the Oakland A's took them over. They are members of the Northwest Short Season League, playing

Montague baseball team
SOURCE: Paul and Leah Reichman

other affiliated teams. In 1997 the name was changed to the Timberjacks but the team remains a farm team of the Oakland Athletics.

Oregon Oddities, WPA; *Semi Professional Baseball in Southern Oregon*, Weinhold (paper); *Medford's 1st Century*, Medford *Mail Tribune*; *110 Years With Josephine*, Sutton

Longest Home Run

BASEBALL CAME TO YREKA in 1884. About ten years later the game began to change. Gloves were starting to be used but they were much smaller than those used today. The first baseman's glove only covered the palm of the hand, leaving the fingers bare. The baseball weighed five ounces and measured nine inches in diameter.

Our story is about the Yreka–Edgewood game. The teams agreed to play three games. Each had won one game and the third was played in Edgewood. The area between the hotel and the railroad track acted as the baseball field. Al Connelly was playing center field for the Yreka team. He came up to bat and hit a long ball that headed for the railroad track just as a freight train happened to be pulling through the yard. The ball went in the open door of a box car and was carried right out of town. Since the train was headed for San Francisco, the home run has to be the longest in history.

Siskiyou *Pioneer*, Spring 1954

Ed Meade

MARSHFIELD (COOS BAY) was the part time home of Ed Meade, actor. Small, dapper, with graying hair carefully combed back and a resonant voice, Meade always wore a horseshoe tie pin set with pearls. He was one of the last of the barnstorming theatrical personalities who traveled the small communities of Southern Oregon and Northern California. In those days, actors played several parts, changing makeup and attaching mustaches and wigs. Meade could play any part, in any kind of hall. When not acting he would load and unload the wagons, play brass with the orchestra, set up for the shows or drive the horses. Sometimes he would go ahead of the company, making engagements and arranging accommodations and a place to perform.

Never playing in the larger towns, the troupes traveled thousands of miles. Audiences were treated to such fare as, *The Fatal Wedding, Beyond the Rockies, Two Merry Tramps, The Rajah of Bhong, Old Kentucky* and, of course, *Uncle Tom's Cabin.*

When traveling shows began to dwindle, Ed Meade stayed year around in Coos Bay but finally went back to Virginia, where he died.

Could I Be Forgetting? Taylor

Silver Lake Opera

THE OLD TIMERS could make any place into an "Opera House." In Silver Lake it was a barn. The landlord of the hotel had an empty barn on his lot. The troupe began sweeping the old hay into the corners and spreading new hay on the floor. A temporary stage was built and the horse stalls, which went down one side, acted as dressing rooms. Lanterns became floodlights and Japanese lanterns on the street side of the barn advertised the playbill. Seats were kegs, boxes or boards set on blocks of wood.

All was ready for the performance but the actors had overlooked the sneeze weed that made up a large part of the hay. As the performance of *The Fatal Wedding* proceeded, the audience and actors began to sneeze. With tears rolling down their faces, the situation became so outrageous the actors and the audience ended up laughing their way through. Everyone enjoyed the joke.

The next night, the hay was wet down and this time all went well.

Could I Be Forgetting? Taylor

Chautauqua – 1893

LAKE CHAUTAUQUA, New York was the home of the first Chautauqua encampment in 1874. By the 1890s groups were traveling around the country bringing music, readings, schools, storytelling, illustrated lectures and entertainments. Ashland, Oregon already had its eye out for ways to attract tourists and Chautauqua seemed like a good idea.

On the 14th of June in 1893, a committee formed to build a building large enough to seat 1,000 people. It had to be complete by July 5th, the day the first Chautauqua was scheduled. In just 21 days the land had to be bought, materials found and the building erected.

The Association of Southern Oregon Chautauqua bought about 10 acres of orchard land along the banks of Ashland Creek, almost in the heart of town. That left 10 days for the building to go up. It was a beehive dome 80 feet across and 40 feet high with no posts or pillars and a dirt floor. A large force of amateur carpenters under the direction of an architect, had the building enclosed, sealed and electrically lighted in time for the opening. The outside was shingled and canvas covered the window openings.

News of the Chautauqua show spread fast. People came to camp in the area that is Lithia Park today. There were two performances a day for 10 days. A season ticket to all of the performances was only $1.

In the 1920s Chautauqua declined and the city of Ashland bought the property. All that remains of the old beehive structure is part of the wall that surrounds the present Elizabethan theater at the Oregon Shakespeare Festival.

The Ashland Story, O'Harra; Southern Oregon Historical Society *Sentinel*, February 1987; *Ashland Oregon*, League of Women Voters

Lithia Park

LITHIA PARK IN ASHLAND really began in 1892 with the idea of Chautauqua. The original park consisted of a few acres where people visiting the Chautauqua show could tent, picnic or just stroll around. It was known as Chautauqua Park and was made up of the lower portion of present day Lithia Park.

On December 15, 1908 the city provided a park board to landscape and maintain Chautauqua Park. The next summer they built the lower lake.

By 1912 pressure was mounting to make Ashland a world famous health center. There were a number of mineral springs in the area. Lithium salts were considered especially desirable and a spring was found near Emigrant Lake and purchased by the city. A bond issue was called providing money to pipe the water to the plaza. The park was renamed Lithia Park.

This was an exciting era everywhere with more people buying cars, roads being improved and travel becoming more common. To take advantage of this, the Lithia Park Auto Campground was opened in 1915. This was located at the top of the park where the Cotton Memorial Area is now. The tennis courts were built at that time also.

The Lithia Park Story, Scripter

Ashland, Oregon, c. 1905
SOURCE: Paul and Leah Reichman

Bowling – 1897

BOWLING ALLEYS OPENED in Ashland and were touted to be one of the finest double alleys in the state. The newspaper said bowling was a fad across the nation and was great recreation for both men and women.

On a Friday in November, 1897, the proprietors of the alleys were going to try to interest the women of Ashland in bowling. Ladies were to be admitted free of charge from 1 p.m. to 4 p.m. If it was popular, an hour on other afternoons would be reserved for women. Men could only come at that time if they accompanied a lady.

Friday proved to be a great success. The lanes were crowded for several hours. It was reported that some of the women made scores that few men could equal.

Ashland *Tidings* (Excerpts, Vol 9) November 4, 1897

Steamer *Winema* – 1905

"Moonlight excursions with bands for dancing.
Round trip $1.00 per person."

WOULDN'T YOU LIKE to read that in the paper? In January, 1905 a crowd turned out for the launching of the *Winema*. A bottle of French wine was broken over the boat's bow and the mayor of Klamath Falls spoke.

It wasn't until the end of April that the first excursion left the wharf with 200 people aboard and the band playing. The newspaper reported the passengers were made as comfortable as at home in the roomy cabins and parlors. The ladies' parlor was called "a delight," the floor covered in Brussels carpet. Comfortable chairs provided a view of the beautiful scenery.

At Odessa they stopped for lunch at the big Griffith hotel. At two p.m. the paddle wheel steamer left for a trip to Pelican Bay and back.

Better roads and railroads gradually took over freight and passenger service on the lake. The novelty and luxury of *Winema* had worn off. She was retired to dry dock in 1919.

Klamath *Echoes*, 1965

Jack and Tim Holt – 1912

ABOUT 1912, A RANCHER near Klamath Falls hired two ranch hands named Fred Starr and Jack Holt. They were conspicuous because of their "drug-store" cowboy appearance and the flashy saddles and trappings of their horses. It even became known the two were Harvard graduates. What had brought them to Klamath County? Together they would ride into Klamath Falls and hitch their horses to a post in front of the most elegant hotel in the region. This was long after hitching posts were used but the two horses would patiently remain there all night.

Just when Starr and Holt went to Hollywood is not recorded. Jack Holt became quite famous as a stunt man in the movies. It is his son, Tim Holt, whose name you are more likely to recognize. He followed in his father's footsteps and became a highly successful actor, playing in at least 140 movies.

It is said Tim Holt was always proud to show off the boots and saddle his father had used in his stunt man days.

Recollections of Percy Dixon and Ruth King

Rural Movies – 1916

RURAL FAMILIES WERE hungry for entertainment. Many had probably only heard of moving pictures when this article appeared in the Klamath *Evening Herald* in 1916.

"A moving picture machine on wheels for the accommodation of rural districts without electric service has been purchased by J.V. Houston, pioneer showman. Last week Mr. Houston showed to a full house in Fort Klamath, and the pictures showed up plainly.

"The machine is small, and can be carried easily in any automobile. A show can be put on any place where it is dark enough. The electric power for the machine comes from the automobile engine, a wire being strung from the automobile to the interior of the building where the show is being given.

"Mr. Houston plans to give motion picture shows in many districts of Klamath County that do not enjoy electric lights and other comforts from electricity."

The quality of the movies may be questionable. Perhaps just seeing this modern wonder was enough to draw a crowd.

Klamath *Echoes*, 1968

Flicker Films – 1910s

FLICKER FILMS WERE the first form of motion pictures made. In Montague they arrived about the turn of the century. They were shown upstairs in Gagnon Hall. A lady took the tickets. When everyone was seated, a man cranked the machine by hand and projected a flickering picture on the screen. A second man provided sound effects that followed the action. His equipment was a one-man band with the harmonica playing the main part. There were drums and stringed instruments, all of which added up to very realistic sounds.

When the flicker was over, a dance was held, the one man band furnishing all the music.

Larger towns were already getting moving pictures but the early flickers were full of excitement for the entertainment-starved small communities.

Siskiyou *Pioneer*, 1980

San Francisco to Grants Pass Foot Race – 1928

CALLED THE REDWOOD–EMPIRE race, this 480 mile race went from San Francisco to Grants Pass. It was meant to encourage tourism along the Redwood Highway. Because there were no bridges at the San Francisco end, the contestants traveled by boat to Sausalito and the race began at 11:45 on the morning of June 14, 1928.

At this time, people believed only Indians were capable of long distance running. The Grants Pass Cavemen, who sponsored the race, selected 15 Indian runners. Each represented a town along the route. The prize was a bucket containing $1,000 in bills.

The race gained international notice as one of the greatest feats of human endurance. The rules were simple. A man could stop when he wanted and run when he wanted. And of course, he must run the entire length. A judge accompanied each entrant to see that he followed these rules. Two others went along to take care of food and lodging.

One hundred sixty-seven hours and fifty-one minutes later, on June 21, 1928, a runner named Flying Cloud crossed the finish line in Grants Pass. He could have arrived sooner but the Chamber of Commerce kept him overnight in Wilderville so he would arrive in Grants Pass during daylight. Thousands lined the streets and the last mile was run in five minutes twelve seconds. Flying Cloud had averaged 70 miles a day.

Southern Oregon Historical Society *Sentinel*, April 1986

Maypole dance
SOURCE: Larry McLane

Dances

THE SATURDAY NIGHT dance was a town's main social event. In Montague, California ranchers would come into town in their wagons with the whole family. The cloak room at the K.P. Lodge was lined with benches. Coats would be laid on the benches and children bedded down with more coats over them. This way the family could stay until the end of the dance at three o'clock in the morning.

In the 1930s, for $1 you could dance from nine to three to the music of Peterson's Orchestra. They were local people and usually about seven of them would turn out. There would be a bass, banjo, saxophone, trumpets, trombone and piano. Between midnight and one the orchestra stopped and the local women put on a spread of homemade foods.

When the orchestra played "Good Night Sweetheart" the girls would dance with their special beaus and the dance would be over.

Interview with Leah Reichman

Demon Rum in the Dance Halls – 1930

DANCES WERE ONE of the few opportunities to socialize in 1930.

In Medford, places like Dreamland and Oriental Gardens were pretty glamorous dance halls. They didn't sell liquor but the practice of going out and coming back in was allowed. As people returned more and more drunk, some pretty unpleasant occasions arose and there were many fights.

The Medford City Council passed an ordinance making chaperones a requirement at all dances. Mrs. Barto, a friend of the mayor, was chosen as a chaperone, but Barto's enthusiasm for her job got a little out of hand. Not only did she keep the intoxicated out, she took it upon herself to inform couples when they were dancing too close.

Earl Fehl was a firebrand editor of the *Pacific Record Herald* at this time and he wrote an outspoken editorial calling Mrs. Barto and Medford officials all sort of names. Fehl was sued and found not guilty but the trial caused quite a sensation.

Dance halls began to lose much of their importance as the movies gained in popularity.

Southern Oregon Historical Society *Sentinel*, June 1983

CHAPTER 18

THE FOOD CHAIN

Horticulture – 1795

SHIPS' LOGS FURNISH valuable historical information. Captains reported every detail of life, including dates and locations.

White men's first attempt to grow anything on Oregon soil seems to have been made by the crew of the ship *Ruby*. On May 24, 1795 the ship's log reported the following:

> "Wednesday I took a small party of our people and cleared a small island which we called Tree Island Possession, and made a garden, planting indian corn, peas, beans, potatoes and several peach stones and sowed radishes, mustard, cresses and celery seeds that we are in hopes on our return from the North we shall have vegetables for our table..."

No further mention is made of the peach stones but a later entry in the log tells us:

> "On our return in October we found the potatoes, abundant large and good, the radishes had gone to seed, ... there were several beans, but no appearance of peas, mustard, cresses or celery. The latter we ascribed to the troop of birds which inhabited the islet."

With the advent of fur trading, the Hudson Bay Company worked extensive farms for provisions.

In California the missions always planted crops and were instrumental in introducing many food varieties to the west coast.

Oregon Oddities, WPA

Kappler Saloon, Montague, California. Emil Kappler tending bar.
SOURCE: Paul and Leah Reichman

Beer, Jacksonville – 1853

ALMOST AS SOON AS the city of Jacksonville came into existence, in 1853, construction of a brewery began. Two of the oldest brewers in Jacksonville were Wetterer and Holman. Holman represented the English style of ale-type beers that could be manufactured in a short time and at warm, more varying temperatures.

Wetterer had come to Oregon in search of gold but was a trained German brewer. His beer represented the popular lager beers that required between two and three months to age at near freezing temperatures. Such ideal conditions were unlikely to be found in Southern Oregon even in the winter.

In order to maintain a near constant temperature, a brewery would be built into the side of a hill with the aging cellar covered with dirt. The malting process was hurried up by the malt being given a quick toasting. This produced a darker beer. A by-product of the brewing process produced yeast which the breweries sold to local housewives. Some breweries operated bakeries as part of their business.

Breweries were often the site of family gatherings. Beer was served on the premises and was promoted as a healthful and moderate drink. The temperance movement was only aimed at saloons and hard liquor. Brewers themselves were respected members of the local society.

Southern Oregon Historical Society *Sentinel*, January/February 1991

Hard to Find Eggs

THE BIRDSEYES FORTIFIED their Jackson County house. When the Rogue Indian War started in 1855, the Savage family came to the fort. The farm work went on as usual.

One of Mrs. Savage's jobs was to collect the eggs. The chickens had been allowed to roam and eggs might be found anywhere. One hen had a favorite spot under the granary floor. Mrs. Savage would crawl under there daily to get the egg. But Mrs. Savage was pregnant and one day, after crawling in, she found she was too large to get back out. Screams were heard. Two women dashed from the house and rushed to the rescue. Each grabbing a leg, they pulled as hard as they could. Mrs. Savage finally popped out, covered with dirt and with her skirts up around her neck. Still clutched in her hand was the egg, uninjured.

Interview with Nita Birdseye

Ice at Forest House – 1863

FOREST HOUSE, NEAR Yreka, was the largest orchard and nursery in California in the early years. It developed many related sidelines. One of these was storing and selling ice. Ice was used for storing their harvested fruits. In the late 1850s a person was well off if he could afford the luxury of owning an ice box.

The very first thing erected by the partners of Forest House was a sawmill built in 1852. This required a pond to raise the level of water that would create the pressure needed to run the mill. In the winter, the mill pond froze and became the source of ice.

The Yreka *Journal* of May 13, 1853 noted that, "Mr. Short of Forest House furnishes an excellent quality of ice to customers in Yreka." The reservoir pond, which produced the ice, was spring fed and was in a ravine where the sun didn't shine. When the ice became eight to ten inches thick, as many as eight men were used to saw blocks of ice about eighteen inches square. These were floated to a chute and slid down into a sawdust pile just inside the ice house. Men stacked the blocks. They would throw buckets of water on the stack and it would freeze solid. Then sawdust was layered on top to act as insulation. The ice house held 300 tons of ice. It would take about three cuttings from the pond to fill it.

For the next 70 years the ice wagon was a common sight as it went up and down city streets delivering ice to every house.

Siskiyou *Pioneer*, 1965

Cattle Terminals – 1887

THE CALIFORNIA AND OREGON RAILROAD opened as far as Hornbrook, California on May 1, 1887. It was a boon to the cattle ranchers in the area. Before the railroad came through, there was a glut of cattle on the market and it was not unusual for them to be sold only for their tallow and hides. The meat was not used.

As soon as cattle could be transported profitably, they were sent to other parts of the country where beef was in high demand. The price of steers and cows was measured at one half their weight. They almost always weighed over 1,000 pounds as they weren't sold until they were three or more years old. That meant one steer would sell for about $25. A whole year's check for a large operation might be only $2,000 or $3,000 a year.

Now, with the train, towns like Montague became shipping centers for cattle. Great cattle drives would come from Scotts Valley and all of eastern Oregon. Towns along the line also profited by the railroad's rules that cattle could not be kept on a train car for more that 36 hours. For eight hours they were taken off, watered, fed, rested and allowed to walk around. Large corrals and feed lots were developed. Twenty-five percent of grains grown in the area were used for cattle in transit.

The majority of cattle were shipped north in the spring as the grass greened and south in the fall to warmer climates. As many as 800 carloads might come by during either season.

Siskiyou Pioneer, 1967

Shipping Cattle, Montague – 1886

MONTAGUE, CALIFORNIA WAS a collecting point for shipping cattle. The Southern Pacific Railroad laid out the town site on March 9, 1886. For years, during the month of August, cattle from Lake, Klamath and Modoc Counties were rounded up and driven to Montague to be shipped to market. Stock yards and feeding pens were strung out along the railroad track. Often it was hard to get these semi-wild cattle into the pens. One trick used was to lead a gentle milk cow into the pen. The wild cattle would follow her.

The gentle cow was again used to lead the cattle onto the train in the late afternoon. About 26 or 27 head of cattle filled a box car. Their destination was the stockyard in San Francisco. Someone went with the train to look after the stock. This man rode in the caboose and handled loading and unloading the cattle.

Sheep and hogs were shipped from Montague also. Usually when sheep were loaded, a billy goat was put in with them. It was the billy goat who led the way and the sheep would follow wherever he went.

When trucks became available, they were popular because they would pick up the cattle right at the ranch. This meant that the long cattle drives to Montague were not necessary, but it also meant that the importance of Montague diminished.

Siskiyou Pioneer, 1986

Splash Dams

SINCE EARLIEST TIMES, humans have been spearing, clubbing, poisoning, snagging, hooking and netting fish. The Pacific Ocean and the rivers that ran into it seemed to hold an inexhaustible supply. In our area, one of the first threats to spawning fish were the splash dams of early logging days. Not only were fish unable to get up the rivers past the dams, the system also removed their shallow water spawning grounds.

What was a splash dam? After felling trees, the lumbermen dumped their logs into a damned lake, called a splash pond. Periodically the dams were opened and the logs sent rushing down the river. The bumping and rolling of the logs scoured the riverbeds leaving bare rock. The gravel bars, vital for spawning, were swept away and water was muddied.

Hundred of splash dams were in operation in the 1800s, mainly on Oregon rivers. The sawmills objected to the system because logs were damaged as they jammed into each other rushing downstream. Early sportsmen and professional fishermen saw the supply of fish dwindling. It was not economy that lead to the use of splash dams but lack of roads or other means for transporting logs out of the back woods. With the improved highway system and logging roads, trucking has taken over and splash dams have been eliminated.

Even though fish hatcheries have done much to keep up the population of fish, natural spawning has always been the preferred way to restock our waters.

Oregon's South Coast, Bain

Orchard Insecticides – 1870s

THE FIRST FRUIT TREES grown in the Rogue Valley sprang from seed brought across the plains. The first commercial fruit orchards were planted by J.H. Stewart of Medford in 1865. Coddling worms were already in the area and quickly spread to the fruit trees. Early suggestions for control included penning hens, pigs or chickens in the orchards. It was thought these would eat the decaying fruit on which the moth eggs were laid. Others suggested sprays such as arsenate of lead or lye and coal oil.

Early insecticides were brushed on the trees. Finally a "power" spray was devised. A fifty gallon tank was put on a wagon with a piston pump by its side. This sucked the liquid and forced it through a hose and rod to a nozzle at 30 or 40 pounds of pressure. The power was supplied by a strong man who pushed and pulled the pump handle back and forth. It wasn't until 1903 that a high pressure spray, working on compressed air, was developed.

The next big step in spray equipment came in the early 1920s. This machine produced pressures up to 100 pounds and the nozzles were adjustable to make a fine or coarse spray. Centrally located spray plants were introduced somewhat later.

Researchers learned the life cycle of the various pests and spraying schedules were adapted to them. Gradually more attention was given to the safety of the sprays and orchardists were required to wash and wipe the fruit to remove any residue of chemicals before marketing the fruit.

History of the Rogue Valley Fruit Industry, Cordy

Minear ranch and orchard, Medford, 1904
SOURCE: Ruth Minear Alborn

W.G. Smith

THE REVEREND W.G. SMITH had big dreams for Wolf Creek, Oregon. He envisioned a sober, happy, industrious community whose vast fruit orchards would make the area self-sustaining. To make his dream come true, he purchased over 2,700 acres of land which he subdivided and sold through brochures mailed back east. Many came.

There were flaws in Rev. Smith's vision. It takes years for an orchard to produce sufficient fruit to be marketable. Even more important, Wolf Creek was in the mountains where fruit developed weeks later than in the valleys. By harvest, the valley orchards had cornered the fruit market. The vision began to fall apart. One orchardist wrote a poem he called "Wolf Creek Lament" part of which goes:

> Long months ago we came up here
> And brought along our plunder.
> Long months we sat and chewed our cud,
> And realized our blunder.

Adversity brought bickering and name calling. Smith became the most unpopular man in town. The plan that had so hopefully started in 1908, floundered and finally died in the 1920s.

You can still see the occasional old fruit tree around Wolf Creek that dates from that almost forgotten era.

From listener Larry King

Fish Lake – 1915

FISH LAKE IN Jackson County, Oregon is a beautiful camping and fishing spot. It was developed to help promote the orchard industry.

In 1897 the Fish Lake Water Company secured a government concession for a reservoir. They built a cribbed-log dam. The resulting lake was fed by springs but this first lake was little more than a widening of the North Fork of Little Butte Creek. The dam was enlarged in 1915. With this, and subsequent development, the lake furnished irrigation water for most of the fruit orchards built to the north of Medford.

Promoters forecast that local towns, such as Lake Creek and Eagle Point, would become large centers for the orchard industry. Indeed, many people flocked to the area, grabbing up land and planting trees.

Water from the Fish Lake reservoir furnished Medford with drinking water until 1926. By that time the growing population required a more dependable source.

Prehistory and History of the Rogue River National Forest, U.S. Forest Service
Medford *Mail Tribune* (Excerpts Weekly, Vol 2)

Carp, Shad and Striped Bass – 1885

IN THE LATE 1870s, 10,000 shad fry were brought to the Sacramento River from Rochester, New York. The released shad stay in the streams until fall when they are about six inches long, at this time they swim out to the ocean. Little is known about a shad's life at sea, but when water temperatures are near 60° the shad swim upstream. They do not have the homing instincts of the salmon who return to their own stream. With a lot of flurry and splashing, they lay their eggs, which hatch in six to ten days. The adult shad returns to the ocean after spawning.

The striped bass is another import from the east coast. As bass fishing declined in Virginia, it was decided to try them on the west coast. In 1879 the first shipment of 132 bass was sent to San Francisco. They thrived in their new environment and by 1914 the first bass was caught in far away Coos Bay.

Dr. James Spence, of Illinois Valley, heard about raising carp for food, so he built a pond on his land. In 1885 he telegraphed for the carp which arrived by rail and were transported to the waiting pond. Several years later high water washed out his pond and the carp escaped into the Illinois River. They soon spread throughout the Rogue River water shed.

Oregon's South Coast, Bain; Grants Pass *Courier,* June 1992

The Sheepman and the Singer – early 1900s

FOR YEARS THE MYSTERIOUS Mr. M.F. Armstrong lived as a sheepman about ten miles east of Klamath Falls.

What puzzled the local people was his obvious education, his resentment of any curiosity and his hatred of music.

With Armstrong lived his son George. The two had come to Klamath County from Texas, in the early 1900s. The father took on the life of the sheepman to promote privacy, but privacy was hard to find. When the father and son went to Portland to meet with the famous opera singer, Dame Melba, it leaked out that she was his former wife. Known throughout the world, she had committed the sin of choosing her career over life with Armstrong.

Young George went off with his mother to further his education and lead a more exciting life. He settled in England and married the daughter of an English peer, even winning a seat in the House of Commons. He returned to Klamath County on a visit in 1939 and spoke fondly of his summers herding sheep in the hills around Olene.

In the meantime M.F. Armstrong, the father, found his privacy invaded and left Klamath for Canada.

Klamath Express, *December 27, 1906; Klamath* Evening Herald, *July 20, 1939;*
Oregonian, June 3, 1934

Rabbit Drive – 1902

ABOUT THE TURN of the century, jack rabbits threatened the farmers and ranchers east of the Cascades. The plague didn't happen overnight. The rabbit population had been building up through the 1890s. Klamath County declared a bounty on rabbit scalps at 5¢ a piece. A scalp consisted of two ears with enough skin to attach them together.

The rabbits consumed entire gardens and fields of grain. The county court reported paying out for 30,000 rabbit scalps and 854 coyote and wild cat scalps. Some communities had rabbit drives. They held them on Saturdays so children could share in the outing . Everyone would gather to form a continuous chain. They would move forward several miles driving the rabbits toward a canyon wall or into a net strung along a fence. The rabbits would try to break through the line of people but were usually clubbed or killed by shotgun fire.

The drives netted between 500 and 2,000 rabbits. The money earned from the bounty would be divided among the participants. A drive was usually followed by a potluck and maybe even a dance. They were considered a popular social event.

Even this method failed to stop the rabbits from multiplying. It wasn't until poison was introduced that they were controlled.

Klamath Echoes, *1972*

Cattle Versus Sheep – 1904

CONFLICT BETWEEN CATTLE interests and sheep ranchers, common everywhere, was bound to erupt in Oregon. It did just that on February 3, 1904 in Lake County.

During the night, five masked men slaughtered 2,000 sheep out of a band of 3,000. Next, J.C. Corn came up missing. It was said Corn leaked some facts about the sheep

Holding corral at the railroad, Montague, California
SOURCE: Paul and Leah Reichman

shooting. His body was found seven weeks later with two bullet holes in it. In April, all but 300 sheep were killed from a band of 2,700. Again the men were masked.

The slaughters spread and there was no success with the idea of establishing separate territories for each group. The cattlemen thought that since they had arrived in the basin first, the sheep men were the intruders.

Klamath County was soon involved with more killings and camp burnings. Arrests were impossible as no one would testify and the majority of sentiment was with the cattlemen.

There was no resolution to the cattle versus sheep problem but, since then, the two sides have learned to live in an uneasy acceptance of each other.

Klamath *Echoes*, 1972

Hops Growing – 1910

FOR MANY YEARS the growing of hops was a major industry from Medford north to Portland.

Albert J. Walcott was the first grower on record in the Rogue Valley. He began in 1855. By the late 1880s there was considerable acreage being grown west of Grants Pass, and by 1910 Oregon was the largest grower of hops in the country.

Growing hops was almost a year around job. First came the cultivation, suckering, twining and spraying. The year peaked with the harvesting which took about four weeks. Then came the curing and baling. When that was done the vines had to be disposed of and the process started again.

In the beginning, hops were trained up tall pine poles. At harvest, one strong man served as the pole puller. He pulled the pole out of the ground and turned the tip end onto a "jack." The picker would strip the hops off the vines and the pole puller would clean the vines off the pole and put it back in the hole. Bales weighed 200 pounds. A good crop would be nine or ten bales per acre.

It wasn't prohibition that put an end to hops growing, it was the lure of big money being made in fruit orchards. Suddenly everyone was growing fruit. So many growers switched to fruit, in fact, that orchards began to harvest more than could be sold. As this became more and more evident, many of the orchardists began pulling up their fruit trees and going back to hops.

As late as 1958, hops were still considered a major crop. For awhile it was hard to find anyone in the business. Now, with micro-breweries, the industry is expanding once again.

Josephine County Historical Highlights II, Hill; *Land of the Umpqua*, Beckman

Egg Laying Record – 1912

BORN ON JUNE 11, 1911, Laura T. of Grants Pass, was a White Rock Hen. She was a pullet eight months old when her owners realized she was a remarkable egg layer. She was penned by herself, with only a macho White Rock rooster for company. Her owners began keeping a record of her egg laying skills on February 19, 1912 and during the remaining 17 days of that month she laid 17 eggs including one for the extra day of leap year.

For the 31 days of March, Laura T. added 31 eggs and continued during April and May, with a grand total of 109 eggs in 109 days.

Following the remarkable four-month performance, Laura T laid 25 eggs in June and only 17 in July. She then became broody and wanted to sit on her eggs. We have no record to show if her offspring were exceptional egg layers as well.

Rogue River *Daily Courier*, June 11, 1911

Sugar Beet Industry – 1916

IN OCTOBER OF 1915 the Oregon–Utah Sugar Company advertised in the Grants Pass *Courier* saying they would build a factory in Grants Pass if Josephine County could sign up farmers to plant 5,000 acres of sugar beets. The town was delighted.

Farmers signed up thinking their future was assured, but not enough farmers signed up to make the 5,000 acre requirement. Even so, the company planned to go ahead. The site of the plant was located and construction began. Almost immediately a problem emerged.

Growing sugar beets requires a lot of water and Josephine County had lagged behind others in development of irrigation. A processing factory would also require a lot of water. A well was drilled which took care of the factory's supply. By May the beets had grown to ten inches in length. The conditions seemed favorable but by mid summer the beets had begun to shrivel. This lowered both the size and the sugar content.

Grants Pass sugar beet factory
SOURCE: Larry McLane

In October the harvest began. The plant employed two shifts of workers. Visitors flocked to inspect the factory in action and they were impressed. Workers dressed all in white gave out samples of sugar at each stage of the processing. Outside, people watched the feeding pens where the waste pulp was given to cattle.

Looking ahead, the sugar company tried to convince the beet growers that they must develop an irrigation system in order to produce large, good quality beets. There was much opposition to the idea of forming an irrigation district even though World War I had begun and the demand for sugar was high. As a last resort, employees were offered incentives to plant beets but still the number needed for a profitable operation was not reached.

The second harvest in October, 1917 produced only enough beets for a 30 day run at the plant.

The next year, bonds were approved for an irrigation system but it was too late. The Grants Pass Sugar Beet Factory had closed.

Josephine County Historical Highlights, Hill

Tule Lake Farming – 1923

KARL AND MARIE GENTRY were two of the lucky people who were awarded farm units acquired from the draining of Tule Lake. Or were they lucky?

The land the Gentrys obtained in 1923 was rich but there were no roads, no telephones, no electricity, no indoor plumbing and no running water. In the winter the mud was knee deep and no one could move except when things were frozen. In summer, after the harvest, the winds sent dust right through the houses. But the worst problem was well water.

Shallow wells smelled of sulfur and methane gas. The iron content was so high, it discolored anything washed in it. Residents would drive into Malin to get barrels of fresh water from people who had deep wells.

A favorite story, often repeated, was about the man who was working in a garage on Main street. On his first day, the worker asked to use the rest room. He was warned not to light a cigarette while he was in there. The man ignored the warning and as soon as he sat down he lighted a cigarette. The match ignited the methane gas that had been released from the water in the toilet bowl. The explosion blew off the restroom door and singed the occupant.

After that, no one questioned that Tule Lake water was really dangerous.

Years of Harvest, History of the Tule Lake Basin, Turner

Pigs For Garbage

THE SUMNER, OREGON school was about ten miles from Marshfield (Coos Bay). There was no garbage disposal. The school offered to buy a little pig for any person who would pick up the scraps from the school lunches twice a week. The Harrisons thought that was a pretty good deal and accepted the challenge.

All went well until the pig developed a rupture. The vet came out and performed surgery. It seems the cook had broken a glass and a piece had inadvertently gotten in the garbage and was eaten by the pig. The pig survived the operation and the Harrisons were told to give her an oil enema once a day for a week. They managed to perform one oil enema but the pig would have no more. He got so slick with the oil they couldn't catch him. He recovered without further enemas.

When June rolled around, the Harrisons had a nice fat pig for slaughter and, for $5 the school had had their garbage taken care of for a whole year.

The Harrisons raised three pigs this way.

Interview with Vurl and Jim Harrison

Worm Cheese

KAY PRICE GREW UP on a ranch near Mt. Shasta. They were almost self sufficient. One of the things they made was cheese.

Cheese rounds would be wrapped and put down in the cool cellar to age. They were cleaned and wiped regularly. A few of the rounds would be left untreated. These untreated rounds would form large worms who ate on the cheese. The worms were fat and white, between an inch and two inches long. This was the favorite cheese of the Italian men who worked the ranch. They would eat the cheese and the live worms together and thought it a great delicacy.

Interview with Kay Price.

CHAPTER 19

HEALTH

Klamath Hot Springs – 1870

ON THE EAST BANK of the Klamath River, near the mouth of Shovel Creek, are the Klamath hot springs. Across the river from the springs sits a large cave. Both sites had been used by the Indians for years before the Hudson Bay trappers found and used the area also.

In 1870 Mr. and Mrs Beswich built a hotel for travelers at the hot springs. It had ten sleeping rooms, a blacksmith shop and a barn for stabling horses. Later a spa and a new hotel with 75 rooms was built. A large bath house was constructed over the springs. The mineral water was piped into drinking fountains and mud baths were prescribed for the arthritic visitors. A large swimming pool was heated to the right temperature by mixing spring water with river water. Fishing was also available. Your catch could be dried and taken home.

Among the famous visitors to Klamath Hot Springs were Herbert Hoover, William S. Hart, the movie star; Zane Grey and Amelia Earhart.

The hotel at Klamath Hot Springs burned down in 1915.

Siskiyou *Pioneer,* 1965

Mountain Balm – 1872

DR. FURBER, OF Rough and Ready (Etna), California, introduced "Dr. Furber's Cordial of Mountain Balm" in the fall of 1869. The medicine, an alkaloid extracted from tar weed, was patented a year later and advertised in *Scientific American.* The Mountain Balm Cordial was supposed to be helpful in the healing of "irritability of the stomach" caused by hard drinking. The Balm Center was the most active place in Rough and Ready. It was a basic drug store with the manufacturing of the balm and a printing office on the side. The doctor and his family lived in a dwelling next door. Upstairs was a temperance hall where the Sons of Temperance met. The doctor was an active member and printed their pamphlets.

The balm business was brisk. So brisk, in fact, that the doctor decided to move to Vallejo, California and build a bigger establishment.

In September, 1872 Furber's family decided to move back to Etna while the doctor stayed behind to conduct business. He had branched out by placing Mountain Balm in saloons to be used as bitters. Just how he reconciled this with his temperance beliefs he didn't explain.

Two years later, Dr. Furber died. He had been a pioneer of Etna and had contributed much to the town but Mountain Balm appears to have died with him.

Saddle Bags in Siskiyou, Jones

Colestin – 1881

A HOTEL WAS BUILT at Colestin in 1881 to offer the tourist the "superior medicinal properties" of the mineral waters found there. It had 25 rooms and a campground to take care of another 100 people. It was built of hand hewn timbers but some elegant features were added to its rustic charm. The great advantage of Colestin was its accessibility on the Southern Pacific Railroad. The train stopped just a few miles north of the California border, high in the Siskiyou Mountains.

The mineral water contained iron and was charged with carbonic acid. The springs had been used by the earliest trappers and travelers. The Indians made medicine pellets of the mud but otherwise avoided the springs. The powers of the water have never been proven but certainly cures occurred.

When not drinking the water, vacationers could sit on the wide veranda, play quoits or tennis or watch the croquet matches. Paths led in different directions for strolling but sociability was the main attraction. Evenings the ladies put on their best dresses for dinner and later gathered around huge campfires for music, story telling and singing. On weekends a dance band played. It was all quite elegant.

The era of mineral spas died out as the quality of professional doctors improved. Colestin's popularity faded also.

Southern Oregon Historical Society *Sentinel*, May 1986

Cinnabar Springs – 1890

A HUNTER BY THE name of Walker, who would be called "homeless" if he were living today, got lost in the Siskiyou Mountains when the hard winter of 1889–1890 struck. Already sick and confused, he found a narrow ravine where he decided to spend the winter. He built a shelter and found a spring of water nearby. He made himself as comfortable as possible, expecting to die in the spot.

All winter Walker lived off the food he had brought and the cold mineral water that bubbled up in the pool. He found himself getting stronger and stronger so that, by spring, he hiked into Jacksonville proclaiming himself cured by the wonderful mineral springs he had discovered.

Waiting for the next train load of tourists, Colestin Springs Resort
SOURCE: Larry McLane

This was an era of great belief in healthful waters. Jobe Garretson took out a patent on the springs. He built a spa and resort that quickly became a popular vacation spot. A bath in a tin bottomed wooden tub cost 25¢ if you brought your own towel. For an additional 10¢ the towel was provided. People claimed amazing cures. The water was bottled and shipped throughout the area.

Soon a general store was built, and a second resort providing for hundreds of campers. The nearby Cinnabar Mine employed 25 to 30 people, so boarding houses were constructed. The town and resort reached their peak about 1910.

Like other mineral spas, Cinnabar Springs faded in the Great Depression of the 1930s. There is nothing to show for this once popular place.

Southern Oregon Historical Society *Sentinel,* May 1986

Babies

DR. WARREN BISHOP came to practice medicine in Medford in 1931. The depression was well underway and starting a practice was slow. Some of the established doctors would pass along a call to a new doctor, especially if the call came at night. Dr. Bishop received one of these calls shortly after he came to town. A woman out in the Applegate was in labor.

Before World War II it was common to deliver babies at home. Because of the depression, it was likely for a delivery to be the first time a doctor saw his patient. Such was the case here.

"It was during the night. When I got up to the cabin, this lady was in labor and it was a breach presentation. I delivered the baby but it was a great big baby and the head got hung up. I worked and sweated, I didn't cuss but I did a little praying inside. Finally I got the baby delivered and it was absolutely limp. I gave it mouth to mouth resuscitation and after awhile it grunted. I kept it up and finally the baby cried. The sweat was just pouring off me. Grandma was there and some of the neighbors and the father. That added to my tension too.

"I still remember how I labored to save that baby."

Before he retired, Dr. Bishop delivered over 3,100 babies. This delivery in the Applegate, is one that he will always remember.

Interview with Dr. Bishop

"Healers" – 1901

ONE-MAN MEDICINE SHOWS were great entertainment in the small western communities. Called "A Healer," a single man traveled hundreds of miles in his medicine wagon. No town was too small for him to stop and put on a show. He would select someone from the audience on whom to perform a miraculous cure using one of his ointments or tonics. Usually these were affected by hypnotism, but the results amused and amazed the town folks. Between sales pitches, the "doctor" performed feats of magic and sang ballads accompanying himself on some sort of musical instrument. The only qualification a person needed to become a "Healer" was to be glib and fast talking.

It is easy today to think of the pioneer as gullible if he or she believed the incredible cures claimed for patent medicines. Remember that these people lived miles from any doctor and even these doctors were sometimes poorly trained and inexperienced. The pioneers were forced to depend on themselves to cure disease and heal injuries. Any information they could glean from a medicine show was to be considered.

'Doctor' was a title the medicine man often conferred on himself. This added veracity to the fast talking pitch. He showed illustrations and diagrams to add any final proof needed.

The medicine shows raked in money but the towns were far apart and few "healers" got rich.

Trooping in the Oregon Country, Ernst

Buckhorn Soda Springs – 1900

INDIANS CONSIDERED mineral springs a manifestation of the Great Spirit. Of all the springs in the Cascade area, the Indians thought Buckhorn Springs the most sacred. It is located on Emigrant Creek ten miles east of Ashland, Oregon.

One-man tent show
SOURCE: Fort Jones Museum

The Modoc and the Rogue River Indians brought their sick to the spot. The medicine man would dig an indentation over a vent hole and make it just large enough for one person. The hollow was spread with boughs and the patient placed on them. Carbon dioxide vapors surrounded him until he passed out and was removed. Under the influence of the Great Spirit, the person was taken to a wickiup and manipulated until he regained consciousness. Immediately the patient was put in a sweat house, while the medicine man made incantations. There the patient drank water and steamed in the sauna. This continued until the person was declared well or was considered incurable.

Around the turn of the century, mineral springs were popular everywhere. Boswell Springs in Douglas County was typical, claiming cures for all types of disorders, rheumatism, stomach trouble, kidney disease, poison oak, sore throat, and anything else that troubled the ill. Dead Indian Soda Springs, and others, sold bottled water to taverns and restaurants. Most spas were located on National Forest Service property but were developed privately as camps with accommodations. McCallister Soda Springs was buried by road fill for the construction of Oregon route 140.

Prehistory and History of the Rogue River National Forest, U.S. Forest Service;
Southern Oregon Historical Society *Sentinel*, July 1988

Dr. G. A. Massey – 1918

WHEN PEOPLE THINK with nostalgia, of the old family doctor, they are thinking of a man like Dr. George Massey. He arrived in Klamath Falls the fall of 1918. He was a young man about to begin his practice at the Blackburn Hospital. He had hardly settled before he was in major surgery and plunged into the 1918 flu epidemic, which hit the population of Klamath County hard.

As soon as possible, the doctor purchased a Model-T Ford to make his house calls. But many of his calls were in the outlying areas of the county and roads were bad. Sometimes only a horse and buggy, or even a sled, had to do. Dr. Massey even made use of the railroad hand cars ordinarily used by the repair crews.

In spring the county roads were notorious for their mud holes. To be prepared, the doctor carried a strong logging chain. When mired, he would take the chain, fasten it to the rear end of the vehicle, take the crank, fasten it securely at the other end and looping it around a nearby tree, slowly but persistently he would crank the car out of the mud hole.

Dr. Massey practiced in Klamath for 57 years, delivering at least 5,000 babies. He was still practicing at age 85 which demonstrated to his own good health.

Klamath *Herald News*, August 13, 1967

CHAPTER 20

NATURE

Wild Animals

SOMETIMES ANIMALS TAKE to a new environment so well, they are soon thought of as native to the area. Such is the case with the Chinese pheasant in Oregon.

Owen Denny was in the U.S. Consular Service, stationed in Shanghai. In September of 1881, he sent his brother, John, of Linn County, a shipment of Chinese pheasants. Due to neglect on shipboard, most of them died. The next spring he sent about 30 more. These arrived safely. They were freed on Denny's farm. Protected from hunters by state law for the first 11 years, they thrived.

The Chinese pheasant can now be found throughout Oregon and Washington and is the state bird of South Dakota.

Another story of animals going wild can be told in Medford. By 1920, streetcars, railroads and automobiles had taken the place of horses. The Medford Livery Stable found themselves with a lot of unwanted horses and nothing to do with them. They finally decided to set them free west of town, thinking they would live out their lives and die. Instead they bred rapidly and soon became known as the "Wild Horses of the Applegate." They began raiding haystacks and pastures, kicking calves to death, breaking down fences and ruining summer ranges.

In the late '30s local stock men waged war on the horses so that by 1946 only about five remained. These too, seem to have disappeared.

Oregon, Homer; Medford *Mail Tribune*, November 23, 1947;
Oregon Oddities, WPA; *Chinese Pheasants, Oregon Pioneers*, Holmgren

Camas Lily

THE BEAUTIFUL CAMAS LILY has deep blue flowers on stems as long as 30 inches. This was one of the most important sources of food for the Indians west of the Cascades. The lilies dominated large fields where Indian women made trips to

Chinese pheasant
PHOTO: Norman Barrett

dig the bulbs. They could be eaten raw but the most popular way of preparing camas bulbs was to bake them. A pit was dug, lined with stones and a fire built in it. When the stones were red hot, the ashes were raked out of the pit. A special grass was laid over the stones and the camas bulbs were spread on top. Grass went over the bulbs and dirt was spread on top of the grass. A fire was kept burning over the pit for two days. Caring for the fire was critical and given to the older, more experienced women.

The death camas grows under much the same conditions as the camas lily. There is no similarity in the blossoms or the leaves but the bulbs look very much alike. The death camas can indeed sicken, or even kill, an unsuspecting eater. It also affects cattle.

Tribes waged wars for possession of camas fields. When the white men came, not only did they plow up fields but they allowed their pigs to run wild. The pigs discovered the camas bulbs and loved them.

While fields of camas are harder to find these day, many places have been named for the lily, Camas Valley, Camas Swale, Camas Lake and Camas Creek are some.

Oregon Oddities, WPA

Wild Man or Big Foot

THE INDIANS BELIEVED there were scattered wild men living in the mountains near Happy Camp, California. So did many of the settlers. In 1886 the Del Norte *Record* printed reports of "wild men." This edition mentioned a sighting by Jack Dover.

"Jack Dover, one of our most trustworthy citizens, saw an object 150 yards from him, picking berries or tender shoots from the bushes. The thing was of gigantic size. About seven feet high, with a bulldog head, short ears and long hair. It was also furnished with a beard, and was free from hair in such parts of the body as is common among men. It's voice was shrill or soprano and very human, like that of a woman in great fear."

A number of other people had reported similar sightings over the years. They all agreed with Dover's description except for the height, which some thought was as much as eight feet. Most people decided that this animal was a herbivore who lived in caves around Marble Mountain.

Del Norte Historical Society

Lower Klamath Birds

IN 1900, LOWER KLAMATH LAKE teemed with birds. It was probably the most important breeding ground on the west coast. In spite of the difficulties of reaching

Kestrel, Lower
Klamath Refuge
PHOTO: Norman Barrett

the shallow lake through the tules, hunters came to harvest plumes for women's hats. During nesting season thousands of gulls, terns and grebes were killed, leaving eggs and young baby birds to die. Grebe skins were made into capes and coats. One summer an estimated 30,000 were killed and shipped.

Suppliers for San Francisco restaurants hunted ducks and geese during the winter months. In 1903, 120 tons were killed and shipped.

In 1917 the Lower Klamath Lake headwaters were closed off and the lake was drained. By 1922 only a pond remained. Cormorants, pelicans and gulls disappeared. Thousands of ducks were killed by the alkali.

In the 1940s it was acknowledged that the draining of Lower Klamath Lake was a mistake. A new reclamation project was initiated and once again Lower Klamath Lake exists and wildlife has found its way back.

Southern Oregon *Heritage*

Snow geese, Klamath Marsh
PHOTO: Norman Barrett

General Crook – 1906

GENERAL CROOK DIED IN 1906 after a brief illness. Maybe you've never heard of General Crook of Lake County, Oregon. He was a horse. He was very special and a much loved buggy horse owned by C.U. Snider. Snider had purchased him for $150 in March, 1873, when he was five years old. A little arithmetic will tell you that he died at age 38 years. He was thought to be the oldest horse in Oregon. General Crook would probably still hold the record.

The name General Crook came from the famous Indian fighter of that name. For 27 years the horse pulled the buggy of Mr. Snider. He covered a mile in three minutes on long trips. He hated to have another horse ahead of him and would trot until he passed it.

General Crook took a liking to one of the Snider's cows who was particularly smart. The two would stay close together. If General Crook wanted to get out he would nudge the cow who unlatched the gate for him.

The horse's hearing and eyesight began to fail as he got older but he was loved and petted by the family. When he died, he was buried in Lakeview in the southwest corner of the courthouse yard.

Lake County *Examiner*, August 2, 1906

Mare's Eggs

IF YOU ARE EVER DRIVING in Oregon between Route 140 and Fort Klamath, stop at the side of the road and look down at beautiful Mare's Eggs Springs. When you look in the clear water you will think you are seeing smooth, round stones that have been dumped into the pond. If you can reach one and touch it you will get a big surprise. Each stone is a form of extremely rare algae, found in only four or five places in the world. They range in size from those barely visible to others the size of a large baked potato. If they are left out in the air, they soon collapse leaving only a thin empty skin.

Scientists call the algae NOSTOC but others know it as "witches' butter," "star jelly" or "spittle of the stars." They are really cells in chains which break apart, each segment forming a new chain. The chains are held together by a gelatinous substance forming a spherical colony protected inside the sac. Mare's Eggs are generally brown in color with lighter tones or even a blue-green tint. Where they are in sunlight they show signs of fading.

The pool that has produced these rare algae covers about an acre of spring fed water. It is extremely clear and cold with little variation in temperature winter and summer. The bottom of the pool is pumice. While it looks deceptively shallow it does, in fact, drop off quickly to about eight feet where the underground spring flows in.

It is said that the Chinese once relished Mare's Eggs in soup.

Pages From the Past, Drew; Sign at the site.

Rooster Crow Champion – 1978

IT WAS A GALA DAY. "White Lightning" had broken Butte Baurn's 25 year record. White Lightning may not have been a thoroughbred, but he was the winner of the 1978 Rooster Crow contest in Rogue River, Oregon. In thirty minutes he had crowed 112 times. He just barely broke the record of 109, set in 1953.

For years the town had held the rooster crow contest. Hundreds turned out in 1978 to see the 114 entrants. Of these, 45 never even got started. The average number of crows was 14. Second place came in way behind White Lightning at 63 crows.

Owner Willie Beck had brought White Lightning to the Saturday festival in a large sack. It wasn't just accident the rooster won the contest, it was wise strategy. Beck had kept the rooster isolated from the hens and other roosters for six weeks. When it was time for the contest White Lightning saw all these roosters and got excited. When the others started to crow he just let loose and kept going and going. Midway through the contest the press became aware that something special was happening. They crowded around the rooster's cage counting and snapping pictures. When the 30 minutes was up Willie Beck pulled his rooster out of his cage to the wild cheers of the crowd.

Medford Mail Tribune, June 25, 1978

Chapter 21

Parks and Forests

Petroglyph Point

Petroglyph Point is in the Modoc Lava Beds National Monument. The rock rim, in places 100 feet high, was once an ancient volcano. Now when the waters of Tule Lake are high they lap against the wall. Drawings are carved into the rock wall as though from a canoe. The stone is a semi-soft volcanic tuff, easy to make an impression on. In dry years when the lake recedes, other drawings appear along the shore of the lake. It is probably the lake itself which has helped to preserve the petroglyphs from the wind and rain. These are some of the most interesting in North America and cover a quarter mile along the shoreline.

It is not known why the ancient Indians drew these pictures. It may just be graffiti, doodling or a kind of self expression. Perhaps someone was relaying a message or offering a prayer. Some of the drawings suggest a scoreboard.

Petroglyphs are drawings cut into rock. There are also pictographs here which are painted on the surface of the rocks. Some of the pictures or symbols have been seen in other sacred Indian sites, suggesting they have a special meaning.

Ancient Times of the Klamath Country, Drew

Mt. McLoughlin – Cascade Mountains

Names of places have a way of changing. Mt. McLoughlin is no exception.

One of the early trappers for the Hudson Bay Company first gave us the name "Mt. McLoughlin" in honor of Dr. John McLoughlin, chief factor of the Hudson Bay Company from 1824 to 1846. He was the most powerful man in Oregon during that time. Later the name was changed to "Mt. Jackson" in honor of President Jackson. "Snowy Butte" or just "Big Butte" was the name referred to locally. Some people still use the name Mount Pitt. In 1905, the legislature restored the name Mt. McLoughlin.

John Darby and Mearl Minear at Oregon Caves, c. 1923
SOURCE: Ruth Minear Alborn

The Cascade mountains also went through name changes. The range was called "Sierra Madres de San Antonio" by the Spanish explorer Manuel Qumpu, in 1790. "Snowy Range" was the name given it by explorer George Vancouver in 1792. Next it became the "Range of Rugged Mountains." "Cascade Mountains" was first applied by David Douglas in 1823 but that gave way to the name "President's Range" in 1830. Finally the Charles Wilkes expedition charted it as the "Cascade Range" and it has been that ever since.

Prehistory and History of the Rogue River Forest; Oregon Geographic Names, McArthur

Crater Lake Discovered – 1853

THOUGH REPORTS DIFFER, John Wesley Hilman is credited with discovering Crater Lake on June 12, 1853. He and a party of prospectors named the lake "Deep Blue Lake."

Twelve years later, the road from Jacksonville to Fort Klamath was built and F.B. Sprague blazed a trail to the lake. He referred to it as "Hole in the Ground." The same year a party of 11 men on a hunting trip found a gentler slope and went down to the lake. Two of them inscribed their names on a rock, James Fay and Herman Helms. In reporting it the Oregon *Sentinel* refers to the lake as "Great Sunken Lake" and "Lake Majesty."

In 1873 six men from Fort Klamath visited the lake and named it "Lake Mystery." In 1883 the name Crater Lake had been settled on. It was at this time that the first U.S. Geographical Survey was made. J.S. Diller advanced the "collapse of the mountain" theory. He reasoned that as the molten lava drained away through subterranean passages, it weakened the support of the peak and occasioned its collapse.

The Smith Brothers' Chronological History of Crater Lake National Park

Oregon Caves Discovery – 1874

MOST CAVES ARE FOUND accidentally and such was the case with Oregon Caves near Cave Junction. The stories vary, but this is one version.

In November 1874, Elijah Davidson wounded a bear and, with his dog, was following him when the bear disappeared into a hole. Davidson went in after the bear and killed him. He was more interested in the bear than in the cave and didn't realize what an extensive cavern he had discovered. It wasn't until three years later that a man named Frank Nickerson, of Kerby, set about an extensive exploration of the three miles of rooms and passageways that make up the caves.

An article in the Grants Pass *Courier* of September 2, 1928 remarks on the growing tourist attraction to the Oregon Caves. The day before the article ran, 303 people had attended with a season total expected to be nearly 20,000. In 1992 it was over 75,000.

Oregon Oddities, WPA; Grants Pass *Daily Courier*, September 2, 1928; Oregon Caves Brochure

Oregon Caves – 1909

JOAQUIN MILLER, "the Poet of the Sierras" was a celebrity when he visited Oregon Caves in August of 1907. With him were two men who were amateurs interested in geology and conservation. The three men were stunned by the damage done by visitors since the cave's discovery in 1874. Countless rock formations had been broken off as souvenirs and initials scratched on the surfaces.

Miller and his friends, along with local residents, began their campaign to save the Oregon Caves for the future. In July 1909, President William Howard Taft proclaimed the caves, and 480 acres surrounding them, a national monument. The Forest Service was to administer the monument "for the enjoyment of the American peoples for all times."

For years there was only one guide at the caves, Dick Rowley. Few came and during the periods when he was not busy, Rowley built crude camp facilities. He began the construction of the walkways that limited the tracks of the public inside the caves. It wasn't until the highway to the caves was opened in 1922 that visitors began to flock there. Openings had been blasted to widen the paths but the caves are so extensive that only a part is open to the public.

Discovery and Exploration of Oregon Caves, Walsh and Halliday; *The Underworld of Oregon Caves National Monument*, Contor

Crater Lake National Park – 1902

WILLIAM STEEL WORKED for 17 years to make Crater Lake a National Park. Finally, on May 22, 1902, President Theodore Roosevelt approved the bill. While we owe much to William Steel for his efforts, it was not preservation of a natural wonder that he had worked for. He wrote in August, 1925:

"...it is only a matter of time when a road will be built inside the rim.... A tunnel should then be bored from the water to the rim road on a grade of five or six percent and the debris used to fill in along the shore line, for parking, turning, boat houses or other conveniences.

"The crowning glory of the park will consist of an automobile road to the top of Mount Scott, 9000 feet high....Walls will encircle the summit, where 200 cars or more can park with perfect safety and the occupants enjoy the entrancing thrills of mountain climbers without their hardships and dangers.

"...Then will come a road inside the rim, near the water, crossing to Wizard island and up to its crater and encircling it.... (the visitor will) depart in peace,... singing the praises of this wonderful lake and its environs."

Thankfully, William Steel's vision never gained wide acceptance. The Portland *Oregonian* was one of his backers and quoted him as saying,

"Crater Lake belongs to the people. If they want to deface the wall, they can do it. What good is scenery if it can't be enjoyed?"

The Smith Brothers' Chronological History of Crater Lake

Old Man of the Lake – 1903

IN 1928 PAUL HERRON, a guide at Crater Lake, sighted "The Old Man of the Lake." The name had been given to a large mountain hemlock log that fell into the lake. What makes it unusual is that it floats in a vertical position with just a few feet of the top sticking out of the water.

It has been explained that the hemlock had been growing with its roots entangled in rocks. When the tree fell into the lake, large rocks were still trapped in the roots, causing that end of the log to sink down into the water.

In 1938 the movement of the "Old Man of the Lake" was charted for three months. It traveled a total of 67 miles, as much as three miles in one day.

The first record of a floating, upright log in Crater Lake was in 1896, reported by a man named Dillar. Again in 1903, William Stell and Fred Kiser saw a similar log and named it "Ilao." Mountain hemlock is a long lasting wood. The cold waters of the lake would add further to preserving wood. Is it possible that this tree that floats around today can be the same one that has been floating since 1896?

Smith Brothers Chronological History of Crater Lake

Forest Service Poster – 1905

IN 1905 THE MANAGEMENT of the forest reserves was transferred from the Department of the Interior to the Department of Agriculture. Gifford Pinchot was the first chief. He was determined to change the image of foresters. New applicants must take written and field examinations. Both tests were considered "challenging."

To recruit these applicants for the new Forest Service, Pinchot authorized posters to be put everywhere possible.

MEN WANTED!

A RANGER MUST BE ABLE TO TAKE CARE OF HIMSELF AND HIS HORSES UNDER VERY TRYING CONDITIONS; BUILD TRAILS AND CABINS; RIDE ALL DAY AND ALL NIGHT; PACK, SHOOT, AND FIGHT FIRE WITHOUT LOOSING HIS HEAD . . . .

ALL THIS REQUIRES A VERY VIGOROUS CONSTITUTION. IT MEANS THE HARDEST KIND OF PHYSICAL WORK FROM BEGINNING TO END. IT IS NOT A JOB FOR THOSE SEEKING HEALTH OR LIGHT OUTDOOR WORK . . . .

INVALIDS NEED NOT APPLY!

SOURCE: U.S. Forest Service

Prehistory and History of the Rogue River Forest; Oregon Geographic Names, McArthur

Lassen Park Forest Preserve – 1905

CREATED IN 1905, LASSEN PARK is in Lassen County and Shasta County. The park was named for Peter Lassen. He was a native of Denmark who came to the United States when he was 29. In 1839 he joined an overland party to Oregon and then went down the coast by boat to Fort Ross. He was one of the first white settlers in the upper Sacramento Valley. In 1848 he brought a party of emigrants from Missouri to California over a new trail that branched off the Applegate Trail and later bore his name. By 1855 he settled in Lassen County and was very important in its development. That same year he found gold in Honey Valley which attracted men to the area, but it was not as rich as other finds and few stayed to develop the country.

Peter Lassen was killed by Indians in April 1859. He was 66 years old and had lived in the west for 20 years.

Shasta County Centennial Edition; Historic Spots in California, Rensch & Hoover

Disappearance of B.B. Bakowski – 1910

B.B. BAKOWSKI WAS a young photographer looking for wintertime pictures when he disappeared. The first alarm was reported in the Medford *Tribune* on February 22, 1910, headlined, "Photographer Lost in Snows of Crater Lake." Bakowski had gone out three weeks before to secure winter pictures of the lake in the snow. When no word was heard from him, a small party went from Klamath Falls to search. They returned to say they had found his sled and shovel a mile and a half from the rim, but nothing else.

Two searchers from Medford returned, having found the photographer's camera and supplies at an abandoned campsite, but no trace of the man. Several trees had been chopped down. In the snow they found a canvas stretched over the opening of a tunnel. The tunnel extended back into the snow about 10 feet. Inside were supplies, provisions and clothing. Also found were 60 unexposed films and three cases of exposed film. No cooking utensils were found.

All sorts of theories were put forth but further search was suspended. It was supposed that with spring, after the snow was melted, the mystery would be solved. It wasn't. No further trace of the young photographer was ever found.

Southern Oregon Historical Society
Sentinel, October 1985

Hallie Daggett, Lookout – 1913

THE ELEVATION AT Eddy's Gulch lookout on Klamath Peak is 6,444 feet. Being lookout was a lonesome job. In June 1913, Hallie Daggett became the first United States Forest Service woman lookout. She and her sister hiked three hours to the station bringing up her supplies on pack mules. The station was new and Hallie's new home was a log cabin 12 feet by 14 feet. She was determined to prove she could do the job as well as any man.

The only instruments needed by a fire watcher in 1913, were a pair of binoculars and a small map of the Klamath National Forest. At first it was hard for Hallie to judge the location of a fire and she was supposed to be on watch 24 hours.

Even being so isolated, most days some hiker would drop by. Many brought water

Crow's-nest lookout, Peavine
Mountain, Galice, Oregon
SOURCE: Larry McLane

which was a problem after the winter snows had melted. Hallie loved the woods and the animals and learned them well. Her telephone was her connection with the other lookouts and the outside world. Her sister continued to come up the mountain once a week bringing the mail and provisions. As the news of a woman lookout spread, much of her mail consisted of fan letters.

Gradually learning , Hallie held the position for 15 years and became the most respected lookout in the district. Her success opened the field to other women and before long, half the lookouts were women.

Siskiyou *Pioneer*, 1961

Forest Service dot and dash blaze
SOURCE: Rogue River National Forest, Historic Photographs Collection

Shorty and the Blazed Trails

THE U.S. FOREST SERVICE took a frisky colt off the range and began training him to pack supplies. They named him Shorty. Even during his first season in service he could follow a blazed trail without guidance. His only training was in being taken out along these trails with one man leading him through the woods. His only reward was to be relieved of his burden at the end of the trail and being given a bag of oats.

As he grew older, it was noticed that Shorty constantly glanced from side to side looking for blazes on the trees. If he could not find a blaze he would stop and look around until he located the next spot no matter how distant or how faint.

Some people maintained that Shorty could distinguish between the distinctive double-notched Forest Service blaze and ordinary blazes. Skeptics doubted this claim but no one doubted that he was a marvel at following a blazed trail.

U.S. Forest Service Radio Script, August 7, 1936

Lassen Peak Eruption – 1914

THERE WAS NO RICHTER SCALE to measure the Mt. Lassen eruption of May 30, 1914. It was strong enough to cause serious concern. A column of steam and ash rose high in the sky. Eighteen more minor eruptions occurred before July 16th when a major explosion took place. Again, in January 1915, violent rumblings and tremors were felt for a radius of 25 miles.

In February an earthquake lasting two minutes took place some 20 miles north of Lassen Peak. New springs burst forth and large rocks disappeared down cracks. In one place it was reported an acre of ground fell 60 feet.

In May the greatest damage of all took place as a result of mud slides. While it was called mud, the dirt was a combination of ash and mud spewing from the crater. It swept down Hat Creek Valley, in places two miles wide. As the mud cooled, it turned into concrete like chunks. Great clouds of smoke hid the peak of Mt. Lassen but no ash fell.

The last mention of trouble was in the newspaper of June 17, 1915 when the 101st eruption was reported. A pillar of ash and smoke rose 100 feet.

Medford *Mail Tribune* (Excerpts, Vol 2, 110 and 165)

Homing Pigeons – 1919

FOREST RANGER STATIONS were very remote. The men were always on the lookout for fires. Rangers were sent out to inspect any smoke rising in unexpected places. Often they found things beyond their control and additional help was needed. Rather than send a man back to bring help, the rangers used pigeons.

By May 1919, every ranger station in the Cascade National Forest was given six pairs of homing pigeons. These were to be trained to carry messages from the men fighting the fire, back to their ranger station. The "fire chaser" took the pigeons with him in cages. After assessing their needs, they would write, telling just how many men and how much equipment was needed. They would then attach the message to the pigeon's leg and liberate it from its cage.

Medford *Mail Tribune,* May 14, 1919

Signal Pits

IN LOOKING FOR SITES for fire lookouts, the Forest Service went into remote regions and climbed many hills and mountains. In the mid 1930s they noticed that the sites they picked often showed evidence that the Indians had used the same location.

Throughout southwestern Oregon Indian signal pits were discovered. While the Forest Service chose the top of a mountain for its lookout, the Indians chose the saddle of a high ridge. The site would have a good view for 15 to 20 miles in either direction. Here a pit was dug about five feet long, two and a half feet wide and a foot deep. The pit was lined with rock to preserve its shape. A hot bed of coals was maintained in the pit. To create the smoke for a signal, green brush and leaves were added. An elk hide held tightly over the pit and quickly removed, produced a series of distinct smoke puffs in a sort of dot and dash code.

Were these Indians sites manned at all times? What kinds of messages were sent? These are question we can't answer.

U.S. Forest Service Radio Script, June 26, 1936

Crater Lake Fish – 1910

FIFTY THOUSAND RAINBOW TROUT were the first fish liberated in Crater Lake the summer of 1910. They thrived in the cold water. Silver salmon, steelhead, kokanee, eastern brook and brown trout were added over the next 31 years. Only the kokanee and rainbows survived in large quantities. The practice was discontinued after stocking rainbow trout in 1941.

Not many people took the long, twisting trail that went down in front of the present lodge. Those who took a rowboat out could count on catching their limit of 12 large trout in just a few hours. The largest on record was a 32 pound rainbow caught below Watchman in the summer of 1932. It was mounted and hung in Sinnot for many years.

Now it is thought that fish may be adding pollution to Crater Lake and there is an effort to rid the lake of all the remaining fish.

Smith Brothers Chronological History of Crater Lake

Lemurians – 1931

LEMURIANS WERE SAID TO BE the survivors of a world lost beneath the Pacific Ocean for thousands of years. They were up to seven feet tall with strong upper bodies. In the center of their forehead was a protrusion with which they could communicate with other Lemurians in telepathic ways. Lights flashing on Mount Shasta were said to be these people carrying on secret ceremonies.

Dr. Spencer Lewis, writing under the name W.S. Curve, wrote a book titled *Lemuria the Lost Continent of the Pacific.* It was published in 1931 and persuaded many to believe the fantasy.

While many believed and searched, no one ever found a Lemurian or proof of their existence.

Siskiyou Pioneer, 1964

CCC Snow – 1932

THE OLD EAST ENTRANCE to Crater Lake Park has long been closed. It used to run from route 97, the Bend/Klamath Falls road, up past the Pinnacles to the rim road. There was a CCC camp midway between the Rim road and Route 97.

The park service had a small ranger station along the road. In the winter of 1932, Mabel and Clarence Hedgpeth, with ranger Rudy Lump, were hired to live for the winter at these buildings. They were to keep the snow shoveled off the roofs of the CCC camp buildings, which had not been built to withstand heavy loads.

In October the couple brought in $250 worth of food. That was as much as their pickup would hold. It would have to last them the winter. As soon as snow fell, they skied the eight miles in from Route 97, to their waiting cabin. Neither had been on skis before, but by the time spring came, they were experts.

All winter, the two men shoveled snow from the roofs of the CCC buildings. Weekends Lump would ski over to the small town of Kirk, to see his girl friend

Sightseeing in the Redwoods
SOURCE: Curry County Historical Society

but the Hedgpeths stayed at the cabin and never tired of the wild beauty of winter in Crater Lake Park.

Interview with Mabel Hedgpeth

Casual Law

HANDLING THE LAW was a good deal more casual in the thirties and forties.

The Mule Creek Forest Service Station was in the Upper Rogue River Valley. Mid summer it was dry as a bone. In fact, it hadn't rained in three months when one of the forest service men came across a young man walking along on a hot sunny day, smoking a cigarette in a very hazardous area. Being an eager young recruit, the ranger promptly arrested the young man. There was no such procedure as reading him his rights. Instead the two marched to the nearest telephone.

The Justice of the Peace in Agnes was Chauncey Fry. When he heard the story over the phone, he asked to speak with the young man. Fry ask him how he pleaded, guilty or not guilty? The fellow said, "Guilty." For this he was fined $5.

It turned out the young man had no money, so he was let go without payment. Not only that, it was later learned that Chauncy Fry's term as Justice of the Peace had expired five years before the incident.

George Morey, Gold Beach

Pack String – 1955

DID YOU KNOW THAT as late as 1955 the Forest Service was still using pack animals? Long after mule trains stopped supplying the gold fields, mules and burros were used to transport supplies to remote lookouts in the forest. The supply point might keep six or eight animals. Mules had a reputation for being sure footed but burros seemed to relate to humans, were easier to handle and less likely to stray if let loose to graze. Rarely were burros and mules used together as they did not like each other.

When a lookout was to be built, all the supplies had to be taken in by pack animals. This included lumber up to 20 feet in length. Many are the stories of taking a mule carrying long boards, around a hair pin turn in the trail. If caught off balance, a mule could lose his footing and roll down a bank. Even if it was not hurt, the animal had to be unloaded, brought up to the trail and the load it was carrying hiked up one piece at a time and repacked.

During World War II, an air warning station was built on Bald Knob in the Siskiyou Forest. All the materials for a two room cabin, including a brick fireplace, were brought in by pack train.

Packers became very attached to their mules and burros. It was a sad day in 1955 when the animals were retired, to be replaced by trail scooters and other mechanical equipment.

George Morey, Gold Beach

‑‑‑

Chapter 22

DISASTERS

Tsunami

THERE HAVE BEEN many tidal waves along our coast but one is part of Native American history.

Somewhere between 500 and 1,000 years ago, legend says a tidal wave occurred that was the greatest ever known. It happened on a calm day, when the ocean was smooth. The water suddenly receded from the shore in a smooth mass, leaving the ocean bottom exposed beyond Mile Rock off the Northern California coast. Fish were left flapping about on the exposed sea bottom. A sand bar outside the mouth of the Klamath River lay uncovered. It ran parallel to the shoreline. Seeing this, the Indians immediately went up into the hills.

Suddenly the ocean moved back in a mass. It totally covered Black Rock, struck the long sand bar at the mouth of the river, dislodging a large pile of logs. The wave moved up the river as far as the Indians could see.

As proof of this tidal wave, old timers remember that there were huge redwood logs and stumps with roots deposited in Elk Valley Slough. These could only have gotten there by some such wave.

The Tolowa Indians also recalled a wave that must have been this same tidal wave. It struck the Crescent City area and went across Elk Valley, destroying an Indian village at the base of what is now Howland Hill. Everyone was killed except two women who had been in the hills gathering hazel sticks when the wave struck.

More recently, in May 1960, a tsunami started off the coast of Chile and traveled north. It was trapped in the bay at Crescent City causing several deaths, destruction and flooding.

Del Norte Historical Society

Crescent City after the tsunami
SOURCE: Del Norte County Historical Society

Port Orford Meteorite – 1861

WHEN DR. JOHN EVANS died in 1861, with him died the information leading to the site of the Port Orford meteorite.

Evans was an explorer and geologist. He found a meteorite while journeying through unexplored country near the Rogue River. He traveled alone and seemed to make friends with all the Indians he met. Wherever he went he gathered samples of rocks. It wasn't until these were examined at a later date, that it was discovered that one specimen was a rare type of meteorite.

Details from Dr. Evans' log book about the sample, plus his own recollections, described the meteorite as being on the western slope of Bald Mountain, in a grassy open area. Unfortunately, names of mountains change but Evans said Bald Mountain was a prominent landmark visible from ships at sea. It was about 40 miles from Port Orford in a wild setting. It sounded easy to find as the rock was reported to show about five feet above ground. Dr. Evans planned to return, but died suddenly before doing so.

The value of the Port Orford Meteorite has been exaggerated over the years. From a scientific viewpoint it is beyond value. It may also be of great financial value, and hunters for the lost rock have been numerous. But it has never been found.

Treasures of the Oregon Country, Dawson

Earthquake, Del Norte – 1873

THE INHABITANTS OF Del Norte County had undergone real struggles and hardships in order to settle the area. Now they added the fear of a more serious earthquake to their list of worries.

On November 22, 1873, an earthquake shook the area. Minor quakes had been
felt before, but this was by far the strongest. The shock lasted about 25 seconds. It
seemed from the noise that the quake came from the north. In Happy Camp it
was said the tin pails hanging in the stores swung back and forth for 10 minutes.
The ground shook strongly enough to ring the bell in City Hall and the one in
the fire department at Crescent City. Houses, some of which were not too well
constructed, jumped around. People rushed into the streets and fear of a tidal
wave panicked many. Dogs howled and frightened horses ran wildly in the fields.

When all was over, the damage seemed surprisingly small. About half the chimneys in town were cracked. More severe damage seemed to have occurred in the
Smith River Valley where cracks six to eight inches wide appeared in the ground.

It was reported that a loud noise was heard off the sea west of Cape Blanco.
There was an upheaval in the water accompanied by boiling and hissing noises,
but no tidal wave developed.

History of Del Norte, Bledsoe; Curry County *Echoes*, November 1989

Hard Winter 1889–1890

ON THE DAY BEFORE Christmas in 1889, snow started to fall west of the Cascades.
This was the beginning of the Hard Winter. In Glendale, Oregon the storm continued with little letup for 52 days leaving the area with seven and a half feet of
snow. Not only did cattle die but so did the deer and elk that settlers counted on
for meat. When the snow finally melted in the spring, it melted so fast it caused
flooding and disastrous land slides. One landslide covered the railroad track
and trains couldn't get through. Mail for Glendale was shipped down the coast
and put on the train at Redding. It would come as far as Grants Pass where it
had to be transferred to stage coaches headed for Glendale.

In California, during the hard winter, the "D" ranch lost between 6,000 and 8,000
head of cattle from starvation. The spot later was called the "Bone Yard." The remaining 1,500 cattle were only saved by driving them through five feet of snow to a
gulch where trees were cut down so the cattle could browse on the branches.

A Klamath County account tells of taking 300 head of cattle to winter on the
Sprague River near Bly. Only 75 survived. The snow had started here in October
and never melted. It was still deep in the middle of March. Some people claimed
it snowed 40 days and 40 nights.

It was said that the keyhole in the front door had to be plugged or the snow
would blow through it during the night. In the morning it would have drifted
right across the room.

Klamath Echoes, 1968 and 1977; Klamath *Evening Herald*, October 22, 1913;
Pioneer Days in the South Umpqua Valley, August 1972

Indian Jacob's Death

MOST INDIANS BELIEVED in the supernatural. Old Jacob was no exception. He was an Indian who lived on the Pit River in California.

Old Jacob told his wife that he had had a dream and was going to die. This was during the Hard Winter and a foot of snow was still on the ground. Winds were blowing fiercely but Jacob took his small dog with him to go hunting.

Jacob stopped at the cabin of a white settler and repeated his story of the dream and the prediction of his death. They considered it just Indian superstition.

Some time later the dog came home alone. The next day searchers went out looking for Jacob but with no luck.

That night Jacob's wife dreamed of finding Jacob. When the searchers came...she led them to the spot. Two miles from their house was a hill with just two trees on it about 10 inches in diameter. The wind had blown them down. Sure enough...Jacob was found buried in snow under a tree trunk with his gun by his side.

Listener Joe Mazzini

Hard Winter

DURING THE HARD WINTER, large haystacks were buried out of sight under huge snowdrifts. The snow was packed so hard that one could easily drive a team and wagon over fences. It was easy to lose a sense of direction and people said they remembered the thermometer congealing in the bulb at −40°. It stayed there for weeks.

Addie Walker said,

"Imagine, ladies having to wear woolen "undies" with sleeves to the wrists and pants to the ankles, under cashmere hose, underskirts crocheted from heavy Germantown yarn, a heavy woolen dress, heavy sweater and heavy overshoes over house slippers. I wore all this load of clothing going about my work for weeks and it was very uncomfortable."

Even cooking took longer. All through the freezing weather it took an hour to thaw steaks, milk and sourdough before cooking. When the morning work was done, the women would stand by the fireplace, turning from front to back, trying to keep warm.

Klamath *Echoes*, #12

Hard Winter, Northern California

DECEMBER 10, 1889 marked the date the snow began around Yreka. The snow stayed on the ground until late February with temperatures as low as −30°. Horses kept some trails open. When it was too deep elsewhere, the deer would use the

Clearing the tracks, Siskiyou Mountains
SOURCE: Paul and Leah Reichman Collection

trails. As the snow became deeper and deeper the trails took on the appearance of tunnels with high walls. The deer were getting weaker from lack of food and couldn't jump out of these tunnels. It was said that some people would trap a deer and club it to death so that they could feed the deer meat to their hogs.

The Stone family lost 28 horses. In the spring the bones were found in two different spots. The horses had milled around tramping down the snow. By marks on the trees it was estimated that the snow reached 18 feet deep. This walled in the horses in the trampled down area where they finally all died of starvation.

Siskiyou *Pioneer,* 1963

Stalled Train, Ashland

THIS IS ANOTHER STORY of the terrible winter of 1889 to 1890.

On January 23, the southbound train from Portland stopped in Ashland and had to remain in the station. No one could get over the mountains. There were 150 people aboard. Southern Pacific offered to return the passengers to Portland and refund their money, but only 50 took them up on the offer. That left some 100 to be taken care of aboard the train. First class passengers were charged 50¢ a meal but second class passengers were fed by the railroad company free of charge.

While the train remained in the station, in the town roofs were collapsing and everything was at a standstill. As the days lengthened into a full week, every passenger had a tale of woe. One couple with a five year old daughter were on their way east to find medical attention for the little girl. While in the station she died and was buried in Ashland. Another man was headed for San Francisco for an eye operation and felt sure he would not get there in time to save his sight. A woman was headed south to find out what was wrong with her husband, who had been hospitalized in San Francisco. Two daughters were trying to reach their dying mother, but she passed away while the train was still snowbound. A partially paralyzed man had to be cared for. Several passengers were on their way to be married.

This was a storm people would talk about for years to come.

Ashland *Tidings*, January 24, 1890

End of the Hard Winter

TEETER'S LANDING WAS on the Klamath River five miles up river from Keno. Here goods and passengers could be moved by boats and barges when the Keno road was under water. Francis Teeter recalled:

"During the hard winter we all went broke; we lost all our stock except one horse. We didn't see the ground from the third of November until the 18th of April except for a few bare patches. Like everyone else around, we were nearly starved out. We got along on wheat and frozen potatoes.... Before our last cow died, Father put a saddle on her and led her 24 miles through deep snow to Linktown (Klamath Falls) to get food at Smith's Grocery. He strapped the food on the cow's back and walked all the way home. It took him three days. He said when he got home, 'I thought I would find you all starved to death.'"

Klamath *Echoes*, #15

Etna Fire – 1896

THE TOWN OF Rough and Ready, California began with the building of a saw mill in 1853. It was followed by a flour mill and a few homes. Because the name was confused with the town of Rough and Ready in Nevada County, the name was changed to Etna in 1874. It grew as a supply point to the Northern California mines. At one time there were 150 mules bringing supplies to the town.

The call of "Fire" roused the town of Etna on March 16, 1896. The fire started in a hotel where the residents scrambled into clothes and rushed out into the streets. There were few brick buildings and it was soon seen that a large block of stores was beyond saving. The bucket brigades, largely made up of women, concentrated on keeping the fire from jumping the street and taking all the rest of the town. Mrs. Lathrop was in labor when the fire commenced. Since she couldn't fight the fire, all the young children were brought to her house to stay while the rest of the family went to help. Fortunately Mrs. Lathrop was married to the town's doctor. She gathered his instruments and sheets together in preparation for the delivery of her baby and he arrived back just in time for the birth of his son.

A few years after the fire, gold was discovered in the Klondike and miners rushed away to make their fortunes there. Even many of the mules were shipped to the new mine fields. Etna and the other mining towns were left with empty buildings.

Siskiyou *Pioneer*, #5, 1961

Butcher Hill – 1906

CHILDREN WITH FIREARMS is not just a problem today. Back on August 19, 1906 a ten year old named Albert Holland went into C.C. Cady's store in Yreka and rented two twenty-two caliber rifles. With his two buddies, one 15 and the other 13, Holland went up Butcher Hill east of Yreka. On the hill were three powder houses, 12 feet by 14 feet, built of sandstone blocks. The houses contained dynamite that was used in gold mining operations. The one nearest town held 25 pounds of powder.

Five minutes before ten in the morning a tremendous double explosion was heard. A dense cloud of smoke rose and stones began dropping over a wide area. James Fairchild told:

> "Small particles dropped all around us at first, then I saw a big stone making a beeline for me. I watched until it was close and stepped aside. it was a piece of concrete the size of a sugar bowl."

The explosion tore up 150 feet of railroad track. Fourteen windows were broken at the high school. Ten year old Albert lived for several days but couldn't tell what had happened. His two friends were never found.

Siskiyou *Pioneer*, 1993

Lassen Peak – 1914

WHEN LASSEN PEAK ERUPTED on May 30, 1914, it attracted sightseers and scientists alike. R.E. Phelps was one of a group who climbed the north side of the mountain after things had quieted down. Or they thought things had quieted

All that is left after the Bandon fire, 1936
SOURCE: Coquille River Museum, Bandon Historical Society

down. When they reached the rim of the old crater, a huge column of smoke shot upwards with a roar and accompanying wind. The air was filled with smoke, ash, and flying rocks. Phelps hid under an overhanging rock. Another man with him ran down the mountain as fast as he could. Coming to a snowdrift, he slid down to the bottom where he found a bush and buried himself in snow. Both men survived even though reports said the smoke was so thick it turned day to darkest night.

One peculiarity was that all the rocks and ashes thrown out by the volcano were cold or only slightly warm. Had they been hot, both men would have burned to death. Even on the inside of the old rim, rocks were seen resting on packed snow without melting it.

Eruptions of Lassen Peak, Loomis

Mud Flood – 1915

MT. LASSEN HAD ERUPTED and it is thought that the lava flow melted great quantities of snow and caused the mud flow of May 19, 1915. Hot gases and rain from condensing steam melted more. The snow pack was exceptionally thick and layered with ash from previous eruptions. Suddenly, down the mountain came a gush of mud.

Red Cross shelter tents after the Bandon fire
SOURCE: Coquille River Museum, Bandon Historical Society

One homesteader was living in a tent near the creek. It was the middle of the night when his dog woke him up. He looked out and saw a wave about twelve feet high headed his way. The boom of tumbling logs and rolling rocks soon became deafening. The wave moved more slowly than a wave of water would have, enabling people to be warned in advance and get to higher ground. When daylight came, the mud was still flowing, looking more like mortar than water. Many homes and barns were destroyed but most animals were able to outrun the flood.

The Forest Service estimated a loss of up to 5 million feet of timber just from the mud flow and hot steam.

Eruptions of Lassen Peak, Loomis

Bandon Fire – 1936

ON THE NIGHT OF SEPTEMBER 26, 1936 fire destroyed the town of Bandon, Oregon. The fire started several miles east of the town. Large crews of CCC fire fighters were sent to combat the flames. It struck near midnight and burned with such intensity that the town was a mass of ruins before morning.

When it became apparent that all attempts to stop the fire were useless, fire fighters turned their efforts toward the evacuation of Bandon. Nine people, all elderly, lost their lives. Some of them apparently became confused or would not leave. Others failed to realize the seriousness of the situation and remained in their homes. Loss of life would have been far greater had not the CCC enrollees and other workers forcibly removed some of the residents from their homes.

The rebuilt town of Bandon today is a tribute to the efforts of its citizens.

CCC Boys Remember, Howell

Columbus Day Storm – 1962

STORM STRUCK THE west coast on Columbus Day, 1962.

Bad weather was expected but no one forecast the disaster that hit. Starting in Northern California, the path of the storm followed just off the coast as far north as British Columbia. Winds shrieked and rain slanted across the land. Waves reached six feet on Lake Shasta. The Squaw Creek area got 12 inches of rain in 24 hours. In Oregon alone, 84 homes were destroyed and over 50,000 damaged. Electricity was off for days. Oregon was declared a disaster area.

Even such a storm had its comic side. Everyone had a story. One family had a yellow plastic patio cover that was blown away in the storm. But, a few gusts later someone else's patio cover blew into their yard. It was green, and the exact size.

So what was this Columbus Day storm? Meteorologists were puzzled and finally called it an "extra tropical cyclone."

West Coast Disasters, Franklin

End of the World – 1892

PROPHETS OF DOOM will probably always be with us.

The second edition of the Talent, Oregon *News* announced the end of the world.

"A very learned minister of the gospel is preaching to the people of Jackson County that the world will surely come to an end on the 29th of March next, at half past eleven p.m. sharp. No mistake in the figures this time as all previous calculations have been carefully revised and corrected.

"We assure our readers, however, that even an event of such magnitude will not interfere in the least with the regular publication of the Talent News."

Obviously the editor was enjoying himself. The follow-up story came out in the April first edition.

"...we awaited the hour... expecting the world would come to an end according to the Morganic prophecy; but the dreaded hour came and went. The sun rose as usual in the morning, the birds warbled their songs of joy, all nature smiled and affairs in general drift along in regular order."

Talent *News,* Vol 1, #2

༝

CHAPTER 23

GROWING UP IN A SMALL TOWN

Ashland Schools – 1854

THE FIRST SCHOOL IN Ashland was also the first school in all of Southern Oregon. Lizzie Anderson taught it in the home of A.J. Emery. It was 1854 and Ashland didn't have the required 13 students necessary to form a school district. This they were able to do three years later by including the name of three year old John Helman.

The first public school house was built in 1860. It was a frame building 18 feet by 24 feet built on a stone foundation. Even with land and much of the labor donated, it cost $600. Anyone could attend the school but they had to have their own books and pay a small fee toward the teacher's salary. Each student worked at his own pace as there were no grades. There were 28 students when the new building opened, the majority between the ages of ten and fourteen years old.

As in most parts of the country, religion was one of the prime motives for a school. The religious attitudes of the teacher and the use of the bible in the classroom was important. In 1870 the Presbyterian General Assembly took the stand that to remove religion from the classroom "would be eminently unwise, unjust, and a moral calamity to the nation."

In 1915 three women teachers in Ashland were required to appear before a special session of the school board to answer charges that they violated board rules that prohibited teachers from attending public dances. Two of the women apologized for having done so and continued to teach. The third teacher stood by her principles and resigned rather than apologize.

Ashland, O'Harra; A.J. Walling; *Religion as an Influence*, Farnham

Ashland Normal School, 1907
SOURCE: Ruth Minear Alborn

Southern Oregon University – 1882

SOUTHERN OREGON UNIVERSITY has come a long way since it was first conceived in 1869. It was at a quarterly conference of the Methodist Episcopal Church, held in June 1869, that funds were allocated for a church school in Ashland, to be called the "Ashland Academy." The money gave out before completion, and the school had to wait until 1872 for refinancing. It was finished, furnished and opened as a private enterprise called "Ashland College." This, too, went bankrupt.

The school revived for a short time in 1878 as "Ashland College and Normal School" but it also failed. It wasn't until August 1882 that the college got another start as a state normal school.

This was not the end of the name changing however. In 1892 the school was known as Ashland Collegiate Institution. In 1895 it was moved to a new site and opened as Southern Oregon State Normal School. Even though the word *state* was used in its title, the state did not help with financing until 1899. Money was withdrawn in 1909 and the college was again closed.

The City of Ashland donated the grounds for a new campus in 1926 and the school reopened. In 1939 it was known as Southern Oregon College of Education, later simply Southern Oregon College. As a result of the rapid growth after World

War II, the institution expanded to become Southern Oregon State College. On April 1, 1997 it was given the title Southern Oregon University.

A.J. Walling; Southern Oregon Historical Society *Sentinel*, November 1984

Cigarettes

LEAH REICHMAN'S FATHER owned a grocery store in Montague, California. She and her friend decided they would go into the store and steal a package of cigarettes and try them out. The girls had the run of the store, so getting the cigarettes was no problem. They went to the outhouse and tried smoking. After one puff, they looked at each other and agreed they didn't like smoking. They threw the whole pack down the hole.

Next the two girls thought they would take a soda fountain straw and fill it with coffee and see how that smoked. This wasn't any better.

With hindsight, Leah decided her father knew what was going on all the time and wisely let the girls find out about smoking for themselves.

Interview with Leah Reichman

Huckleberrying – 1900+

THERE MAY BE many Huckleberry Mountains but the one Frances Pearson went to was near Union Creek, Oregon just south of Crater Lake.

When Frances was a child in the 1890s, the family packed up the wagon and went on an outing that was a combination of play and work. Each summer in August, when the huckleberries were ripe, the Pearsons went to Huckleberry Mountain. Here year after year, they met other families doing the same thing. The wagons could only go as far as "Wagon Camp." Horses were packed to carry the equipment up the mountain. The family pitched camp and went to work.

Every member of the family went out and picked huckleberries all day long. The children were expected to pick about two gallons each. Frances' father could pick five gallons in a day. Back in camp they would bake huckleberry pies in dutch ovens.

The Indians from the Klamath reservation would spread their huckleberries on canvas sheets to dry. Some of the others had brought jars and bottles and would can berries right in camp. Frances and her family took their berries home fresh and bottled them at home. They would use wine and beer bottles that had been well washed. The huckleberries were cooked and put in a bottle with a tight cork. They dipped the top of the bottle in melted wax to seal it.

It was not all work in the huckleberry camps. Evenings were full of music, dancing and just visiting.

Recollection: *People and the Forest*, Vol III

Canning berries, Huckleberry Mountain
SOURCE: Rogue River National Forest, Historic Photograph Collection

Root Beer

IN A ONE-ROOM school house it often happened that one teacher was hired to teach as many as 40 children, grades one through eight. It wasn't possible to keep track of everyone and the older boys often took advantage of their opportunities.

An often used trick was to put .22 bullets in the wood stove. The stove was usually in the middle of the room and the exploding bullets caused plenty of commotion but no damage.

Almost as noisy was the time the boys in Scott Bar Elementary School made root beer. It was bottled and stored in the school attic to age. Since the stove chimney went up through the middle of the attic, it wasn't long before the root beer was aged and bottle tops began blowing off. Root beer came dripping down in the classroom, a surprise to the teacher who was unaware there was anything in the attic.

Siskiyou *Pioneer*, 1989

Bathing

THE SATURDAY NIGHT BATH was a ritual that went on in nearly every household during our pioneer days.

Some wood cook stoves had a fairly large tank attached to the back. This was filled with water and could be warmed while the cooking was going on during the day. When supper was cleaned up and dishes put away, the kitchen became the bath room. Hot water was drawn from the hot water tank and used to half fill a large wash tub. If you weren't lucky enough to have a tank on your stove, the water had to be heated on the stove top.

Usually the youngest child was the first one in the bath tub. When the child was washed, he or she was dried while standing in the heat of the cook stove, then sent off to bed. The next youngest took over. When the water looked too dirty, it was taken outside, dumped and the tub refilled. The mother and father were the last to bathe and the washtub was left sitting in the middle of the kitchen floor to be emptied in the morning.

You know the old saying, "Everyone had to take a bath on Saturday nights whether they needed it or not." It was true in most homes.

George Morey, Gold Beach

Juvenile Depravity – 1866

AN EDITORIAL APPEARED in the Jacksonville *Sentinel* on September 29, 1866.

[Juvenile Depravity] "seems to be on the increase. Frequently we see a crowd of boys in front of our office, of ages ranging from eight to fifteen, who indulge in obscenity and profanity to a degree that does not indicate much exercise of parental authority. They can swear with great volubility and seem to want only a few more years of street education to qualify them for the penitentiary or gallows. Why don't parents send their children to school and keep them there? Do they forget that the lessons of childhood are those that make the most lasting impressions, and that the vicious training received in the streets is hard to eradicate? We frequently hear parents moan that they had no opportunities for education, yet we see their children, surrounded by educational advantages, following in the parental footsteps. Take our advice and patronize the school, it may save many an hour of sorrow."

With a slight change in vocabulary, that could have been written today.

Oregon Sentinel, September 29, 1866

Early Schools – 1892

PARENTS HAD TO WANT an education for their children. Any district could have a school provided they had a building and enough money to pay the teacher $40 a month plus room and board.

In Southern Oregon the first school started in 1853. From then until the end of the century, a "public school" meant a school that anyone could attend provided he or she could pay a small tuition. Once counties were formed and taxes raised, some money might be given to a school but it was never enough to cover the needs. Families had to pay "rate bills" which is just another word for a tuition charge. Curriculum consisted of grammar, spelling, reading and arithmetic.

Griffin Creek schoolhouse
SOURCE: Ruth Minear Alborn

Many pioneers felt that education was not necessary, which was reflected in the fact that only about 40 percent of children attended school in the 1870s and 1880s. The quality of education was usually low. The teacher most likely was an older student, who might not have even finished eighth grade and was hired for only a quarter term. Schools could run three months, six months or nine months. Vacation depended on the harvest season, when all hands were needed on the farm.

Eight years of school was enough for the early settlers. It wasn't until 1892 that the first high school was built in Siskiyou County.

It was a rare teacher who could make learning stimulating. However, it provided many children their only opportunity to be with other children who were not in their own family.

Religion As An Influence, Farnham; Scott Valley Bank calendar

School Punishment

SCHOOL DISCIPLINE WAS as much of a problem in the one room school house as it is today. Emmet Esteb was nine years old and went to the Antioch school north of Medford. His teacher was Miss Hattie Bliss. What Emmet did to warrant her disfavor we don't know, but Hattie whipped him.

It was an accepted practice for a teacher to strike a child's hand with a ruler and boys were often whipped, especially the older ones. Teachers felt they needed to have control and many were not as old as the oldest pupils. Apparently Emmet got a severe whipping and his parents took exception to it, calling it "unprovoked cruelty." The school board heard the case but since there were only nine more days in the school session, they decided to let Miss Bliss finish out the term.

Mr. Esteb was not satisfied, so he went to court. The case was tried before a jury in 1896. Hattie Bliss was charged with assault and battery but she was acquitted.

The reasons for acquittal would shock many people today. The court said Miss Bliss acted within her rights. Teachers should be allowed great discretion in matters of discipline.

Ashland *Tidings* (Excepts Vol 8, June 8, 1896)

Purse Trick

WHEN THE OLD MODEL T Fords hit the market there was very little traffic on the region's rural roads and only a few cars went over the Montague–Grenada Bridge. Young boys thought up all sorts of tricks to play on the passing motorist but the "purse trick" was a favorite. One old timer remembers how they would fill a medium sized lady's purse with gravel. With a string attached, it would be placed in the middle of the road part way up the Montague bridge. The string would be covered up with dirt and the end thrown over the side. The boys would disappear under the bridge, grab the end of the string and wait until they heard the putt, putt of an oncoming Model T. Sure enough, the driver would see the purse and stop the car. Timing was important. As the driver pulled over and put on the hand brakes, the boys jerked the string and the purse went over the side of the bridge.

The fun part was listening to the driver walking around in search of the purse and talking to himself. Eventually the driver would realize he had been tricked and go on. As one old timer remembered it, the boys were never caught and no one ever told on them.

Siskiyou *Pioneer,* 1986

Montague–Grenada Bridge
SOURCE: Paul and Leah Reichman

Interior of Agnes school
SOURCE: Curry County Historical Society

To School by Boat

IN THE EARLY 1930s Jim Harrison lived outside Sumner, Oregon on Catching Inlet. Sumner was at the head of the tide coming into the inlet. A boat would make the rounds of the slough in the morning picking up children and taking them to school. They picked up the milk at the same time. The boat made other trips throughout the day bringing up supplies for the Sumner store and hauling anything anyone wanted moved. In the evening the boat picked up the children and brought them home again.

Harrison wanted to play football so he boarded in town when he could. At one time he was allowed to sleep at the fire house in return for keeping the fire going. He did the same thing at the Armory and worked at a restaurant for his meals.

As roads improved, school buses replaced the boats that had picked up and returned the children living along the sloughs.

Interview with Vurl and Jim Harrison

Spitballs

WHEN LEAH REICHMAN was in elementary school in Montague, California, she was disciplined by a very wise teacher.

One of the boys was throwing spit balls at Leah and, of course, she retaliated by throwing some back. The teacher saw what was going on. When recess time came she told the two to stay in. She brought a big wastepaper basket and said,

"Now I want you to make spitballs and fill this up and I want you to put plenty of spit on them." The two went to work making spitballs as fast as they could.

When recess was about half over the teacher said, "Now I want you to throw those spitballs up the aisle and I want you to pick every one of them back up and put them in the basket."

The two never threw spitballs again.

Interview with Leah Reichman

Rules for Teachers

THE FOLLOWING RULES for Siskiyou County teachers are dated 1872.

Each day the teacher will:

- Fill the lamps and clean the chimneys.
- Bring a bucket of water and scuttle of coal for the day's session.
- Make pens carefully.
- Men teachers may take one evening a week to go courting or two evenings to go to church.
- Women teachers who marry or engage in unseemly conduct will be dismissed.
- Any teacher who smokes, uses liquor, frequents pool or public halls will give good reason to suspect his worth, integrity and honesty.
- The teacher who performs his labor faithfully for five years will be given an increase of 25¢ per week.

Along Our Histories Trail, Hayden

PUBLISHED BY AUTHORITY

STATE OF OREGON

LOCAL OPTION LIQUOR LAW

ENACTED BY THE PEOPLE

UPON

INITIATIVE PETITION

AT THE

GENERAL ELECTION

HELD

JUNE 6, 1904

SALEM, OREGON
J. R. WHITNEY, STATE PRINTER
1905

SOURCE: Kerbyville Museum

CHAPTER 24

PROHIBITION

Sons of Temperance – 1855

WE TEND TO THINK of the prohibition movement as being a women's movement. But the Sons of Temperance was the oldest and most powerful organization of its time.

There is no question the gold rush of 1849 attracted many who were lawless drunks. Saloons were the only gathering place and many lonely men turned to drink whenever they had enough gold to pay for it.

Temperance speeches began right from the start of the Gold Rush. In 1855 I.S. Diebl toured the mining camps and organized eleven new Sons of Temperance groups. The Scotts Bar Division #198 was chartered in 1855 and remained active for 25 years. The men built a log cabin at the lower end of Scotts Bar for their headquarters. This gave men who did not want to go to saloons a place to gather. Ladies were allowed, but only "refined" ladies.

Siskiyou Pioneer, 1978

Prohibition, Oregon – 1914

THE CONTROVERSY OVER prohibition in Oregon came to a vote in the November election of 1914. The war in Europe had started but it took a back seat to the heated arguments in Oregon for and against prohibition. Many counties had already "gone dry" but the November vote affected the entire state. When it passed, the saloons had until December 31st to close down. Doctors could prescribe liquor after that date but each was allowed to distribute only two quarts a month. If the limit was violated, the doctor was subject to a fine of $500 or six months in jail.

On the night of December 31, the saloons were packed. Even non-drinkers showed up to join the final party. At midnight they closed their doors. The state was dry years ahead of national prohibition.

The Coos Bay Region, Doughit

Leland Saloon closed when Josephine County went dry, July 1, 1908, reopened 1 1/2 years later only to close again when the state went dry.
source: Larry McLane

Prohibition – 1920

BEFORE THE STATES VOTED in prohibition, specific counties and cities were allowed to vote whether they wanted to be "wet" or "dry." Several communities printed big cards for people to place in their windows announcing, "This House is Dry." One newspaper editor suggested they should have another sign reading, "This House Leaks a Little."

The Volstead Act took effect January 1, 1920 bringing in prohibition. During the next years, grocers stocked such things as sweet grape juice. The bottles bore a warning label on them saying, "Do not loosen cork or this will ferment and became illegal." Often the grocer had already loosened the cork when the customer came to buy a supply of sweetened grape juice.

Local bars sold glasses of cider for 25¢. People were known to get very drunk indeed on saloon cider.

Along Our Histories Trail, Hayden

Moonshiners in Scottsburg Bridge – 1929

EVERY AREA HAS SOME good stories about prohibition times. This one happened during construction of the Scottsburg, Oregon bridge. For years a ferry had taken traffic across the Umpqua River. In 1929, with the bridge being built,

Copper still
SOURCE: Curry County Historical Society

the ferry's days were numbered. One morning, when the bridge workers were coming on the job, they saw the ferry stopped out in the river. An enclosed truck was sitting with the front two wheels on the ferry and with the back end under the water. The chain holding it in place had broken. The truck was loaded with sugar.

It was obvious to everyone that the only use for a truck load of sugar was for moonshining. Manufacturing illegal liquor was a big business. Everyone thought the driver had been caught red-handed and was in bad trouble.

It took several hours for the truck to be righted and brought to shore. By then, all that was left of the contents of the truck was empty sugar sacks. The sugar had dissolved and gone down the river.

Undaunted, the truck owner sued the county for the lost sugar and he won the case. He was never tried for moonshining.

Umpqua Valley Oregon, Minter

Moonshine – 1931

IT WAS CHRISTMAS EVE and most people were thinking about Santa coming down the chimney, but not the Medford Sheriff's Department. The week before, the sheriff and his men had confiscated a ten gallon barrel of extra fine moonshine that had been sitting at the railroad station waiting to be picked up.

The address label was to F.H. Burke of Central Point and the shipment had come from Montague, California. The contents claimed to be shrubs.

An agricultural inspection team was required to look over any incoming plants for the weevils or Florida flies. The inspector realized he was not dealing with shrubs and alerted the sheriff's department. No F.H. Burke was found in the telephone book so the sheriff staked out an agent behind a boxcar ready to seize anyone coming to pick up the barrel. Word must have leaked out because several people came inquiring about the shipment. When the station agent warned them that they would have to remove the barrel at their own risk, they all backed off.

At the end of ten days it was Christmas Eve and time to confiscate the ten gallons of moonshine and dump it into Bear Creek. It makes you wonder if all ten gallons got in the creek.

Medford *Mail Tribune*, December 24, 1931

Ice House Liquor

WHEN NEW OWNERS took over the run down Klamath Hot Springs Hotel in the 1930s, they decided to burn down the old icehouse. As the fire burned hotly, small explosions popped like fire crackers. The smell of whiskey was in the air.

It seems the ice house hid a secret door leading to a room where cases of whiskey were stored. The Hot Springs were in California, just over the line from Oregon. When Oregon went dry, the hotel was even more popular than usual. In fact, the following song was sung:

> It's a long way to California,
> It's a long way to go.
> It's a long way to California
> To the first saloon I know.
> Good bye Tom and Jerry,
> Farewell Rock and Rye,
> Its a long way to California
> Since Oregon went dry.

Siskiyou *Pioneer*, 1965

CHAPTER 25

DEPRESSION YEARS

Shasta Soda Springs – Early 1900s

SHASTA SODA SPRINGS was one of the most famous and fashionable mineral spas. It sat halfway between Dunsmuir and Mount Shasta on the railroad line. The spring water was naturally carbonated and very popular. Soon after the soda Springs opened, the owners began bottling the soda water and sending it to the San Francisco markets. To keep up with the expanding trade, they began sending the water by tank car. However, going this way, the water lost its carbonation and had to be recarbonated in San Francisco. Now when you buy Shasta Soda you will be buying tap water that has been carbonated and no longer comes from the Shasta Soda Springs.

Shasta Springs died with the depression, as did all the resorts in the area. A religious group, calling themselves the Saint Germains, bought many acres of land including the Mount Shasta Springs resort and have maintained it as a private facility.

Interview with Kay Price; Sisson Museum Tourist Information

Applegate Fish Hatchery – 1936

THE APPLEGATE FISH HATCHERY opened in 1912 where Jackson Creek joins the Applegate River. It was Jackson Creek that furnished the water that flowed through a series of troughs at the hatchery. From the troughs, the water went into one of three ponds and out again into Jackson Creek.

Salmon were trapped below the dam and kept in holding ponds until time for spawning. When ready, they were killed and the eggs taken from them. The eggs were fertilized and put in the hatchery troughs. The parent fish was not wasted. As many as 500 people would line up waiting with their gunny sacks. One salmon was doled out to each person.

Drinking fountain, Shasta Springs, California. Note ladles on rim of fountain.
SOURCE: Paul and Leah Reichman Collection

In 1930 the practice of killing the fish before taking their eggs was discontinued. It had been found that the fish could be "milked" and when put back in the river, they would recover to lead a normal life.

Extra men were hired to "pick eggs" in spring. They looked them over and, with special tweezers, picked out all the white eggs which had died. The eggs were then measured into shipping trays. Eggs from the Applegate Fish hatchery were shipped all over the world, to England, South America, Canada and to all the United States.

Another casualty of the depression, the Applegate Fish Hatchery closed in 1936.

Grants Pass *Courier,* July 15, 1991

Black Tuesday – 1929

OCTOBER 29, 1929 WAS "Black Tuesday," the day the stock market crashed and plunged the country into the years of the "Great Depression." Most people in the State of Jefferson were blissfully unaware of what had happened. Life went on pretty much as usual — for a short time.

In Medford, the film *Romance of the Rio Grande* was showing at the beautiful Craterian theater. A ticket cost 50¢. Down at the Isis theater it only cost 10¢ but they showed silent films like *Uncle Tom's Cabin*. The Fox was showing Joan Crawford in *Untamed*. Admission was 35¢. These prices were to go down as the depression deepened. When even that failed to help, the theaters competed by offering free dishes and glassware.

As the depression worsened, money grew scarce in small towns. People then resorted to bartering and odd jobs. Many a family looks back with gratitude to the local food stores who would allow charge accounts to build up indefinitely. Children moved back in with parents or parents moved in with their children. Young men joined the Civilian Conservation Corps and many moved away to try their luck in the big cities.

It wasn't until the buildup to World War II that the economy began to improve. It had taken almost ten years.

Southern Oregon Historical Society *Sentinel*, November 1982

Hoboes

MANY SUCCESSFUL AND WEALTHY men spent the depression years as hoboes traveling the rails.

Montague, California was a stop-off place for hoboes traveling the trains. They would knock on doors and ask for food in exchange for work. They were not considered dangerous, simply out-of-luck men. They soon learned where they could get a handout and the word spread.

One favorite meal began at the Mount Shasta Mill where they could always count on a bit of flour. The next stop would be the Montague Creamery for milk and maybe some butter. With luck someone might produce an egg or two. Pancakes would be made down in the hobo jungle at the railroad tracks.

Interview with Leah Reichman

Pot Liquor Soup

DURING THE DEPRESSION, one of the ways to save money on food was to have pot liquor soup. This is how it was made.

Every time a vegetable was cooked, the remaining juice was poured in a pot on the back of the stove. When there was sufficient fluid, vegetables from the garden would be added, chopped carrots, potatoes, greens and anything else available. A piece of fatback salt pork was sliced and fried. A little chopped onion and potato were added and fried with it. Then everything was put together and simmered.

The results were delicious as well as nutritious. Many families lived on variations of pot liquor soup.

Interview with Ross and Billie Youngblood

Harvest Camp Workers

SEASONAL WORKERS HAD a particularly hard time during the depression. Near Merrill, Oregon a tent town grew that was home to many. The campground consisted of homes of all sorts. A circus type tent was the largest. Several spaces were designated by sheets tied to poles in the ground. Packing cases were used and tents of every size and description. Some homes were well kept, with rock borders designating well swept paths, and a few even had potted flowers. Others were filthy, with litter strewn around. Car doors yawned open to show those sleeping inside. Water was heated over open fires for bathing, laundry and cooking.

Who lived here? Migrant workers of all ages. In one tent housing ten people, lived an old Irish grandmother. Another elderly man admitted picking potatoes just to keep off relief. A couple with a baby were hitch-hiking up to Yakima and stopped to try to earn some money picking potatoes. College students who had run out of money for schooling were trying to pick up a meager existence.

The camp had a camaraderie about it. People shared news and information with transient strangers. Worries and hopes were exchanged. A few people moved on each day but others took their places.

Klamath Herald News, October 29, 1935

Civilian Conservation Corps, CCC

WHEN THE CIVILIAN CONSERVATION CORPS was formed in 1933, the Army took on the job of organizing and running the camps. Usually this took two Army officers and an Army doctor.

To qualify for membership in the CCC, a male had to be single and between 17 and 28 years old. He must be a citizen of the United States, physically fit and not otherwise employed. Applicants were often recommended by state relief agencies or the Veteran's Administration.

The camps were set up with the rank of Leader wearing three stripes. His assistant wore two stripes. The job was to keep order and enforce rules. For instance, if a fight started, it was quickly stopped and the boys signed up for three rounds of boxing or wrestling. On the appointed night, the whole camp would turn out to watch.

To keep track of the boys, they lined up for roll call at 7:30 a.m. They lined up again at 5:30 p.m. for a second roll call in full uniform. The flag was saluted and

Civilian Conservation Corps camp
SOURCE: Del Norte County Historical Society

lowered. They marched to the mess hall where they stood behind their seats until a whistle blew allowing them to sit down and eat.

Thousands of men and boys benefited from the CCC discipline, learning hard work and a trade that they could use the rest of their lives.

CCC Boys Remember, Howell

CCC Camp

A TYPICAL CCC summer camp was made up of tent barracks with wooden floors. The walls were four feet high all around, angling into a center ridge pole. Candles provided light. Headquarters, infirmary and the mess hall-kitchen were usually long, simple wood buildings. In these areas, cooking and heating was generally done with wood stoves. These more permanent buildings would have oil lamps, or possibly electricity. Pit toilets were the rule.

A large, main camp might oversee many smaller outpost camps. Whenever possible abandoned Army camps were used.

Each CCC boy was responsible for his own clothing which he washed in old fashioned wash tubs using scrub boards. No one was allowed to have a car in camp. However, some boys might pool their money to buy an old car which they would keep at a nearby farm house. These provided a rare trip to town.

CCC Boys Remember, Howell

CCC Men

THE CCC, OPERATED under military authority. When enlistees arrived in camp, they were issued World War I uniforms, blankets, a bag filled with straw for a mattress and a mess kit.

When small groups went out on jobs, only a supervisor accompanied them. They would set up camp and remain until their job was done. Ross Youngblood was a supervisor in charge of about 40 boys one summer. He remembers that most were from the south and most had to be trained for the kind of work that was needed. Their job was to grub out current and gooseberry bushes that grew wild in the forests. The bushes were host to a disease that was killing the sugar pines and other valuable lumber trees.

CCC boys were paid $30 a month. Of this, $25 was sent back to the boy's family, while he received $5. Considering how much a dollar bought during the depression, and that each CCC man was provided room and board, $5 was a lot of spending money. When they were paid at the end of each month, dice and card games flourished. Soon some of the boys would be flush while others were left penniless until the next pay day.

Interview with Ross Youngblood

CCC Camp Rand

IN 1933, 275 INEXPERIENCED boys were sent to Camp Rand. Their main duties centered around road construction.

George Morey, one of the new enrollees, was given the duty of "powder man unlimited" and made head of a crew blasting trees from the right of way along the road they were building. Morey studied the manual and approached a Douglas fir 50 inches in diameter. It was near the edge of the road. The idea was to blast it down in such a way the entire tree and stump would roll down the mountain. He and the men dug the required holes and put in the proper amount of powder. When that was done Morey began to worry that maybe it wasn't enough powder to do the job. Just to be on the safe side, he dug two more large holes and tamped down another box of blasting powder in each. When the blast went off, the tree went down the mountain all right, but, with it went about 10 feet of the road.

It took several days to repair the road, but the men learned to follow the manual's instructions precisely after that.

George Morey, CCC member

CCC Boys and the Bear

BOYS OF THE CAMP RAND CCC had an unusual experience with a bear. The group was detailed to cut wood for winter, and they went out into the woods to establish a tent camp. They had only been there a few days when they were vis-

CCC Camp Rand
SOURCE: Diane (Morey) Harper

ited by a large bear. The cook heard a noise in the mess tent and went to investigate. He came face to face with a bear. The bear was just as scared as the cook and took off. There being no door in the opposite end of the tent, the bear dragged the tent down and everything with it. The men were called out in the middle of the night to repair the damage.

The bear returned every night and got bolder and bolder. The CCC boys thought of an idea to scare the bear. They got an old oaken barrel, the 52 gallon type, and bored holes near the open end. Through these they inserted spikes with the sharp ends slanting towards the inside and the bottom of the barrel. The idea was that the bear would be able to squeeze her head past the nail points to get at the food, but would not be able to draw back out.

The barrel was baited and placed in front of the tents so everyone could watch what happened. Sure enough, the bear came, stuck her head in and ate the bait. When she tried to get her head out she panicked. With her head and the barrel held high, she started to run and ran right into a large fir tree. The barrel broke open, strewing staves and binders several feet in all directions. That freed the bear and allowed her to get away.

George Morey, CCC member

CCC and the Deer

George Morey while in the CCC
SOURCE: Diane (Morey) Harper

CAMP RAND WAS A FEW miles from Galice, Oregon. One early summer day, a truck load of CCC men saw a doe and two fawns crossing the road . They jumped off the truck and caught the two fawns and took them back to camp. The commanding officer was furious and ordered the men to return the fawns to exactly where they were caught. His order was ignored and the men gave the fawns to a woman living in Galice.

The community fell in love with the fawns who were now called "Sweet" and "Sweety." As they grew up, they had the run of the town and the CCC camp. This was great until Sweet and Sweety both had twin fawns who also came to be petted and fed. That worked out pretty well until the third generation. Now the deer herd numbered 14, semi-tame but unafraid. As they grew older, they became more aggressive and less friendly. Children were afraid to go outside, gardens were trampled and eaten and even dogs were in danger.

Just when things seemed out of control, Camp Rand closed and the deer took to the wilds again.

George Morey, CCC member

CCC in the Klamath Basin

ONE OF THE MANY CCC camps was built on the west side of Tule Lake. From here crews went out to build roads, kill problem weeds, fence and clear land. They were also on call in case of any forest or range fires. In 1936 a dike broke and flooded 1,400 acres of grain. The CCC was called out to harvest the remaining grain and fix the dike.

The Civilian Conservation Corp was disbanded at the beginning of World War II. This left the camp available for use as a Prisoner of War Camp. In the spring of 1944, Italian prisoners were brought in to repair and restore the buildings in preparation for the first Germans.

When the German prisoners arrived, they worked in small crews to help harvest crops on the farms nearby. Some of the men ate meals with the farmers and their families and made lasting friends with them.

On May 1, 1946 the War Department returned the camps to Wildlife Refuge management. A few buildings from the old Camp Tule Lake are still standing and used as storage buildings.

The Years of Harvest, A History of the Tule Lake Basin

ംുുു •❧• ുുു

CHAPTER 26

WARTIMES

Spanish-American War – 1898

OREGON TROOPS WERE the first to enter the walled city of Manila in the Philippines, during the Spanish-American War. George Newell wrote to his mother in July 1898,

> "I know now what hardship, cannon and rifle balls are, and ain't stuck on having them shot at me either, even if they don't hit me.... We came across the bay...in an open scow.... The rain just poured down on us,...everything was just soaking wet. We were in camp ten days before we took Manila."

In a later letter he wrote:

> "The insurgents attacked us during the night. We repulsed them until daylight and then we made a general attack.... The Fourteenth lost thirteen killed, an officer and forty-eight wounded."

It was two years before Newell returned to San Francisco. The Oregon troops fought in 42 battles. They traveled 536 miles in three months, fighting the whole time.

Oregon Oddities, WPA

Yoemanettes – 1917

DID YOU KNOW THAT women served in the Armed Forces during World War I? On March 29, 1917, Bertha Loftus became the first woman to enlist in Jackson County and probably the first to enlist on the entire West Coast. The Naval Reserve received applications from 17 women in Medford. They were given what the service referred to as a "modified" physical examination and tested for proficiency in typing and stenographic skills.

Entries in the journal of Emma Minear, Spanish-American War, April, 1898
SOURCE: Ruth Minear Alborn

Two weeks after enlistment, Bertha was ordered to report. In Portland, she was assigned to the drafting department at the Navy yard. The girls were housed in private homes. They had no naval uniforms so they wore their civilian clothes for the first year.

It is interesting what kind of girls were the first to enlist:

Most of the women already worked outside their home.
Ages ranged from 17 to 36.
Eight of the fifteen were telephone operators.
Several were married.

At the time of enlistment, a Yeomanette received $28.75 per month base pay, with 20¢ deducted for hospitalization. Because the Navy had no housing for women, they were given $1.25 a day to cover room and food.

Southern Oregon Historical *Society*, March 1990

World War I in Klamath County – 1917

THE BEGINNING OF World War One didn't go smoothly in Klamath County. A series of unexplained fires in Klamath Falls gave rise to rumors that a certain labor organization was causing them. The membership of the organization included many German sympathizers. Feelings were running high. The crisis came in July, 1917 when the Martin Brothers Mill and Grain Storage was burned. The following morning there was a call for all law enforcement officers to meet at the courthouse and bring their guns. Reprisals were planned. Fortunately calmer minds prevailed and order was restored.

WWI soldier
SOURCE: Kerbyville Museum

Meanwhile, the local draft board began calling up boys. On August 13, 1917, young J. Howard Boggs of Langell Valley was one of the first to go. He was sent to Camp Lewis but by December was in France. In July, after less than a year in service, he was killed. This was the first Klamath County life lost in World War I.

Herald News, July 1984

Grants Pass Honors War Dead – 1917

GRANTS PASS TURNED OUT, en masse, to pay tribute to the first soldier to lose his life in service during World War I.

Joseph Borough was born in Wilderville in 1897 and lived all his 20 years in Josephine County. When volunteers were called for, at the beginning of the war,

Joseph enlisted in the Aviation Corps. He was assigned to Company B, First Corps which was headquartered in Fort Sam Houston, Texas.

Grants Pass left no leaf unturned to honor Boroughs. Banks and business houses closed for the hour between two and three to pay tribute to his memory. The Red Cross and the Girl's Honor Guard attended and citizens turned out in such numbers it was the largest funeral ever held in all of Southern Oregon. Everyone declared it a fitting tribute.

Private Borough had been in service for only two months when he died. How did this young, honored patriot die? He caught measles which developed into pneumonia.

Josephine County Historical Highlights, Hill

Air Craft Warning Service – 1941

EVEN BEFORE PEARL HARBOR, the United States had formed an Air Craft Warning Service. In Oregon the first volunteers were organized in August, 1941. By the end of the war about 15,000 had served, working 24 hours a day. In built up areas, stations used existing buildings but the National Forests began building lookout towers located throughout the public lands. These remote towers were staffed by paid personnel who watched for both aircraft and fires day and night. It was demanding work requiring long periods of isolation with only one or two fellow watchers for company. Tempers would begin to fray after about one week.

Radar was just being developed during World War II and while it was used in many places along the coast, it could not possibly cover all the area. The Japanese were launching incendiary balloons that drifted across the Pacific and were expected to land as they met the coast. Some did, even as far inland as Klamath Falls. All reports of sightings had to be followed up. Many proved false.

Since no real invasion occurred on the West Coast, it is easy to underestimate the need for the Air Craft Warning Service but, at the time, the threat seemed very real.

George Morey, Gold Beach

Coast Guard – 1942

IN EARLY AUGUST, 1942, the Commander in Chief of the United States Fleet ordered the Coast Guard to patrol the beaches and inlets along the Pacific Coast. It was a tremendous job and one the Coast Guard had little or no preparation for. Nevertheless, only three weeks later, they were able to report that 13 lifeboat stations and 26 coastal lookout stations in Washington and Oregon were being maintained on a 24 hour basis.

The stretch of coastline beginning about three miles north of Cape Blanco and extending beyond the Coquille River was considered the most vulnerable section along the entire coast. The beach was unobstructed and the inland area had

Dutchman Peak Lookout
SOURCE: Rogue River National Forest, Historic Photograph Collection

plenty of vegetation to cover a landing enemy. Many small roads filtered through the area.

It was decided to locate a Coast Guard Station at nearby Lake Floras at the old town site of Lakeport. The town had been abandoned but a resort had been built on the lake consisting of a two-story hotel, a store and several cottages. There was even a gas station, boat house and dock. The Coast Guard moved in. The unit grew until there were some 85 men, the largest unit on the Northwest Coast.

The Floras Lake station was abandoned as the tide of war changed. The facility was given back to its owners.

Lakeport, Webber

Tule Lake Internment Camp – 1942

THE INTERNMENT CAMPS for the Japanese-Americans during World War II are a blot on the history of our country.

Camp Newell was to be built in 30 days according to the Klamath *Evening Herald* of May 23, 1942. It was to be a 1,000 building detention center to house some 18,000 Japanese–Americans during World War II. The first group of 300 arrived there on May 28, 1942.

The camp was surrounded by barbed wire with guard towers and armed guards. Although quickly built, water, sewage, heating and utilities were provided as were schools, hospitals and recreation centers. The internees were almost all American citizens. Two months after Pearl Harbor, President Franklin Roosevelt ordered the military to set up these camps. They were for everyone of Japanese ancestry under the theory that these people might be pressured to help our Japanese enemy. Within a few months the entire Pacific Coast population of Japanese–Americans was relocated without a trial or hearing.

There was only one way the young men of the detention camps could get out. That was to join the armed services. Many did, and formed some of the most decorated regiments in service. Surprisingly enough, the Japanese who were subjected to this humiliation seemed to accept it philosophically and did not bear any lasting grudge against their country. However, when the war was over, only one family remained in the Tule Lake area.

Siskiyou *Pioneer*, 1977

Camp Newell – 1942

WHEN THE WAR WAS OVER there was no need for Camp Newell, the Japanese-American internment camp. There were 1,000 buildings and equipment housed in them.

At the same time hundreds of returned veterans were taking up land claims from the land that had been uncovered when Tule Lake was drained. These homesteaders were living in tents or poor houses because no lumber or materials were available. The Bureau of Reclamation made arrangements to sell surplus equipment from Camp Newell at the time it closed in 1946. Each homesteader was declared eligible to receive one barracks building 20 feet by 100 feet. These buildings were moved all over the Klamath basin on flat bed trucks. With the narrow roads it was quite a traffic hazard and a problem for ranchers. As the barracks jolted down the roads thousands of nails vibrated loose and scattered over the roads. It was impossible to go anywhere without the danger of getting a flat tire.

Many of these Camp Newell buildings are still being used.

Klamath *Evening Herald*, May 24, 1942; *Years of Harvest, History of the Tule Lake Basin,* Turner

Camp White – 1942

WHITE CITY, OREGON, located just north of Medford, began as Camp White during the second World War. Named for Major General George White, Camp White was dedicated in August 1942. The camp commander said he wanted to train his troops so that "they would have a chance to come back alive." That training was hard. The camp soon gained the reputation of being the "Alcatraz of Training Camps." During the war years more that 200,000 men swam the Rogue River in full combat dress, took 90 mile hikes and suffered through tank battles using live ammunition.

Cape Blanco Lighthouse
SOURCE: Curry County Historical Society

When the war ended in 1945, the army pulled out, taking with it all the guns and supplies that could be used elsewhere. The government declared the camp surplus in 1946. The buildings were moved or torn down. The materials and furnishings were sold at auction. Almost as fast as it had risen, the camp had disappeared. All that remained were a few barracks, the roads, utilities and the medical complex which is now a Veterans' Domiciliary.

Camp White was larger than the nearby town of Medford and dominated both it and the small surrounding communities. When the camp was dismantled, the area which had become used to the government money went into a short local depression.

Besides the Domiciliary, much of the Camp White land has been converted into an industrial park. The rest has become home to over 5,000 people.

Southern Oregon Historical Society *Sentinel,* August 1988

Submarine I-25

DURING WORLD WAR II there were several incidents of strategic attacks on our Pacific Coast. Cape Blanco lighthouse, in Oregon, figures in one story. A Japanese submarine surfaced off the Oregon/California coast. A small reconnaissance plane was assembled on its deck and put into the water. The plane took off and, using the Cape Blanco light as a guide, flew a little southeast and dropped two 170 pound incendiary bombs on Wheeler Ridge, east of Brookings.

The Japanese thought that if they set big forest fires it would cause the American people to panic, anticipating further Japanese attacks. Only small fires resulted from the bombs.

On the 29th of September the small bomber was again sent out, this time to Grassy Knob east of Port Orford where two bombs were dropped. No evidence of fire was found.

The submarine was more successful when it torpedoed the oil tanker, S.S. *Camden,* which caught fire and eventually sank. Another oil tanker, the *Larry Doheny* was also a victim of the same Japanese sub. It sank off Port Orford on October 5th. This was the final attack on American ships along the West Coast in World War II.

A Guide to South Coast History, Doughit

ᕙᕗ

AS IT WAS

BIBLIOGRAPHY

Applegate, Sharon and Terence O'Donnell. *Talking on Paper*. Corvallis, Oregon. Oregon State University Press, 1994.

Atwood, Kay. *An Honorable History*. Medford, Oregon. Jackson County Medical Society, 1985.

Bakken, Lovola. *Land of the North Umpqua*. Grants Pass, Oregon. Te-Cum-Tom Publisher, 1973.

Bain, Bill. *Oregon's South Coast*. Flagstaff, Arizona. B. Bain, 1970.

Bancroft. *Bancroft's Works, XXII History of California, Vol VI.* .

Beckham, Stephen Dow. *Coos Bay, The Pioneer Period*. Coos Bay, Oregon. Arago Books, 1973.

_____. *Land of the Umpqua*. Roseburg, Oregon. Douglas County Commissioners, c 1986.

Bledsoe, Anthony Jennings. *History of Del Norte County, California*. Eureka, California, 1971.

Boggs, Mae Bacon. *My Playhouse Was a Concord Coach*. Oakland, California. Howell-North Press, 1942.

Bradford, June Ann. *State of Jefferson*, 197?

Bureau of Land Management (BLM) Department of the Interior. *Homestead Law*.

Carey, Charles H. *A General History of Oregon Prior to 1861*. Portland, Oregon. Metropolitan Press.

Contor, Roger. *The Underworld of Oregon Caves National Monument*. Crater Lake National Historical Association, 1963.

Cordy, C.B. *History of the Rogue Valley Fruit Industry*. Central Point, Oregon, 1977.

Dana, Julian. *Sacramento, River of Gold*. New York, Toronto. Farrar and Rinehart Inc., c. 1939.

Dawson, Maynard C. *Treasures of the Oregon Country*. Salem, Oregon. Dee Publishing Co., 1974.

Dodge, Orville. *Pioneer History of Coos and Curry County*. Oregon. Western World Publishers, 1969.

Doughit, Nathan. *A Guide to Oregon South Coast History*. Coos Bay, Oregon. River West Books c. 1986. *Coos Bay Region*. River West Books, c. 1981.

Drew, Harry J. *Pages From the Past*. Klamath Falls, Oregon. Klamath County Museum, 1979.

Duncan, Janice K. *Minority Without a Champion*. Portland, Oregon. Oregon Historical Society, 1972.

Ernst, Alice Hensan. *Trouping in Oregon Country*. Portland, Oregon. Oregon Historical Society, 1961.

Farnham, Wallace D. *Religion As An Influence in Life and Thought*, Jackson County, Oregon, 1955.

Franklin, Dorothy. *West Coast Disasters*. Gamm Publishing Co., c. 1962.

Friedman, Ralph. *In Search of Western Oregon*. Caldwell, Idaho. Caxton Printers, 1990.

Gilmore, Jesse Lee. *History of the Rogue River Valley, Pioneer Period*, 1952 .

Gray, Dennis J. *Takelma and the Athapascan Neighbors*. Eugene, Oregon. Department of Anthropology, University of Oregon, 1987.

Gudde, Erwin Gustov. *California Gold Camps*. Berkeley California. University of California Press, 1975.

Handbury, Joan. Research paper 501, SOC. *Chinese in the Rogue Valley, 1850-1890*.

Hegne, Barbara. *Country Folk, Butte Falls Derby Dudley*, 1989.

Helms, Marhorie Neill. *Early Days in Phoenix*. Grants Pass, Oregon. Bulletin Publishing Co., 1954.

Hill, Edna May. *Josephine County Historical Highlights II*. Grants Pass, Oregon. Josephine County Library System, 1979.

Holmgren, Virginia C. *Chinese Pheasants, Oregon Pioneers*. Portland, Oregon. Oregon Historical Society, 1964.

Homer, John B. *Oregon, Her History, Her Great Men, Her Literature.* Corvallis, Oregon. Press of the Gazette-Times, 1919.

Howe, Carrol B. *Ancient Tribes of the Klamath Country.* Portland, Oregon. Binfords and Mort, 1968.

Howell, Glenn. *C.C.C. Boys Remember.* Medford, Oregon. Klocker Printery, 1976.

Hult, Ruby El. *Lost Mines and Treasures.* Portland, Oregon. Binfords and Mort, 1957.

Jewitt, Dick. *Medford's First Century.* Medford Mail Tribune, 1985.

Jones, Alice Goen and Richard Krieg. *Trinity County Historic Sites.* Weaverville California. Trinity County Historical Society, 1981.

Jones, James Roy. *Saddle Bags in Siskiyou.* Happy Camp, California. Naturegraph, 1980.

Kirchhoff, Theodor. *Oregon East, Oregon West.* Portland, Oregon. Oregon Historical Society Press, 1987.

Klamath County Historical Society. *History of Klamath Country.* Klamath County Historical Society, 1984.

Knudtson, Peter M. *Wintu Indians and Their Neighbors.* Happy Camp, California. Naturegraph Press, c. 1977.

Kreb, Helen. *With Her Own Wings.* Portland, Oregon. Beattie and Co., 1948.

Laird, Irma Williams. *The Modoc Country.* Alturas, California. L&A Kennedy, 1971.

LaLande, Jeffrey. *First Over the Siskiyous,* Portland, Oregon. Oregon Historical Society Press, c. 1983.

League of Women Voters. *Ashland Oregon.* League of Women Voters, 1971.

Levy, Jo Ann. *They Saw the Elephant.* Hamden, Connecticut. Archon Books, 1990.

Lion's Club Book Committee. *Pioneer Days in Canyonville.* Lion's Club Book Committee, 1968.

Lockley, Fred. *Across the Plains by Prairie Schooner.* Seattle. Shorey Book Store, 1968.

_____. *Oregon Journal.* Portland, Oregon. The Oregon Journal, 1934.

_____. *Oregon Folks.* New York. The Knickerbocker Press, 1929.

Loomis, Benjamin Franklin. *Eruptions of Lassen Peak.* Mineral California. Loomis Museum Association, Loomis Volcanic National Park, 1966.

Mayo, Roy F. *Gold Mines of Southwest Oregon.* Snumclaw, Washington. Nugget Enterprises, 1987.

McBeth, Frances Turner. *Pioneers of Elk Valley.* Angwin, California. Pacific Union College Press, 1960.

_____. *Lower Klamath Country,* Berkeley, California. Anchor Press, 1950.

McCormack, Win; Dick Pintarich editors. *Great Moments in Oregon History, A Collection of*

Articles. Portland, Oregon. New Oregon Publishers, 1987.

McLagan, Elizabeth. *A Peculiar Paradise, a History of Blacks in Oregon 1788-1940.* Portland, Oregon. Georgian Press, 1980.

Minter, Harold Avery. *Umpqua Valley Oregon and Its Pioneers.* Portland, Oregon. Binford's and Mort, 1967.

Nichols, Claude W. *The South Road; Its Development and Significance,* 1953.

O'Harra, Marjorie. *The Ashland Story.* Ashland, Oregon. Lewis Osborne, 1971.

_____. *Southern Oregon.* 1978.

Palmberg, Walter H. *Copper Paladin.* Bryn Mawr, Pennsylvania. Dorrance, 1982.

Peterson, Emil and Alfred Powers. *A Century of Coos and Curry County.* Portland, Oregon. Binfords and Mort, 1952.

Pfeiffer, Ida. *A Lady's Second Trip Around the World,* c. 1858.

Rensch, Hero and Ethel; Mildred Hoover, William Abeloe. *Historic Spots in California.* Stanford, California. Stanford University Press, 1966.

U.S. Forest Service. *Prehistory and History of the Rogue River National Forest.* U.S. Forest Service, Pacific Northwest Region. Portland, Oregon. U.S. Department of Agriculture, 1990.

Robinson, Fayette. *The Gold Mines of California.* New York. Promontory Press, 1974.

Roseburg, Oregon. Douglas County Commissioners, 1986.

Scripter, Charles, Eldon. *Lithia Park Story.* Ashland, Oregon. Pilot Rock Publications, 1975.

Snedicor, Jane. *Founding of Medford.* Medford, Oregon, 1935.

Spreen, Christian August. *A History of Placer Gold Mining in Oregon,* 1939.

Stearns, Orsen Avery. *Reminiscences of Pioneer Days, 1921-1922.*

Street, Willard. *Sailors' Diggings.* Wilderville, Oregon. Wilderville Press, 1973.

Stumpf, Gary D. *Gold Mining in Siskiyou County 1850-1900.* Yreka, California. Siskiyou County Historical Society, 1979.

Sutton, Jack. *110 Years With Josephine.* Josephine County Historical Society, 1966.

_____. *Mythical State of Jefferson.* Medford, Oregon. Klocker Printery, 1967.

Trinity County Historical Society. *Trinity County Historical Sites.* Trinity County California.

Tucker, William Pierce. *History of Jackson County,* 1931.

Turner, Stan Eugene. *Years of Harvest, A History of the Tule Lake Basin.* Eugene, Oregon. 49th Avenue Press, c. 1987.

WPA. *Oregon Oddities,* 1939-1941.

Walling, Albert G. *History of Southern Oregon.*

_____. *Indian Wars of Southern Oregon.*
Portland, Oregon. A.G. Walling, 1884.

Walsh, Frank K. and William R. Halliday.
Discovery and Exploration of Oregon Caves.
Grants Pass, Oregon Te-Cum-Tom
Enterprises, 1971.

Webber, Bert. *Oregon's Great Train Holdup.*
Fairfield, Washington. Ye Galleon Press, 1973.

_____. *Oregon's Seacoast Lighthouses.* Medford,
Oregon. Webb Research Group, 1992.

Webber, Bert and Maggie. *Railroading in
Southern Oregon.* Fairfield, Washington.
Galleon Press, 1986.

_____. *Lakeport, Ghost Town of the South
Oregon Coast.* Medford, Oregon. Webb
Research Group, 1990.

~~~

Periodicals

Bakkam, Lavola. *Umpqua Trapper.* Summer 1975.
Douglas County—Years of History, Aug 12, 1882.

Ball, Lottie A. (as told to) *Siskiyou Pioneer.* 1956.
The Charles F. Kappler Brewery, p.33.

Bandon Historical Museum placard "Elizabeth."

Beeson, Welborn. Talent (Oregon) *News.* Vol 1,
#12, July 3, 1853. *Fourth of July Reminiscences.*

Bondinelli, Carl. *Morning News* (Central Point,
Oregon). Mar 3, 1979. *History of Jackson
County.* Same. May 12, 1979.

Boyle, Lawrence. *Pioneer Days in the South
Umpqua Valley,* 1974. *The Rock.* p.3.

Brown, Natalie. *Table Rock Sentinel.* Sep/Oct
1991. *Then and Now,* p.11.

Burton, Fred W. *Siskiyou Pioneer* Abstracts. 1965.
Shasta-Scott Valley Bar Turnpike Toll Road. p.24.
Last Lynching of the West, p.34.

Bussert, Wendell. *Siskiyou Pioneer.* 1978. *Before
the Gold Rush,* p.5.

Childers, Lida and Ruby Lacy. Ashland *Tidings*
Excerpts:
Vol 4. Jul 5, 1889. *Lost Cabin Victims.* p.107. *The
Census Machine.* Supplement.
Vol 6. Oct 7, 1892. *Dunsmuir "601,"* p.64. Oct
28, 1892. *Divorce,* p.68.
Vol 8. Feb 17, 1896. *The Isolation of the Oregon
Pioneers,* p.12. Jun 11, 1896. *Untitled,* p.43. Sep
7, 1896. *A Mystery Cleared,* p.66-67.
Vol 9. Nov 4, 1897. *The Bowling Alley,* p. 53.
Vol 10. May 22, 1899. *Smith's Approaching
Doom,* p.53. May 25, 1899. *The Doom of Frank
Lawrence Smith,* p.57. May 27, 1899. *Jacksonville
Items,* p.65.

Childers, Lida and Ruby Lacy. *Oregon Sentinel,*
various 1856-1873. Sept 29, 1866. *Juvenile
Depravity,* p.124.

Clark, Ella E., Oregon Historical Quarterly, Dec.
1960. *Indian Thanksgiving in the Pacific
Northwest,* Vol 61, p.437.

Crescent City *Courier.* Jan 16, 1873.

Curry County *Echoes.* Mar 1985; Nov 1989, May
1993.

Curry County Historical Society Monthly Bulletin.
April 1974.

Davis, Hazel. *Siskiyou Pioneer.* 1972. *Scott Bar,*
p.62.

DeWald, Oral; Jennie and Emma Bealman and
others. *Pioneer Days in the South Umpqua
Valley.* 1971. *The John Weber Story,* p.12.

Dexter, Francies Teeters. *Siskiyou Pioneer.* 1957.
Teeters Landing, p.70.

Dill, Thomas. *Southern Oregon Heritage.* Summer
1995. *Riding the Rails,* p.4.

Dreyer, Anna Soule. *Siskiyou Pioneer.* 1988. *From
the Writings of Anna Soule Preyer,* p.60.

Evening Herald (Klamath Falls), Shasta Forest
Clips, Nov 23, 1940. *Remmes Great Ride.*

Flower, Jean (Churchill). *Siskiyou Pioneer.* 1980.
The Montague Box Factory and Lloyd Churchill,
p. 46.

Foulke, Lewis M. *Siskiyou Pioneer.* 1963. *Beef!
Beef!* p.1.

Foster, Doug. *Southern Oregon Heritage.* Summer
1995. *"Send Chiliquin Up."* p.22. Fall 1995.
"Refuge Reclaimed," p.22.

Grants Pass *Courier.* July 15, 1991, Jan 23, 1992.

Grants Pass *Daily Courier.* Sep 2, 1928.

Harris, Ellen. *Pioneer Days in the South Umpqua
Valley.* 1972. *A Short History of Blendale,* p.3.

Helfrich, Devere. Klamath *Echoes.* 1965. *As Told
to me by Ray Telford.* p.25. 1967. Part 1, *The
Founding of Linkville,* p.13. 1967. Part 2,
Courthouses of Klamath County, 1-9. 1968. *Fort
Klamath,* p.1. *The Telephone and Telegraph of
Linkville,* p.49. 1973. *Stage Coach to Linkville,*
p.1. 1977. *White Lake City,* p.25.

Hennigh, Larry. *Pioneer Days in the South
Umpqua Valley.* 1976. *The Lost Soldiers' Mine,*
p.13. *Klamath Express.* Dec 27, 1906.

Hessig, Alice. *Siskiyou Pioneer.* 1965. *Ice,* p.14. *The
History of Klamath Hot Springs,* p.63.

Jacobs, Cecile. *Siskiyou Pioneer.* 1957. *The Late
Sam Clary,* p.52.

Jacobs, Gordon. *Siskiyou Pioneer.* Spring 1954.
Longest Home Run On Record, p.41.

King, Ruth. Klamath *Echoes.* 1960. From the
Herald News. Nov, 6, 1960. *Election Board
Customs.* 1970. *Growing Pains of Malin,* p.48.

King, Larry. *King Mountain Advocate.* Spring
1992. *Who Was W.G. Smith, Anyway?* p.1.

Klamath *Echoes.* 1968. *Movies,* p.75. 1970. *Tule
Lake Valley Post Offices,* p.51. 1972. *Cloverleaf
Country Cattle Drives.*

Klamath *Evening Herald.* Oct 22, 1913; Nov 14,
1914; Apr 18, 1919; May 24, 1942.

Klamath *Express.* Dec 17, 1906. Jul 20, 1939.

Klamath Falls *Herald.* Jan 28, 1962.

Klamath Falls Historical Society *Newsletter.*
Summer 1990.

Klamath *Herald News*. Oct 29, 1935; Jul 1984; Aug 3, 1959.

Klamath *News*. Aug 5, 1962, p.2.

Klamath *Republican*. Nov 8, 1906.

Korbulic, Mary. *Table Rock Sentinel*. Nov/Dec 1992. *Romancing the Rogue*, p.3.

Kostiz, B.H. *Siskiyou Pioneer*. 1986. *The Stockyards*, p.94. *The Purse Trick*, p.106.

Kramer, George. May/Jun 1990. *Medford's Carnegie Library*, p.22.

Lake County *Examiner*. Aug 2, 1906.

Lange, Harold (Bill). *Siskiyou Pioneer*. 1963. *Holdup on Borrowed Horse*, p.71.

Lathrop. *Siskiyou Pioneer*. 1961. From the *County Reporter*, Fort Jones, Mar 16, 1896. *The Old Etna and the New*, p.37.

Lelande, Jeff. *Table Rock Sentinel*. Jan/Feb 1993. *Politics and the Klan*, p.3.

Lewis, F.E. *Siskiyou Pioneer*. 1967. *Original Town of Weed*, p.5. *Depot and Railroad*, p.54.

Lewis, Raymond. *Table Rock Sentinel*. Jan 1883. *Madame Holt, The Lady and the Hotel*, p.3. *Ed Schieffelin*, p.13. Apr 1983. *Lan Kee Finds His Treasure*, p4. *A Few Chinese Became Part of the Community*, p.11. Jun 1983. *Earl H. Fell in a Courtroom Drama*, p.3. Sep 1883. *Knights of the Ku Klux Klan in Southern Oregon*, p.10. Nov 1984. *The Chappell-Swedenburg House*, p.3. Jan 1985. *Indian Remedies*, p.16. *Troupers*, p.18. Feb 1985. *Tillie*, p.3. Mar 1986. "The Jacksonville Cannonball," p.17-30. Apr. 1986. *The Big 1928 Foot Race*, p.20. May 1986. *Cinnabar & Colestin Revisited*, p.18. Aug 1986. *David Linn, Master Builder*, p.3. Feb 1987. *Chautauqua, The Way It Was*, p.19. Apr 1987. *Judge Hanna*, Aug 1987. *Madame Holt and the President*, p.17. Sep 1987. *Medford's First Railroad Office Robbery*, p.22.

Lockley, Fred. News Item in the Southern Oregon Historical Society File. p.44.

Loosley, Willeska. Klamath *Echoes*. 1968. *A Pioneer Family*, p.13.

Love, Roger. *Table Rock Sentinel*. July 1988. *Trouble With Healing Waters—The Turbulent History of Buckhorn Springs*, p.4. August 1988. *City of Industry, City of Dreams*, p.5.

Lovell, Leo Brown. *Siskiyou Pioneer*. 1980. *Personal Communication*, p.125.

Luecke, Mary. *Siskiyou Pioneer*. 1982. *Catholic Church Paradise Flats 1853*, p.13. *Deadwood*, p22.

Mathews, W.D. Sr. *Siskiyou Pioneer*. 1960. *Comical Happenings at Solemn Affairs*, p.60.

Mazzini, Joe. Excerpts from Northern California Newspapers.

McKinney, J.O. *Siskiyou Pioneer*. 1964. *Callahan Store and Bar*, p.62. *One October Day*, p.48.

McMurry, Alan. *Siskiyou Pioneer*. 1993. *George Decker*, p.85.

McNeill, James. *Siskiyou Pioneer*. 1969. *Bunion Derby*, p.5.

McNeill, Jim. *Siskiyou Pioneer*. 1964. *That Old House*, p.59. 1983. *The Saga of the Salmon River Lifting Rock*, p.1.

Medford Mail Tribune. *Necessity for Water Pointed Out by Landowner*, Jul 10, 1915. p.2. *Homing Pigeons in Cascades to Report on Fires*, May 14, 1919. p.5. *Suspect Arrested, Establishes Alibi*, Oct 23, 1923. Page 1 headline, *Barrel of Cheer Lays Unclaimed, Sheriff Take It*, Dec. 24, 1931. p.5. *Kidnap Money Recovered Here*, Nov 8, 1934. Page 1 headline, *Upper Applegate Wild Horse Band*, Nov 23 1947. p.8. *Shale City, A Reminder of Jackson County's Great Oil Venture*, Aug 22, 1965, Sect. B, p.1. *New Champ at the Crow*, Jun 25, 1978. Sect D, p.1. *Voyager Survives Jupiter's Radiation*, Mar 5, 1979. p.1. Oct 20, 1991. Apr 23, 1993.

Nesbitt, Virgil. *Siskiyou Pioneer*. 1988. *Fun Times at Scott Valley Bar Elementary School*, p.14. *Pioneer Days in the South Umpqua Valley.*

Odell, Ida Momyer. Klamath *Echoes*. 1964. *Water Snakes and Water*, p.4.

Otey, Emma. Klamath *Echoes*, 1977. *Hard Winter*, p.72.

Pendleton, Carl. *As told by* —. Schminck Museum Scrapbook #4, #5, #12. Lakeview, Oregon.

Pinkham, Bernice Jacobs. *Siskiyou Pioneer*. 1992. *A Trip Down Memory Lane*, p.13.

Pollock, Hazel (Schultz). *Siskiyou Pioneer*. 1969. *The Electric Tree*, p.53.

Robison, Edward (Eddie). Talent *News*. Vol 1, #2. Feb 15, 1892. *End of the World*. Vol 1, #20. Nov 15, 19982. *Literary Societies.*

Rogue River Daily *Courier*. Aug 7, 1912. Dec 2, 1912.

Rogue Valley Communities, selected writings. Rogue River section. Unidentified Spokane, Washington newspaper clipping. Jul 29, 1924. *Norse Explorers.*

Rosborough, Alex J. *Siskiyou Pioneer*. 1957. *California's Gold Find*, p.62.

Sacramento *Bee*. May 28, 1974. *Pilgrimage of the Japanese-Americans to the Tulelake Internment Camp*. Reprinted in *Siskiyou Pioneer*, 1977, p.139.

Schroder, Isabel. *Siskiyou Pioneer*. 1964. *Mount Shasta*, p.1.

Shasta *Courier*. Mar 24, 1888, Dec 17, 1892.

Shasta County *Centennial History Edition*. P. 21, p.22, p.152, p.285.

Siskiyou *Daily News*, Aug 25, 1953. *Sailor Jim*. Reprinted in *Siskiyou Pioneer*. 1993. p.98. Aug 24, 1992.

Siskiyou Pioneer. 1978. *Sons of Temperance*, p.84.

Smith, Hubert. *Table Rock Sentinel*. Jan/Feb 1991. *Ancient Ales and Later Lagers*, p.16.

Smith, Joe. *Siskiyou Pioneer*. 1980. *The West Coast Air Transport Company*, p.100.

Sorensen, Mary Wagner. *Siskiyou Pioneer.* 1969. *Banking in Shasta County,* p.41.

Soule, Ruth. *Siskiyou Pioneer.* 1963. *The Snow of 1889-1890,* p.15.

Southern Oregon Historical Society *Sentinel.* Jul/Aug 1980. *Jack London's Crater Lake Trip Reviewed,* p. 3. *Shale City Oil Well Proves To Be Disaster,* p.6. Aug 1982. *The Broom Brigade Revisited,* p.13. Nov 1982. *The Age of Innocence Revisited,* p.9.

Stone, Mrs. Leland. *Siskiyou Pioneer.* 1967. *First Schools of Weed,* p.43.

Sweet, Chuck. Apr 1986. *The John Beeson Story,* p.11. Dec 1987. *Gin Lin and the Mountain of Gold,* p.5.

Table Rock Sentinel. Jul/Aug 1980. *Jack London's Crater Lake Visit Reviewed,* p.3. *Shale City Oil Well Proves to Be Disaster,* p.6. Aug 1982. *The Broom Brigade,* p.13. Nov. 1982. *The Age of Innocence Revisited,* p.9. Jun 1983. *Earl H. Fell in A Courtroom,* Nov/Dec 1990. *Seventy-eight Years Ago,* back of cover.

Tickner, Bernita. *Siskiyou Pioneer.* 1961. *Hallie Daggett, First USFS Woman Lookout,* p.71.

United States Forest Service, *History and Prehistory of the Rogue Valley National Forest, A Cultural Overview.*

Wacker, George. *Siskiyou Pioneer.* 1993. *A Bad Day on Butcher Hill,* p.101.

Waldron, Sue. *Table Rock Sentinel.* Mar/Apr 1990. *Yeomanettes,* p.2. Sep/Oct 1991. *Passing Through the Gap,* p.2.

Wyatt, Steve M. *Table Rock Sentinel.* Mar/Apr 1992. *Buffalo Bill, Stampeding Into Southern Oregon,* p.3.

Interviews and Correspondence

Beckham, Dow Sr.

Birdseye, Nita.

Bishop, Dr. Warren.

Harrison, Vurl and Jim.

Hedgpeth, Mabel.

Morey, George.

Perry, Diane. BLM geologist.

Peyton, Cal.

Price, Kay.

Reichman, Leah.

Youngblood, Ross and Billie

As It Was

INDEX

About the Author

Carol Barrett moved to Eagle Point, Oregon in 1974. She became involved in local history when the Southern Oregon Historical Society gave the city a grant to survey their historic buildings. The society again contacted her when they were proposing a program with Jefferson Public Radio. She took on the project little realizing where her commitment to *As It Was* would lead.

In 1993 Carol self-published *Women's Roots* incorporating stories used on Jefferson Public Radio Women's History Month. She is also the author of the radio series on the Oregon Trail, the Applegate Trail, World War II and the Ten Days of Christmas.

Carol lives at the Rogue Valley Manor in Medford, Oregon.